Student's Guide to Writing College Papers

Chicago Guides
to Writing, Editing,
and Publishing

Student's Guide to Writing College Papers

4TH EDITION

Kate L. Turabian

REVISED BY GREGORY G. COLOMB,
JOSEPH M. WILLIAMS, AND THE
UNIVERSITY OF CHICAGO PRESS
EDITORIAL STAFF

The University of Chicago Press   Chicago and London

GREGORY G. COLOMB is professor of English at the University of Virginia. He is the author of *Designs on Truth: The Poetics of the Augustan Mock-Epic.*

JOSEPH M. WILLIAMS was professor emeritus in the Department of English Language and Literature at the University of Chicago. Professor Williams died in 2008.

Together Colomb and Williams have written *The Craft of Research*, currently in its third edition (University of Chicago Press, 2008). They also revised the seventh edition of Kate L. Turabian's *A Manual for Writers of Research Papers, Theses, and Dissertations* (University of Chicago Press, 2007).

The University of Chicago Press, Chicago 60637
The University of Chicago Press, Ltd., London
© 2010 by The University of Chicago
All rights reserved. Published 2010
Printed in the United States of America

19 18 17 16 15 14 13 12 11 10   1 2 3 4 5

ISBN-13: 978-0-226-81630-2 (cloth)
ISBN-10: 0-226-81630-3 (cloth)
ISBN-13: 978-0-226-81631-9 (paper)
ISBN-10: 0-226-81631-1 (paper)

Library of Congress Cataloging-in-Publication Data

Turabian, Kate L.
    Student's guide to writing college papers / Kate L. Turabian.—4th ed. / rev.
by Gregory G. Colomb, Joseph M. Williams, and the University of Chicago
Press editorial staff.
      p.   cm.—(Chicago guides to writing, editing, and publishing)
    Includes bibliographical references and index.
    ISBN-13: 978-0-226-81630-2 (cloth: alk. paper)
    ISBN-10: 0-226-81630-3 (cloth: alk. paper)
    ISBN-13: 978-0-226-81631-9 (pbk.: alk. paper)
    ISBN-10: 0-226-81631-1 (pbk.: alk. paper)   1. Dissertations, Academic—
Handbooks, manuals, etc. 2. Academic writing—Handbooks, manuals, etc.
I. Colomb, Gregory G. II. Williams, Joseph M. III. Title.
    LB2369.T8   2010
    808'.02—dc22   2009031583

⊗ The paper used in this publication meets the minimum requirements of
the American National Standard for Information Sciences—Permanence of
Paper for Printed Library Materials, ANSI Z39.48-1992.

Contents

Preface for Teachers

This book was written in the belief that research matters and that your students can, and should, do it.

We have what we think are good reasons for those beliefs. Research matters because

- it is ubiquitous in the workplaces of our information age, especially among those who do not think of themselves as researchers;
- the experience of doing research is the best preparation for a world in which we constantly depend on the claims of experts;
- the questioning mind-set of a researcher fosters the kind of critical thinking that students need now more than ever;
- the ability to do research can free us from the tyranny of false authorities, including our own prejudices.

We believe students can do research because

- the core activities of research—finding information to solve a problem—are a part of everyone's daily life;
- the core elements of a research argument—giving good reasons and evidence to convince someone to act or think differently—are also a part of everyone's daily life;
- the two of us have taught thousands of students to do it, starting as early as the eighth grade.

Why then do so few students actually do it well? Because, we think, the research they do in school is framed in a way that cuts off, rather than enables, students' intuitions about how one uses information to solve a problem or to convince others to change what they do or think; also because schools have not, for the most part, helped students understand why the distinctive forms of research and argument we expect in school are rational applications of what they already know how to do.

This book "repurposes" the ideas, principles, and practical wisdom in two earlier guides we wrote for advanced students and practicing researchers—*The Craft of Research* (3rd ed., 2008) and the Turabian guide to theses and dissertations (*A Manual for Writers of Research Papers, Theses, and Dissertations*, 7th ed., 2007). We describe what we've done with that odd, new-media verb *repurpose* because we have not approached this "beginners'" text in the usual way: We have done more than simply translate our advice from researcher-speak to student-speak, though we have done that. We have done more than eliminate what is beyond the experience or resources of beginners, though we have done some of that too. But, most of all, we have refused to redefine the task of research, distorting it in the interests of simplifying it.

Too many students have arrived in our classes with false—and damaging—ideas of research: that its core activity is collecting information; that the writing that researchers do is pure report and the writer pure conduit; that in the workplace researchers are those who look up information for other, more important people to use; that in the academy, the only reason to do research is some quirky "interest" in a subject no one else cares about. These views, predominant among the students we see, handicap them not just for writing what their college teachers ask of them, but for their entire career as learners, citizens, and workers.

Research is above all about having a purpose, about solving problems. Its most important activities happen before and after collecting information. And it depends far more on thinking than on doggedness in the library or lab, or over a keyboard, though it does also depend on that. Although this book will help students write papers more pleasing to their teachers, its chief design is to lead students to develop a truer, more useful, and more attractive understanding of research.

We will confess to harboring a quiet hope that we might inspire some impressive careers in research. But chiefly we aim to set students off with a way of thinking about research—and some tools for doing it—that will enable them to live and work thoughtfully in an age of information, too often of misinformation. Research is learned by doing, so this guide (though not a traditional textbook) is firmly based in the how-to. We have designed it so that a student can, if our appeals to a larger understanding fail, interact with it with only one practical question in mind: *What do I do next?* But we have also designed it so that such a practical student might have gained a new mind-set at the end of the process.

In repurposing our earlier work, we have reconceived it to suit the beginning researcher. Most of the topics are the same, as are all of the principles and some of the advice, but everything has been recast. Because they have seen so little research writing, students will find many more examples, models, and templates to make the principles more concrete. They will find many more explanations of the rationales behind academic research practices and more examples of how they relate to other practices more familiar to them. Where we emphasized options for advanced researchers, for these students we emphasize the prototypes against which advanced researchers measure those options but that these student do not yet know. But in all of this, we have preserved those core activities and practices that make research what it is.

This book has three parts:

Part 1, "Writing Your Paper," is a guide to producing the paper, from assignment to debriefing a teacher's comments. This part is designed so that students can engage it in three ways: to gain an overview of the research process and its rationales, to learn about the specific stages of that process, and to perform the specific actions that go into those stages. We present this material as a coherent sequence but emphasize throughout the true messiness of the process.

Part 2, "Citing Sources," offers guidance on issues of style in bibliographic citations. It presents models for three common citation styles: Chicago, MLA, and APA. This part is intended for reference, to be consulted as the need arises. It does include, however, one chapter on the general theory and practice of citation. We have limited its coverage significantly, to those sources students are most likely to find. Where a style offers options, we have usually presented the simplest or the most common and ignored the rest.

Part 3, "Style," offers guidance on issues of style ranging from spelling and punctuation to the forms of numbers. It generally follows the *Chicago Manual of Style* (16th ed., 2010). This part is intended only for reference, to be consulted as the need arises. Here, too, we have limited the coverage to those matters we judge to be most useful to students.

An appendix covers the format for class papers. A second offers a glossary of grammatical and other technical terms used in the book. A third is a guide to reference works that students can use to get their work started.

There is a teacher's guide available at www.turabian.org. We do hope you will consult it.

Gregory G. Colomb
Joseph M. Williams

Acknowledgments

This book is in the lineage of *The Craft of Research* and *A Manual for Writers*. Those began as the work of a triumvirate: Wayne Booth, Joe Williams, and myself. Now I alone am left. Wayne Booth died in 2005, while this book was barely an idea; Joe Williams in 2008, while it was in very early drafts. Two better writers, teachers, scholars, colleagues, and companions I cannot imagine. Their influence is everywhere in this book and, where I've been lucky, in me.

In *The Craft of Research,* we tell the story of a dream reported by one of Wayne's students, decades after he left school: "You were standing before Saint Peter at the Pearly Gates," the student said, "hoping for admission. He looked at you, hesitant and dubious, then finally said, 'Sorry, Booth, we need another draft.'" After Wayne's death, Joe and I wrote that Wayne's draft had been "better than most, so much more than good enough." Well, Joe was even more obsessed with revision than was Wayne. His draft was damned good too.

Because of its lineage, this book inherits the debts we mentioned in *The Craft of Research* and *A Manual for Writers*. They are too many to list here, but they know who they are and I thank them again.

New to this book was the help we received from Christine Anne Aguila, Jo Ann Buck, Bruce Degi, Laura Desena, Joe Flanagan, Robin P. Nealy, Kathleen Dudden Rowlands, and Joseph Zeppetello. Among them, I want to single out Joe Flanagan, who guided our thinking about a book like this for more than a decade; thanks also to his colleagues at York High School, who spent a sunny afternoon indoors, educating Joe Williams and me. I also want to thank Robin Nealy and her class at Wharton County Junior College, especially those who corresponded with me about their experience with the manuscript: Dionna Austin, Drew Brenk, Jenni Buyer, Leslie Carcamo, Ashleigh Hernandez, Amber Jennings, Ashley Lockin, Heather Miller, Marcus Pantoja, Kortney R., Julia Smith, and Stephanie Ward. I can assure them that the book is better for their help.

At the University of Chicago Press, David Morrow was as helpful as any editor I've had and always a pleasure to learn from. Mary Laur, who now feels like an old friend, was a mainstay in the development of parts 2 and 3. Moreover, she has been a major contributor to each of the projects that led to this one. Kira Bennett did invaluable work on parts 2 and 3.

Finally, though Joe is not here to say it, I know what his closing sentiments would be: "I thank those who contribute to my life more than I let them know: Oliver, Michele, and Eleanor; Chris and Ingrid; Dave, Patty, Owen, and Matilde; Megan, Phil, Lily, and Calvin; and Joe, Christine, Nicholas, and

Katherine. And at beginning and end still, Joan, whose patience and love flow more generously than I deserve."

And to my own family, words cannot do justice to what they have meant to me. Robin and Kiki, Karen, and Lauren have put up with much and blessed me with more. And for more years than either of us wants to acknowledge, Sandra has been the center of it all.

Gregory G. Colomb

Introduction: Why Research?

Who Does Research

What comes to mind when you think of research? Those hours you spent collecting random information on some assigned topic for a high school "research paper"? Or maybe you picture a scientist in a lab coat, peering into a microscope? Perhaps a white-bearded professor silently taking notes in a hushed library? You might, however, have pictured Oprah, planning her next show or business venture. Or Fred Smith, founder of Federal Express, who developed the idea for his business in a class research paper. Or what about Sig Mejdal? He's the chief researcher for baseball's St. Louis Cardinals, whose manager, Tony La Russa, has had researchers on his staff for decades.

Research is everywhere in the professional world. If you know a lawyer, a doctor, a business executive, a marketer, an event planner, a construction manager, or any other professional, then you know someone whose job depends on research. In our aptly named "age of information" (or, too often, *mis*information), more jobs than ever require you not only to find information, but to evaluate it, sort the good from the bad, and then report it clearly and accurately. In the age of the assembly line, workers had to learn one set of tasks that they performed the same way, over and over. These days the key to most jobs is not just how much you know, but how good you are at finding out what you don't. In this new century—*your* century—the skills of research are essential for just about anyone who wants to succeed.

Did you also think of yourself as a researcher? The fact is you do research almost every day. You are a researcher whenever you dig up the information you need to accomplish a goal—from selecting the most popular chemistry teacher, to finding an affordable apartment that allows pets, to figuring out which laptop is best for gaming. Typically these searches are too quick to feel like a research "project," but you are doing what good researchers always do: collecting information to solve a problem or answer a question.

When you thought of researchers, did you also think of your teachers? We college teachers teach, but we also do research. That research begins in our area of expertise, with what we know, but what gets us excited are the things we *don't* know but wish that we did: *What's the connection between morality and the biology of the brain? Will knowing grammar rules make you a better writer? Can we reduce global warming by removing the greenhouse gases already in the atmosphere? Did the prehuman Neanderthals die out naturally, or did our human ancestors kill them off?* We teachers spend much of our working lives with research questions like those, either asking and answering our own or studying the questions and answers of our colleagues.

Why should the research experience of teachers matter to you? For one thing, it's good to know that we practice what we teach. More importantly, our lives of research color the kind of learning that we value most—and that we expect from you. New college students are often surprised to discover that just knowing the facts is not enough for most teachers. It's not enough in our own work: more than knowing things, what energizes us is our habit of seeking out new questions, the cast of mind that drives all research. And it's not enough in yours: more than checking that you know the facts, we want to see what you can *do* with the facts, what new questions, combinations, possibilities, or puzzles you discover—or invent. We value and reward good answers, but we reward good questions more.

When your teacher asks more from you than just rehashing the facts, she is looking for signs of a critical mind with a questioning bent. She's looking for a mind-set that is keen to find out not just what is already known but what no one knows and perhaps never even thought to ask. The two of us hope that our book can inspire most of you to try on that mind-set, at least for a while. It won't be a waste of time, even if the fit is not right. For even if you are certain that questions are not for you and that what you like are settled answers—and many successful people do—you'll still need to know how to find those answers, and we'll help you do that too.

Why Professionals Do Research

Research in the workplace takes many forms, but the basic structure of every research project is the same. Someone has a problem or a goal, and they cannot decide what to do about it until they figure out something they don't know: *A business is losing customers to a competitor but cannot respond until it researches why customers are leaving. A shipping company wants to reduce its insurance costs, so it researches OSHA requirements for federal safety certification. A local volleyball league wants to raise money to build a practice facility, but it cannot approach potential donors until it has research showing that it can cover ongoing costs by renting the facility for other sports.*

The need for this kind of research is greater now than ever. Whenever a business or professional organization takes an action that might affect the value of its stock or the well-being of its employees or customers, it faces legal requirements for "due diligence." That is, it must thoroughly research the likely consequences or be liable if things go wrong. But beyond those legal requirements, that kind of research is now considered standard practice. No responsible professional these days makes a major decision without knowing all they can about it.

Researching Research in the Workplace

Here's a useful way to start thinking about research: Professionals do research because they need the answer to a question in order to accomplish some goal. Let's suppose that you have a goal—to motivate yourself to care enough about your research assignments that you will do good work on them. And to achieve that goal, you need the answer to a question: *Is research really that important in the workplace?*

So your first mini-assignment is to research the answer. Find five people you know with jobs that you might like to have—not your perfect job, but work that you can imagine doing. Ask them about research on their job. Don't just stop with those activities they call research. Ask about any tasks that require them to find out something they didn't know in order to accomplish some goal. Also ask how much those skills matter in their evaluations of their colleagues. Share your results with your classmates.

Why You Should Learn to Do Research Now

Research is at the heart of every college curriculum, and it will show up in your classes in both obvious and hidden forms. Colleges have been this way for centuries, but it's not just tradition that explains why we expect you to learn research.

The first reason is practical: it concerns your economic future more than your current education. You may not yet be a practicing professional who depends on research, but the chances are good that you will be. The research you do now will prepare you for the day when your job depends on your ability to find answers for yourself or to evaluate and use the answers of others. It will also prepare you to *get* that job in the first place: although potential employers care about what you know, the workplace changes so quickly these days that they care more about how prepared you are to find out what you don't yet know.

A second reason has to do with your education, now and for a lifetime of learning. When you understand research, you are better able to avoid the trap of passive learning, where your only choices are to absorb, or not, what some textbook or teacher says. Doing research, you'll discover how the knowledge we all rely on is only as good as the research that supports it. You'll also discover that what you learn from the research of others depends on what questions you ask—and don't ask.

The greatest problem in research today is not finding information—we are awash in it as never before—but finding information we can trust. The

Internet and cable flood us with "facts" about government, the economy, the environment, the products we buy. Some are sound; most are not. Your own research will let you experience the messy reality behind what is so smoothly and confidently presented by experts on the job, in the press, or on TV. As you learn to do research, you'll learn to distinguish unsupported assertions from reliable research reported clearly, accurately, and with appropriate qualification.

Our third reason you might think idealistic. We teachers ask you to do research because it is the most intellectually exciting part of any education. We hope you too will experience the sheer pleasure of solving a research puzzle: research can spark all the excitement of unraveling a mystery. (TV's Adrian Monk is an amazing researcher, as are Sherlock Holmes, Miss Marple, and all the heroes of detective fiction.) We also hope you can experience the self-confidence that comes from discovering something that no one else knows. When knowledge is king and businesses—and countries—are valued on their intellectual capital, the one who knows is a special person. If we can teach you to love the hunt for knowledge, we'll have given you a gift you'll long treasure.

We must be candid, though: doing research carefully and reporting it clearly can be hard work, consisting of many tasks, often competing for your attention at the same time. And no matter how carefully you plan, research follows a crooked path, taking unexpected turns, sometimes up blind alleys, even looping back on itself. As complex as that process is, we will work through it step-by-step so that you can see how its parts work together. When you can manage its parts, you can manage the often intimidating whole and look forward to your next research project with greater confidence.

Our Promise to You

We have based this book on a lifetime—two lifetimes—of research into how experienced researchers do their work, how experienced writers put together effective texts, what readers look for and what they need in a research report, and what a developing writer needs to know to write better and struggle less. Rest assured that what you read here is grounded not in our opinions or preferences but in our best efforts to know what there is to know about doing and reporting research.

We have also based this book on two lifetimes of helping writers learn to writer better, not just beginners but some of the most distinguished and successful professionals. So you can also rest assured that what you read here will be the most practical advice we know how to give. We know what it is to have to get a paper out the door, and we'll respect your need to get your papers done.

We have written this book to inspire some of you to experience not just the work but the joys of research. We have written it to educate most of you about the nature of research and its reporting, so that you can understand the reasons for the advice we give. And we have written it to give all of you our best practical, step-by-step guidance on how to do your best research and write the best paper you can—now and for the rest of your career. We hope that every one of you will go with us as far down each of those roads as you can or will. But we are confident that if you commit to do your part, we'll help you get that paper out the door—done, and done right.

PART I
Writing Your Paper

We know how anxious you may be feeling if you are facing your first big research project. *What should I write about? How do I find information on it? What do I do with it when I find it?* But you can handle any project if you break it down into its parts, then work on them one at a time. In the first part of this book, we show you how to do that.

You may think that some matters we explain are beyond your immediate needs. We know that a five-page paper differs from a PhD dissertation. But both require the same skills and habits of thought that experienced researchers began learning when they were where you are now. In that sense, this book is about your future, about starting to think in a new way—like a researcher.

We have organized this book as though you could create a research paper by progressing steadily through a sequence of steps, from selecting its topic to drafting and revising it. But we have not written the book that way. No researcher, no matter how experienced, ever marches straight through those steps. They move forward a few steps, go back to earlier ones, even head off in an entirely new direction. So while our sequence of chapters looks like a steady path, when you read them you'll be reminded regularly that you can't expect to follow it without a few detours, perhaps even some new starts. We'll even tell you how to check your progress to see if you might need to go back a step or two.

But you can manage that kind of looping, even messy process if you know that behind it is a series of tasks whose order makes sense, and that with a plan based on them, you can work your way toward a successful paper. There are four stages in starting and completing a research project.

- In chapters 2–3, we focus on how to find a topic and then in it a research question whose answer is worth your time and your readers' attention.
- In chapters 4–6, we show you how to find information from sources and how to use them to back up an answer.
- In chapters 7–11, we show you how to plan and draft your report so that you make your best case for your argument.
- In chapters 12–14, we show you how to revise that draft so that your readers will think that you based your answer on sound reasoning and reliable evidence.

Several themes run through those chapters:

- You can't jump into a project or even a part of it blindly. You must plan, then keep in mind the whole process as you take each step.
- A researcher does more than find data on a topic and report it. Your job is to gather *specific* data to answer a *specific* question that *you* want to ask.
- From the first day of your project to its last, you must keep in mind that your report is a conversation with your readers. You have to bring them into that conversation by asking on their behalf the questions that they would ask if they were there in front of you. And then you have to answer them.
- You should try to write every day, not just to take notes on what you read but to clarify what you think of it. You may not use much of this early writing in your final draft, but it prepares you for that scary moment when you have to begin writing it.

At times you may feel overwhelmed by what you read here, especially because we are asking you to think about research and its reporting in ways that you will only need years from now. But we have designed this book so that when you get confused or lost, you can hunker down with our mini-guides and checklists just to get the job done. Then, when you begin to move forward again, you can step back to reconsider the larger issues of the nature of research and the papers we write to report it. Ultimately—probably not today, and maybe not next month or next year, but someday soon enough—you will find that your success on a job or in life will depend on your understanding of that mind-set of a researcher.

How to Use Part 1

In part 1, we lay out all the goals, plans, strategies, steps, models, formulas, and everything else we know that will help you to understand, first of all, the mind-set you need to do research well, then the processes and forms you must master to manage a research project, and finally the specific things you must do to get your paper done. We hope that each of you will engage our book in all three ways. Here's how we suggest you do that:

1. Read all of part 1 to get an overview. Read the introduction and chapter 1 carefully, then the rest as quickly as you can. Slow down when we explain what research is like, how researchers think, what the stages are, and why you need them. Speed up when we cover small details that you won't remember anyway.
2. Before you start a new stage in writing your paper, reread the chapters that cover it—for instance, read chapters 2 and 3 before you pick a research question, chapters 7 and 8 before you outline a draft. Use this reading to create a mental plan for how you will get through that stage.

3. As you work on your paper, look in the relevant chapters for checklists, models, and other guides (printed in blue) that will help you go step-by-step.

If your deadline looms and you cannot squeeze out the time for this big-to-little-picture approach, you can work the other way around: start from the checklists, models, and guides. If you understand what to do looking at them alone, do it. If not, read the surrounding text until you do. We hope you won't be so pressed for time that you have to take this shortcut, but we designed this book so that you can. If you do, go back and read the sections you skipped after you turn in your paper. You'll be glad you did.

Go to www.turabian.org to find supplemental materials related to part 1.

1: What Researchers Do and How They Think about It

Every successful researcher does at least two things in a research report: she raises a question that readers want an answer to, and then she answers it. In this chapter, we show you how to get started by finding or inventing a research question interesting enough for readers to care about and challenging enough that you have to research its answer. Then we show you how to plan your project by mapping out the parts of the argument you will need to support that answer.

1.1   How Experienced Researchers Think about Their Questions

All researchers gather facts: we'll call them *data*. But they use those data in different ways. Some people gather data on a topic just to satisfy their curiosity: for example, there are history buffs who collect *stories about the Battle of the Alamo* because the history of the Alamo is their hobby. In that case, they don't have to care whether others are interested: they can research in whatever way they want and needn't bother to write up what they find.

Most researchers, however, do their research in order to share it—because their colleagues or clients need it, because they think their question and its answer are important to others, or just because they want others to know something interesting. But when researchers share their results, they have to offer more than just random data they happened to dig up on their topic. They look for and report only certain kinds of data—those that they can use to show that they have found a sound, reliable answer to a research question, such as *Why has the Alamo story become a national legend?* In other words, they look for and report data that they can use as evidence to support a claim that answers a question.

The best researchers, however, try to do more than just convince others that their answer is sound. They also show why that answer is worth knowing by showing why their question was worth asking in the first place. In a business setting, researchers usually show why their research helps someone decide what to do:

If we can understand why our customers are moving to the competition, we can know what we have to change to keep them.

But in an academic setting, researchers usually show how the answer to their research question helps others understand some bigger, more important issue:

Historians have long been concerned with how we Americans developed our sense of national identity. If we can figure out why the Alamo story has become a national legend, then we might better understand how regional myths like the Battle of the Alamo have shaped that national identity.

But even if you cannot imagine yourself appealing to historians, you can locate that larger issue in the context of your class:

A major issue in this class has been how we Americans developed our sense of national identity. If we can figure out why the Alamo story has become a national legend, then we might better understand how regional myths like the Battle of the Alamo have shaped that national identity.

You can find out whether your question is a worthy one by describing your project in a sentence like this one:

1. I am working on the topic of stories about the Battle of the Alamo,
    2. because I want to find out why its story became a national legend,
        3. so that I can help my classmates understand how such regional myths have shaped America's sense of a national identity.

In its second and third parts, this sentence takes you beyond a mere topic to state a question *and* its importance to readers.

When you state why your research question is important *to your readers,* you turn it into a research problem. A research problem is simply a question whose answer is needed by specific readers because without it they will suffer a cost. That cost is what transforms a question that is merely interesting to you into one that you expect others to care about.

TQS: How to Identify a Worthy Research Question

You can help yourself think about your project by describing it in a three-step sentence that states your TOPIC + QUESTION + SIGNIFICANCE (or TQS):

TOPIC: I am working on the topic of _____,

    QUESTION: because I want to find out _____,

        SIGNIFICANCE: so that I can help others understand _____.

Don't worry if at first you cannot find a worthy significance for the third step. As you develop your answer, you'll find ways to explain why your question is worth asking.

Note: Like all of the formulas you will find in this book, the TQS formula is intended only to prime your thinking. Use it to plan and test your question, but don't expect to put it in your paper in exactly this form. You will use its information in your introduction, but not the sentence itself (see chapter 13).

That three-step TQS sentence is worth a closer look because the success of your project will depend on your ability to discover or invent a good research question.

1.1.1 Topic: "I am working on the topic of . . ."

Researchers often begin with just a topic, something that sparks their curiosity, such as *the Battle of the Alamo*. But if you stop there, you've got problems. Even a focused topic is a poor guide to your work. You can only mound up notes on the facts you happen to find on your topic. You will have no principled way to decide which facts to look for, which ones to use in your paper, and which to discard. When that happens, students typically run into trouble, in the form of a *data dump*. They dump everything into a report that reads like a grab bag of barely connected facts. Most readers quickly become bored, asking, *Why are you telling me this?* They might read on, but only if they are already interested in the topic. But even readers fascinated with your topic will want to know: *What do these facts add up to?*

1.1.2 Question: ". . . because I want to find out how or why . . ."

Experienced researchers don't start their research until they have not just a topic but a question about it, such as *Why has the regional story of the Alamo become a national legend?*

Researchers know that readers want the facts they read about to add up to something. Specifically, they want those facts to back up some main finding—a claim that adds to their knowledge or understanding. But they will think that claim is worth reading about only if it answers some research question. Without such a question to guide their reading, your readers will struggle to see what, if anything, your research adds up to.

At the same time, you need such a question to guide the research leading up to your paper: without one you will struggle to know what information you need. All you can do is discover everything you can about your topic and hope you can pull it together at the end. But with a research question, you can know what facts to look for and, when you find them, which ones to use in your paper—those facts that are relevant to your question. (As we'll see later, you'll need not only the facts that support your answer but also any ones that might seem to discredit it.)

You may have to do some preliminary reading about your topic to come up with a question, but in every research project, formulating that question is the crucial first step.

1.1.3 Significance/So What: ". . . so that I can help others understand how or why . . ."

Experienced researchers also know, however, that readers won't be interested in just any research question. They want to know why the answer you have found is worth knowing. So once you find a question that you like, expect that readers will ask you a question of their own: *So what?*

You could ask the question *How many cats slept in the Alamo the night before the battle?* but who would care about its answer? All but the most fanatical cat-lovers would want to know: *So what? Why should I care about those cats?* Readers ask *So what?* about all research questions, not just the off-the-wall ones. If you tell readers that you want to research the question *Why has the regional story of the Alamo become a national legend?,* you should expect them to ask in turn: *So what? Why should I care that you can explain that?* Your answer must point them to the significance of its answer: *If we can find that out, we might better understand the bigger issue of how regional stories shape our national identity.* Experienced researchers know that readers care about a question only when its answer might make them say not *So what?* but *That's worth knowing!*

Of course, professional researchers have a big advantage: they already know what issues their readers care about. Students, especially beginners, have less to go on. So don't worry if at first you cannot find some great significance to your research question. Keep hunting for a good *So what?,* but all won't be lost if you don't find one. As long as you find a question in any way relevant to your class, you can always explain its significance in terms of the class (for more on this, see 13.1.3):

. . . so that I can help my classmates understand how such regional myths have shaped America's sense of a unified national identity, which has been an important issue in our study of American diversity.

1.2   Two Kinds of Research Questions

Research questions come in two varieties. One kind of question concerns what we should do to address a tangible problem. We call such questions *practical*. Practical questions are common in the professions, business, and government. The other kind of question concerns what we should think. We call such questions *conceptual*. Conceptual questions are also common in the professions, business, and government, when their answers help us understand what causes a practical problem. But conceptual questions are most common in the academic world. You will need to distinguish the two kinds of research questions because your teachers usually expect you to address conceptual questions rather than practical ones.

1.2.1   Practical Questions: What Should We Do?

The answer to a practical question tells us what to do to change or fix some troublesome or at least improvable situation. You can recognize a practical question by looking at the third step in the TQS formula: that step states both the practical problem and something we should do to change it.

> T: I am working on the topic of A, (*What's interesting about that?*)
>> Q: because I want to find out B, (*So what if you do?*)
>>> S: so that I can help others know **what to do** to fix C.

Suppose, for example, someone asked about your research as an intern in the Dean of Students' office:

T ⎡ Q: *What are you doing for your internship?*

A: As part of our binge-drinking project, I'm researching incoming students' assumptions about how much their colleagues drink.

Q ⎡ Q: *What do you want to know about that?*

A: We know that first-year students assume that college students drink more than they really do, but we don't know whether they develop that false assumption before they arrive on campus or after they begin to hear drinking stories from their upper-class colleagues.

S ⎡ Q: *So what if you know that?*

A: Then our office can know how to give students a more realistic picture in our safe-drinking orientation.

What makes this *practical* research is that you are interested in the question chiefly because you want to use the answer to decide what to do about a troublesome practical problem, in this case binge drinking by students.

1.2.2   Conceptual Questions: What Should We Think?

Academic researchers ask a different kind of question. Its answer doesn't tell us what to do to change the world, but only how to *understand* it better: *How does the irreverent sitcom* The Simpsons *reinforce traditional, conservative values? Why do unwed teen mothers keep their babies? When does a cult become a religion?*

You can recognize a conceptual question because its significance in the third step concerns not what we do but what we understand:

> T: I am working on the topic of A, (*What's interesting about that?*)
>> Q: because I want to find out B, (*So what if you do?*)
>>> S: so that I can help others **understand** how/why/whether C.

Suppose, for example, that you had to ask your teacher's approval for the topic of your research paper:

T
> Q: *What are doing for your paper?*
>
> A: I want to write on the early years of Motown Records.

Q
> Q: *What do you want to know about that?*
>
> A: I want to find out how and why Motown "smoothed out" African American roots music for white audiences.

S
> Q: *So what if you know that? What does that tell us?*
>
> A: If we can explain how Motown was able to appeal to those audiences, we can better understand how the so-called "mainstream" culture was really a composite of ethnic cultures.
>
> Q: *Now that would be interesting.*

1.2.3   The Challenge of Answering So What? for Conceptual Questions

Students can be impatient with conceptual questions because they seem irrelevant to the genuinely serious problems in the "real" world. Many can't even imagine an answer to a *So what?* question like this one: *So what if we don't understand why Shakespeare had Lady Macbeth die offstage?* (No one asks *So what?* of a researcher trying to understand how to cure Alzheimer's.) Even if you share that impatience, do not try to build your project around a major practical problem. You can't expect to solve the world's problems in the classroom. For now, keep in mind that you are just getting started in your career as a researcher and that the modest questions you can answer in a few pages are likely to have modest consequences.

You can also look forward to a day when you can answer conceptual questions relevant to the practical problems that beset us. Before we can solve an important practical problem, we almost always have to do conceptual research to understand its causes and effects. We often use the answer to a conceptual question to solve an unanticipated practical problem, as when the Pentagon recently used historical research on the fall of empires to create a plan for the future of the U.S. military.

Try to be patient if at the start of your project you cannot think of any good answers to *So what?*—even the most experienced researchers sometimes have to find their results before they can say why they are worth knowing. Remember that you'll need *some* answer by the end, and keep your eye out for larger issues as you do your reading. (We'll show you what to look for in chapter 4.) The more often you imagine others asking *So what?* and the more often you practice answering it, even if only to your own satisfaction, the more confident you can be that you can succeed at every researcher's toughest task—convincing others that your work is worth their time.

1.3   How Researchers Think about Their Answers/Arguments

Students are often surprised to realize that what they had thought was the main job of research—looking up information on a topic—is a small part of a successful research project. Before you start looking things up, you have to find a good research question to guide your reading and note taking: what you look for is information that will support and/or test an answer to that question. But once you think you have found an answer, your work has just begun. Readers won't accept that answer just because you believe it: you have to give them good reasons to believe it too. And they won't just take your word that your reasons are good ones: you have to support each reason with reliable evidence. In short, readers expect you to offer a complete and convincing argument that uses the information you have found to explain and support your answer.

1.3.1   Think of Your Readers as Allies, Not Opponents

By *argument,* we do not mean anything like the heated exchanges you see on TV or among your friends, where anything goes because all anyone cares about is winning. Unfortunately, many students imagine all arguments are like that, partly because the loud and angry ones are so memorable but also because the language we use to describe argument makes it sound like combat:

I will *defend my position* from the *attack of my opposition;* then I will *marshal* my most powerful evidence to *counterattack.* I'll *probe for weak spots* in the other position, so that I can *undermine* it and *knock down* its key claims. We will *fire away* at each other until one or the other of us *gives up* and *surrenders,* leaving only the *victor* and the *vanquished.*

Experienced researchers know that they would be foolish to treat readers like enemies to be vanquished. To succeed, a researcher must *enlist readers as allies* who agree to do or think what the researcher claims they should. If you hope to win over your readers, you must adopt a stance that encourages them not to be defensive but receptive, because you treat their views, beliefs, and questions with respect. That does *not* mean telling them only what they already believe or want to hear—after all, your ultimate goal is to change their minds. But you do have to attend closely to what you know (or imagine) your readers already believe, so that you can move them from where they are to where your new claim would lead them.

CAUTION

Don't Pander to Teachers

Many students are rewarded in high school for writing papers that tell teachers what they want to hear by repeating what the teacher has already said. But that can be a grave mistake in college: it bores your teachers, who think it is not enough that you just rehash what's said in class and in the readings. They want to see not only that you know the class material but that you can use that knowledge to think for yourself. If your papers, especially your research papers, merely summarize what you've read or repeat back your teacher's ideas, you will get that dreaded comment: *This does not go far enough.*

When your teacher says that you must *make* an argument to support your answer, don't think of *having* an argument, in which everyone battles for their position and no one changes their minds. Instead, imagine an intense, yet amiable conversation with people who want to find a good answer to your question as much or even more than you do. They don't want to hear about your opinions but about reasoned claims you can support. They want to know what reasons led you to your claim and what evidence makes you think those reasons are true. Because this is a conversation, they'll expect you to consider their point of view and to address any questions or concerns they might have. And they'll expect you to be forthcoming about any gaps in your argument or complications in your evidence. In short, they want you to work *with* them to achieve the best available answer, not for all time but for now.

1.3.2 Think of Your Argument as Answers to Readers' Questions

To create that kind of argument, you will have to answer the questions that any rational person would ask whenever you ask them to do or believe something new. Each answer corresponds to one of the parts of argument.

1.3.2.1 The Core of an Argument: Claim + Reasons + Evidence

Your answers to the first three questions constitute the core of your argument.

1. **Claim:** *What's the answer to your question?* Once you raise your research question, readers naturally want to know the answer. That answer is what you claim and then support.

Although many people think that black musical artists of the 1950s and 1960s were harmed when white performers "covered" black records by creating their own versions to sell to white audiences, I claim that the practice of racial covering actually helped the original artists more than it harmed them.*claim*

2. **Reasons:** *Why should I believe that?* Unless your answer is obvious (in which case, the question was not worth asking), readers will not accept it at face value. They'll want to know why they should accept your claim as true.

Although . . . , I claim that the practice of racial covering actually helped the original artists more than it harmed them*claim* because without covers white teens would not have heard or bought the original recordings,*reason 1* because covers gave white audiences a taste for blues, R&B, and gospel,*reason 2* and because white teens then began to seek out the work of black performers.*reason 3*

3. **Evidence:** *How do you know that?* Even when your reasons seem plausible, responsible readers won't accept them just on your say-so. They expect you to ground each reason in the factual evidence you collect from sources.

Although . . . , I claim that . . .*claim* because. . . .*reasons* My evidence that white teens would not have heard or bought the original recordings is as follows: [sales statistics, information on record distribution and radio play, quotations from performers and producers at the time, etc.].*evidence for reason 1*

1.3.2.2 Acknowledging Readers' Voices

You'll have the basis for a sound argument once you can offer readers a claim that answers your question, reasons to believe that they should accept your claim, and evidence showing that those reasons are true. These three elements make up the core of every argument. But if you offer only the reasons and evidence that you think support your claim, thoughtful readers may feel that you have not dealt with them fairly. They want to know not only what you found that supports your claim, but also what you found that might work against, or at least complicate it—especially if they have views that are different from yours.

So in addition to the reasons and evidence that you pull together to support your claim, you should answer questions that might seem to challenge it:

4. **Acknowledgment and Response:** *But what about this other view?* You cannot expect your readers to think exactly as you do. They will know things you don't, they will believe things you don't, and they may even distrust the kind of argument you want to make. If you adopt a genuinely cooperative stance, then you are obliged to acknowledge and respond to at least some of the questions that arise because of those differences.

I claim that. . . .*claim + reasons + evidence* To be sure, there were many elements of exploitation in racial covering. The white performers, not the black artists, received the money and fame. And many artists of the 1950s never received any of the benefits that came later.*acknowledgment* But covers helped to bring about a situation in which black artists are among our most popular, influential, and wealthy pop musicians.*response*

1.3.2.3   *Explaining Your Logic*

In some cases, researchers make arguments in which they have to explain not only their reasons and evidence, but their principles of reasoning. Suppose, for example, you were visiting your friend Paul in Cajun country. It is a warm July evening, so he invites you to go for a walk on the levee, and then he adds, "You might want to put on long sleeves." This makes no sense, so you ask, "Why?" "Because the sun's going down," he replies. Now you are truly baffled. You understand Paul's claim, and you can see the sun going down. But you just cannot understand why that means you should wear long sleeves on a warm July night. His reason is true, and his evidence is good. But his argument so far fails.

That's when we need a warrant, when readers understand our claim and accept our reason and evidence, but do not see why the reason (the sun going down) supports the claim (you need long sleeves). So now you ask again: "Why does the sun doing down mean that I need long sleeves?" As it happens, Paul has a good answer in the form of a warrant: "Ah," he says. "You don't know about swamp country. When the sun goes down, the mosquitoes come out. If you don't cover up, they will eat you alive."

Now it all makes sense. As an expert in swamp-country living, Paul knew a principle of reasoning that you did not: *When the sun goes down, you should protect your skin from mosquitoes.* Once you learn the principle, you can accept the claim (though you might wonder why anyone would go walking among mosquitoes that want to eat you alive).

A warrant states a principle of reasoning of the form: When this condition is true, we can draw this conclusion. They are used most often when an expert (Paul) makes an argument about something he knows well (swamp-country living) for someone who is not an expert (you). The expert (Paul) needs a warrant if the non-expert (you) understands a claim (put on long sleeves) and accepts the truth of its supporting reason (the sun is going down) but doesn't see how the reason supports the claim. The warrant supplies the missing connection: "When the sun goes down, the mosquitoes come out, and you must protect your skin from bites. So wear long sleeves to protect your arms."

5. **Warrant:** *Why does that evidence support your claim?* When readers see the world in ways that are very different from yours, they may not recognize what general principle of reasoning connects your reasons and your claims. This situation rarely arises when you write a paper for a class, but it might. For example, you would have to supply a warrant if some readers asked, *But why*

does it matter that white teens would not have heard R&B without covers? How does that show that covers helped more than harmed black artists? To which you would have to reply with a general principle:

An artist benefits from any product that expands his audience for future sales, even if he makes no money off the sale of that product._{warrant}

For the most part, only advanced researchers need warrants, most often when experts write for readers who are not experts, when they use a new or controversial research method, or when they address a controversial issue. You probably won't have to explain your logic in a paper for a class, so we will not dwell on this fifth question. But you should know that readers might ask it.

1.3.3 Use the Parts of Argument to Guide Your Research

A research question helps guide your research because it tells you generally what information to look for: whatever is relevant to answering your question. But in the parts of argument you have an even better guide. As you search for and read your sources, remember that you will need information to answer at least four questions that every cooperative argument must address.

Plan Your Research Around the Questions of Argument

Every argument must answer the three questions that define the core of a research argument, and cooperative ones must also answer a fourth.

c ⌈ 1.	*What's the answer to your research question?*	**Claim**
o | 2.	*Why should I believe that?*	**Reasons**
r | 3.	*How do you know that reason is true?*	**Evidence**
e ⌊ 4.	*But have you considered this view?*	**Acknowledgment**
	[or this evidence, complication, objection, etc.]	**& Response**

Create a plan to search for and read sources so that you have good answers to each of these questions:

1. **Claim:** If you begin without a plausible claim that answers your research question, start by reading general treatments of your topic in order to get ideas for possible answers.
2. **Reasons:** Once you have a claim that can serve as an hypothesis, make a list of the reasons why you think that claim is true. If you think of too few plausible reasons, do some more general reading. If you still can't find any, look for another claim.
3. **Evidence:** Once you have a list of reasons, search for specific data that might serve as evidence to support each one. Depending on the kind of reason, that evidence might be statistics, quotations, observations, or

any other facts. If you cannot find evidence for a reason, then you have to replace that reason. If you find evidence that goes against a reason, keep the evidence. You may need to acknowledge it in your paper.

4. **Acknowledgment & Response:** As you read for claims, reasons, and evidence, keep a record of anything that might complicate or contradict your argument. You will need to acknowledge it if you think it might also occur to your readers.

We discuss these steps more fully in chapters 6 and 7.

1.4 How You Can Best Think about Your Project

You have learned a great deal new about writing research papers, and it's only the end of the first chapter. We'll cover this ground again in later chapters, where we'll go step-by-step through the process of planning, researching, drafting, and revising your paper. Don't expect to walk though those steps exactly as we lay them out—research is too messy, with lots of looping back and jumping forward. But if you stay flexible and take it one step at a time, you'll get through the process easily enough.

1.4.1 Focus on Convincing Readers, Not on Filling Pages

For now, we would like you to focus not on the steps but on creating an overall mental picture of research that you will keep in mind as you work. Unfortunately, the two most popular pictures are ones we hope you will avoid. In the first, you think of your project as no more than looking up information. All that matters is the hunt. What comes after is an afterthought:

Q: *How's your project coming?*

A: Good. I dug up lots of information from lots of sources (even including a bunch of print sources from the library). All I have to do is figure out how to organize my notes and then I can just write it all up.

In the second picture, you think of your project as filling up pages. All that matters is mounding up enough information to fill the assigned number of pages:

Q: *How's your project coming?*

A: Good. I have a four-point outline and I've found three pages of stuff on the first two points. All I need is three more pages on the second two points and I'm done.

If you think of your project in these ways, you'll doom yourself to failure.

Although you and your teacher might say that your assignment is to write a research paper, we urge you to think instead in terms of a research project. Writing a research paper is only one step in a complex process in which (1) you find a research question important to you *and* to your readers; (2) you decide what information you need to find based on the question you ask; (3) you use the information you find to select and then test the best answer to your research question; and (4) you finally present that answer and its support in a way that anticipates readers' questions.

As you begin to plan for your project, let these principles be your guide:

- Don't think that your primary task is to collect and organize information from sources (though you will have to do that). **Your task is to ask and answer a research question that interests you and your readers.**
- Don't think that when you write your paper your goal is to fill up a certain number of pages with the information you've found. **Your paper is what you say to your readers, what you use to communicate your question, its answer, and your argument supporting that answer.**
- Most importantly, don't think of research as a solitary endeavor. **Keep your readers with you from start to finish.**

If right from the start you focus on *asking and answering questions,* you'll find it easier to do the things that will produce a successful paper. Focus on finding stuff to fill pages, and you're sure to go wrong.

1.4.2 Picture Yourself in Conversation with Your Readers

As you plan, research, and draft your paper, picture yourself in an imaginary conversation with your readers. Imagine those readers as interested and inquisitive colleagues, even partners, who want an answer as much as you do. You welcome their questions because they help you know what to say and how to say it. If you can do that, your paper will be better. But just as importantly, you'll be preparing yourself for the day when your readers are indeed colleagues who need from you the best answers you and they can find.

Imagine that conversation taking place not in a classroom, but sitting around a table. Your question grabs their attention because they recognize that they'll be worse off if they can't find an answer. You share not just your answer, but all the information you can find that is relevant to deciding whether your answer is a good one. In sharing that information, you try to anticipate their questions. You are candid enough to acknowledge any information that challenges or complicates your answer, and you address objections they might have. Even so, they have many more questions, alternative explanations, and other issues—each of which you consider and address as fairly as you can. In short, you join with your readers in working through the task of finding and testing the best answer you can find. If you think of your project in these terms, you'll make more good decisions and waste less time as you write your paper. You'll also find that in making your work matter to your readers, you make it matter to you as well.

> **WORKING IN GROUPS**
>
> **Find Surrogate Readers**
>
> You can help yourself think of your paper as a conversation with readers if you talk about your work to your family, friends, and classmates. Later we will suggest that you form a writing group for testing your storyboard and draft. But it may not be too early to form an informal group even before you find a question. Recruit three or four classmates who will join you for coffee or lunch just to talk over your earliest ideas. At this point, you don't need suggestions, just a sympathetic ear. You will also learn just from listening: the more *you* experience what your readers will, the easier it will be to imagine them.

1.5   **How to Plan Your Time (No One-Draft Wonders Allowed)**

Have you ever heard the tale of the one-draft wonder? That's the student who starts writing a paper at midnight before the deadline, knocks out one quick yet perfect draft, and then receives the best grade in the class. The one-draft wonder is one of the more enduring school-based urban legends: the two of us hear such tales all the time, but we've never seen the real thing. We couldn't pull it off when we were in school, and we've never taught a student who could do it either—though we have taught too many students who hoped they could fool us with weak drafts that were all too obviously written the midnight before.

You can't hope to write a decent research paper if you begin the night or even the week before it's due. This is confirmed not only by the thousands of students we've known but by studies of successful and unsuccessful writers. This research shows that the most successful writers tend to share some writing habits:

- They start drafting as soon as possible, before they think they have all the evidence they might need.
- They write in regular short periods rather than in marathon bursts that dull their thinking and kill their interest.
- They set a goal to produce a small number of pages every time they write, even if those pages are not very good.
- They report their progress to someone else if possible, or on a chart if not.
- They anticipate that everything will take longer than they think it should.

To make these insights work for you, you'll have to back-plan from your due date to set interim goals with specific deadlines. Start by giving yourself at least one working session to proofread; then set aside time for a final revision—at least two working sessions for a paper under seven pages, twice that for a longer one. Depending on how long your paper is and how quickly you draft, set aside enough time to compete a draft, then add 20 percent. You'll need at least a day before that to review and revise your argument. Next, set aside the time you'll need for finding and reading sources, then add 20 percent. Finally, you'll need a day or two to find and test your research question. Plot these interim deadlines on a calendar, and keep track of your progress as you go. If you need a deadline to motivate you to work, find someone who will get on your case if you miss one of these interim deadlines.

One of the pleasures of a research project is the opportunity to discover something new, at least to you, perhaps to everyone else. It's a *thoughtful* process that requires you to consider and reconsider what you learn, both when you first find it out and again when you pull everything together. That kind of reflection takes time. To get the time you need, you need a plan that lets you start early, progress steadily, and reflect regularly.

2: Finding a Research Question

A research project is a lot more than collecting data. You start it before you log on to the Internet or head for the library, and you continue it long after you have all the data you think you need. In that process, you complete many tasks, but they all aim at just five general goals:

- Find a question worth answering about a topic you care about.
- Find an answer that you can support with good reasons.
- Find reliable evidence to back up your reasons.
- Write a first draft that makes a good case for your answer, explains its significance, and anticipates your readers' questions.
- Revise that draft until readers will think you have been clear, complete, and convincing.

(You might even post those goals over your desk.)

A research project would be easy if you could march straight through those steps. But as we've said, research is looping, messy, and unpredictable. You can manage it with a plan, as long as you are prepared to depart from it. The first step in that plan is one you cannot put off: to find a good research question.

CAUTION

Start with a Question, Not Your Favorite Answer
Students sometimes think that a short cut to a research paper is to argue for something they already believe so strongly that nothing could change their mind. Big mistake. Not only will you lose the benefits of the research experi-

ence, but you'll come to your paper with the wrong frame of mind: to say whatever's necessary to support your position rather than to find out what will help you discover the truth. Even when they are confident that they know what the answer will be, true researchers follow where the facts lead them rather than force the facts to go their way. Plan to answer a question, not defend an opinion.

2.1 Questions and Topics

Most students start a research project without a good question, often without even a topic. That puts them a couple of steps behind most professionals, who start with their research question in mind.

Often researchers start with a question that others in their field already think is worth answering: *Did Native Americans cause the extinction of North American woolly mammoths?* Because it's a familiar question, they also know why their colleagues think it is important. *So what? Well, if we knew why the woolly mammoths disappeared, maybe we could answer a bigger question that puzzles many historical anthropologists: Did early Native Americans live in harmony with nature, as some believe, or did they hunt its largest creatures to extinction? (And if we knew that, then we might also understand . . .)*

Other times researchers start with a question that just pops into their mind with no hint of where it will lead, sometimes about matters so seemingly trivial that only the researcher thinks they're worth answering: *Why does a coffee spill dry up in the form of a ring?* Such a question might lead nowhere, but you can't know that until you see its answer. In fact, the scientist puzzled by coffee rings discovered things about fluids that others in his field thought important—and that paint manufacturers used to improve their products. So who knows where you might go with a silly question like *How many cats slept in the Alamo the night before the battle?* You can't know until you answer it.

> **QUICK TIP**
>
> A researcher's most valuable asset is the ability to be puzzled by seemingly obvious things, like the shape of coffee rings or that the hair on your head keeps growing while body hair doesn't. Cultivate the ability to question the commonplace and you'll never lack for research projects. Questioning the obvious is also the first step in critical thinking, which is a skill much prized in the workplace. But you won't do it well then if you don't start practicing it now.

If your assignment allows it, you too can start with a question that's been eating at you, especially if you can discover something of use to someone you know. One source of questions might be a problem that you or a family member has faced. If your neighborhood is near a chemical plant, research the health risks. If you know someone afflicted with a disease, research any new or experimental treatments. Another source might be a cause to which you are devoted. If you volunteer for Habitat for Humanity, research how well those houses suit their owners ten years after they are completed. A third source might be something you love to do. If you are addicted to fashion and hope to be a designer, research the economic challenges for a start-up design company.

If you begin with only a topic, you should still consult your interests. Is there some mental itch you'd like to scratch? *I've collected Mardi Gras masks for years, but I have no idea where they came from.* You might not know exactly what will puzzle you about the origins of the masks, but your project gives you a chance to find out, to scratch that itch. Even if you must begin with a topic so unfamiliar that you can't imagine what could be puzzling about it, look hard for something that sparks your interest. The more *you* care to have an answer to your research question, the easier it will be to show why your readers should care too, and the longer you can work on finding it before you weary of the search.

How to Use the Rest of This Chapter

If you are reading this chapter before you start your project, to learn how research questions work, read on from here to the end. But if you are using it to develop a question for a project, go to the section designed for your stage in the process:

1. If you already have a promising research question, skip to 2.5 to learn how to test it.
2. If you are working from a text, skip to 2.4 to learn how to find a research question in your response to it.
3. If you have a general topic, skip to 2.3 to learn how to find a question in it.
4. If you are starting from scratch, move on to the next section.

Watch for the blue examples. You will find lots of questions in this chapter. Some are questions you should ask to help yourself find a good research question: those are in regular type. Some are examples of the kind of research questions you might use in your paper: those are in blue. Your goal is to find a question of the sort you find in the blue examples.

2.2 How to Choose a Topic

Most teachers and handbooks tell students that what they must do with a topic is to narrow it. That's not wrong, but it is misleading. What makes your paper work is a focused research question, not how narrow your topic might be. So as you work through this section, keep in mind that at every stage you are looking for a good, focused research question. As soon as one comes to mind, skip to 2.5 to test it. Until you find a question, keep narrowing that topic—a specific topic is a better source of questions than a general one. But remember, it's the question, not the topic, that matters most.

> **QUICK TIP**
>
> **The Value of Surprise and Disagreement**
>
> Keep in mind as you look for a research question that what is surprising or wrong catches our attention most easily. Look for ideas, claims, facts, or anything that makes you think, *Wow, I didn't know that!* or *How can that be true?* Not only will those matters hold your attention longer, but they will make it easier to get the attention of your readers.

2.2.1 How to Work with an Assigned Topic

In most cases, you will be expected to find a research question related to the subject matter of your class, no matter what your plans or interests. Even if you are passionate about military history, you may be hard-pressed to write about it in a class on Buddhism. But you should still look for a topic that might engage you, even if only for a short while.

If your assignment specifies a general topic—for example, *Buddhism and war*—skip to section 2.2.3 to narrow it. But if you are free to choose any topic related to the theme of your class, look for one that interests you in the following places:

· Do any of your personal interests overlap with the class theme?
· Review your books and notes. What has surprised or irritated you?
· Look over any books or chapters that your teacher skipped.
· Skim other books by the authors of your assigned texts, looking for matters related to your class. Did an author write an earlier work that is inconsistent with the assigned text? Did she apply some of the same ideas in a wholly different context?
· Skim a textbook for a more advanced class on the same or a related subject.
· Look through the archive for an online discussion list that covers the subject of your class. What topics have been discussed?

> **CAUTION**
>
> **What Teachers Say and What They Really Mean**
>
> Some teachers walk with you step-by-step through the process of developing a research question, so that you can't miss finding a good one. Other teachers will give you just a written assignment sheet and expect you to find a

question on your own. If so, you'll have to learn to read between the lines of your assignment.

When experienced researchers like your teachers talk to one another, they use a shorthand that can mislead those with less experience. You'll know that your teacher is using that shorthand in your assignment sheet if you see phrases like these:

explore X	*discuss X*	*analyze X*
explain X	*critique X*	*investigate X*
compare X with Y		*discuss X in light of Y*

In each case, your assignment will really be something more like this:

Find an issue in X that raises a question about a specific aspect of X, whose answer will help us understand some larger theme, feature, or quality of X.

In using the shorthand, your teacher is not trying to fool you. She's just assuming that you already understand what she means. If you keep our advice in mind, then in fact you will.

2.2.2 How to Find a Topic Based on Your Personal Interests

If you can pick any topic, look for things that surprise, irritate, or otherwise interest you.

- What do you love to think about—sailing, the blues, finches, old comic books? The less common, the better. Investigate something about it you don't know: its origins, technology, place in another culture, and so on.
- What would you like to know more about? A place? A person? A time? An object? An idea? A process?
- Is there an important problem you can't solve now, but you can learn more about? Would you like to know more about twelve-step programs? About affordable green housing? About the health risks of gluten-heavy diets?

Look in these places for things that spark your curiosity:

- Wander through a museum with a special collection—cars, dinosaurs, photography. If you can't go in person, browse a "virtual museum" on the Internet. Stop when something catches your eye.
- Wander through a shopping mall or store, asking yourself, *How do they make that?* or *I wonder who thought up that product?*
- Browse a large magazine rack. Look for trade magazines or those that cater to specialized interests. Investigate what catches your eye.
- Use a search engine to find websites about something people collect. (Narrow the search to exclude dot-com sites.) You'll get hundreds of hits, so look only at the ones that surprise you.

You might find a topic in your disagreements with others:

- Is there an issue you have debated with others, then found that you couldn't back up your views with good reasons and evidence?
- Is there a common belief that you suspect is simplistic or just wrong? Do research to make a case against it.
- Tune in to talk radio or interview programs on TV until you hear a claim you disagree with. Can you make a case to refute it?

You might also find a topic if you think about your future:

- What courses might you take later? Find a textbook, and skim its study questions.
- If you have a dream job, what kind of research report might help you get it? Employers often ask for samples of an applicant's work.

Keep in mind that you may be living with your topic for a long time, so be sure it interests you enough to get you through the inevitable rocky stretches.

2.2.3   Make Your Topic Manageable

If you pick a topic whose name sounds like an encyclopedia entry—*bridges, birds, masks*—you'll find so many sources that you could spend years reading them. You have to carve out of your topic a manageable piece. You can start by limiting it: What is it about, say, masks that made you choose them? Think about your topic in a special context that you know something about, then add words and phrases that name what's special about that context:

masks
    masks in religious ceremonies
        Hopi masks *as symbols* in religious ceremonies
            Hopi *mudhead* masks as symbols *of sky spirits in fertility* ceremonies

You might not be able to focus your topic until after you've read something about it. That takes time, so start early. Begin with a general encyclopedia like the *Encyclopaedia Britannica* or even *Wikipedia* (but see the caution, below). Since you are just looking to prime your thinking, you can search the Internet for ideas without too much concern for the reliability of what you find (which, however, will be crucial later if you want to use a source as evidence). Your goal here is to put your topic into a context of what others think is important about it.

> **CAUTION**
>
> **Watch Out for Wikipedia**
> When you need information quickly, *Wikipedia* can be a godsend. You can access it from any browser, and studies show that it is generally reliable. But it

is usually incomplete, and it does have errors, sometimes outrageous ones. As a result, many teachers ban its use as a source. If you have easy access to an established encyclopedia such as *Britannica,* use it. Otherwise, feel free to use *Wikipedia* for ideas or citations to pursue. But do not use it for information you must cite. When you access a *Wikipedia* article, check out its "Discussion" tab, which will help you decide how much confidence to place in that article.

2.3 Question Your Topic

This is a crucial step. Once you have a topic, question it. Make a list of all the questions that you can imagine answering.

2.3.1 Ask Your Own Questions

Here are some questions you can ask for yourself. The categories are loose and overlap, so don't worry about keeping them straight.

1. Start by asking how your topic fits into larger contexts: a larger history, a larger system, or a category that includes things like it.

   • How does your topic fit into a larger history?

   What came before masks? How did masks come into being? What changes have they caused in their social setting? Why have masks become a part of Halloween? Have masks helped make Halloween the biggest American holiday after Christmas?

   • How does your topic work as a part of a larger system?

   How do masks reflect the values of specific societies and cultures? What roles do masks play in Hopi dances? In scary movies? In masquerade parties? For what purposes are masks used other than disguise? How has the booming market for kachina masks influenced traditional designs?

   • How does your topic compare to and contrast with other things like it?

   How are masks like or unlike other things that cover the face—masks to prevent disease, welders' masks, hockey masks, snorkeling masks? How are masks and cosmetic surgery alike? Is face-painting at sports events a kind of mask?

2. Next, ask questions about the parts of your topic.

   • How do the parts of your topic work together as a system?

   What parts of a mask are most significant in Hopi ceremonies? Why? Why do some masks cover only the eyes? Why do so few Halloween masks cover just the bottom half of the face?

- How many different categories of your topic are there?

  What are the different kinds of Halloween masks? What are the different qualities of Halloween masks? What are the different functions of Halloween masks?

3. Next, set your imagination loose with speculative questions.

   - What's *not* true about your topic?

     Why are masks common in African religions but not in Western ones? Why don't hunters in camouflage wear masks? Why don't Catholics wear masks when they go to confession?

   - Ask *What if?* questions:

     What if no one ever wore masks except for safety reasons? What if everyone wore masks in public? What if movies and TV were like Greek plays and all the actors wore masks? What if it were customary to wear masks on blind dates?

4. Finally, turn positive questions into a negative ones:

   Why have masks not become a part of Christmas? How do Native American masks not differ from those in Africa? What parts of masks are typically not significant in religious ceremonies?

2.3.2 Borrow Questions

Researchers often study questions first raised by others. Unless your teacher specifically says you must devise your own question, you too are free to find your question wherever you can. If you are concerned about plagiarism, you can cite the source of your question, but you do not have to.

Some questions you can find online:

- Find a web discussion list on your topic, then "lurk," just reading for the kinds of questions those on the list raise. If you can't find a list, ask a teacher or visit the websites of professional organizations. Look for questions that also interest you.
- Look for study guides related to your topic. You can find them both in textbooks and online. Many questions will be unsuitable because they ask for a rehash, but some will be thought-provoking.
- Find online syllabi for classes on topics like yours. Some of them will list proposed questions for papers.

You can also find questions in your classroom. Listen for issues that are left unresolved in discussions, matters on which a classmate seems confused or mistaken, things that you cannot accept. All of these can be turned into potential research questions.

2.4   **How to Find a Topic and Question in a Source**

You may need to find your topic and question in relation to something you read, either because your teacher assigned a text or because you have found a writer or a work that interests you. In that case, look for surprises, puzzles, or disagreements. Or you can also look for ways to make the text itself your guide.

2.4.1   **Look for Creative Disagreements**

Nothing motivates us to argue more than disagreement, and our quarrels with a source often generate some of our best ideas. But your readers won't like disagreement for its own sake, and you don't want them to think you are merely disagreeable. But they will, if you set out only to show that a source is wrong, wrong, wrong. So look for *creative* disagreements, the kind that lead you to think hard not just about what your source says, but also about what you think in response. You'll know you've found a creative disagreement when you show not just that a source is wrong but that something else is right.

USEFUL FORMULA

Smith claims . . . , but I will show . . .

When you find a creative disagreement, you state your research question in terms of the difference between what a source says (in the first blank) and what you will show (in the second):

Smith claims that _____ is true, but I will show that _____ is really the case.

(In all of these examples, our generic name for the source will be *Smith*.)

Here are a few of the many ways you can create a research question based on your disagreements with a source, grouped by the kind of disagreement:

Kind

1. Smith claims that _____ belongs in category A, but I will show that it really belongs in category B.

    Smith claims that fringe religious groups are "cults" because of their strange beliefs, but I will show that those beliefs are no different in kind from standard religions.

2. Smith claims that _____ is normal/good/significant/useful/moral/ etc., but I will show that it is really _[something else]_ .

    Smith claims that organized religion does more harm than good, but I will show that it is the misuse of religion that does the harm, not religion itself.

(You can reverse all of the forms in this list: Smith claims that a religion is not a cult, but I will show that its beliefs are too strange to count as religious.)

Part-Whole

3. Smith claims that __[whole]__ always has __[part]__ as one of its defining features/components/qualities, but I will show that __[part]__ is not essential.

    Smith claims that competition is the essence of sport, but I will show that, even by her standards, competition is only incidental to the way most people actually play sports.

Change

4. Smith claims that _____ is changing in a certain way, but I will show that it is really the same as it was.

    Smith claims that the Internet will kill off newspapers, but I will show that newspapers will find ways to survive because people still want what only newspapers can offer.

5. Smith claims that _____ is changing in a certain way, but I will show that it is really changing in a different way.

    Smith claims that individualized marketing tools will let consumers get the products they want and need, but I will show that those tools will really let companies manipulate their customers more than ever.

6. Smith claims that _____ is a stage/process in the development of _____, but I will show that it not.

    Smith claims that alcoholics must hit rock bottom before they can commit to change, but I will show that new early intervention programs can save people before they bottom out.

Cause and Effect

7. Smith claims that _____ causes _____, but I will show that it really causes _____.

    Smith claims that persistent poverty causes crime, but I will show that it really causes despair, which sometimes leads to crime and sometimes does not.

8. Smith claims that _____ is caused by _____, but I will show that it is really caused by _____.

    Smith claims that the collapse of the banking system was caused by greed and a lack of government oversight, but I will show that the real cause was that financial instruments became so complicated that no one could evaluate their risks.

9. Smith claims that _____ is sufficient to cause _____, but I will show that _____ is also necessary.

Smith claims that big-time athletics programs always debase the educational mission of a college, but I will show that athletics alone is not enough: there also have to be alumni and other stakeholders who are more passionate about success on the field than in the classroom.

2.4.2 Build on Agreement

If you find a source whose problem you care about and whose argument you find convincing, you can't create a paper out of that agreement alone. "Me too" is not a very interesting claim. But you may be able to build on that agreement by using the argument in your source as a model for a paper on a different, but closely related problem.

> **USEFUL FORMULA**
>
> **Smith claims . . . about this, and I will show . . . about that.**
> When you build on agreement, you apply the problem and answer of a source to a different object of study. You state your research question in terms of how you can show that what Smith has shown to be true about one thing is also true (or not) about another:
>
> Smith claims that _____ is true in the case of _____, and I will show that it is/is not true in the case of _____.

In one typical case, you replay the research of a source on a new subject. Suppose Sue reads an article about how med students learn and it interests her because she is premed. The article makes the following claim:

Medical students learn physiological processes better when they are explained with many analogies rather than by just one.

This result is interesting because it surprises her: Wouldn't it be confusing to get many different explanations rather than one good one? So she wonders, Could this be true of all professional students? And with that she has her research question. She starts with the general pattern:

S. claims that _[many analogies are better than one]_ is true for _[med students]_, and I will show that it is also true for _[engineers]_.

Then she adds her own details:

In his study of medical students, Spiro shows that complex processes are learned better when they are explained with many analogies rather than just one. In my paper, I will show that the same principle of learning applies to engineering students.

Another typical case is when you read an essay that analyzes a creative work in a way that you find convincing, so you apply it to a different work. Suppose John is a gamer who finds an interesting article arguing that the computer game Age of Empires II has racist tendencies in the way it defines its characters. John is persuaded by that analysis, so he uses it as model for his paper analyzing other computer games:

S. claims that __*[racist characterization]*__ is true for __*[Age of Empires II]*__, but I will show that it is not true for __*[three other computer games]*__.

In his study of Age of Empires II, Golumbia shows that there are elements of racism in the depiction of the characters. In my paper, I will show that there are several popular games that do not exhibit the same tendency to harmful stereotypes.

This approach involves lots of borrowing, but as long as you fully acknowledge the source, you are in no danger of plagiarism. Your paper may be less original than if you had thought up the problem yourself, but that is rarely a problem for beginners. In fact, professionals create research questions in this way all the time.

2.4.3   Look for Surprises

When you work from agreement or disagreement, you build on the *argument* of your source text. But you can't do that if you are working from a text that does not make an argument or if what interests you is not its argument but how it is put together. In that case, rather than ask whether you agree with the text, look for what seems puzzling, confusing, out of place, or otherwise a surprise.

When you look for surprises, try the three-step approach we call E-S-P:

E: When I first read this text, I **expected** to find _____.

S: So I was **surprised** when instead I found _____.

P: I have a **problem** because my old understanding of this text/author/ argument makes sense only with __*[what you expected]*__, not with __*[what you found]*__.

This kind of problem gives you four ways to create an argument:

• Figure out how you have to change your understanding of the text:

At first it made sense to understand the text __*[the way you did]*__, but I will show why we should really understand it in a different way.

- Figure out how and why you were wrong to expect what you did:

  At first it made sense to expect the text to do ___[what you expected]___, but I will show why that is based on a mistaken understanding of the text.

- Figure out how and why what you found actually fits in:

  When the text did not do ___[what you expected]___, I first thought that I was wrong to expect it. But I will show that ___[what you expected]___ would have fit perfectly.

- Show that the text would have been better, or at least more consistent, if the author had done what you expected rather than what you found:

  At first it seemed surprising that the text did not do ___[what you expected]___, but I will show that it would have been better if it had.

Among the advantages of this approach is that it gives you an easy way to create a context that shows why your question is significant: you can use what you expected to set up a contrast that defines your question. Here is a compressed version (to learn how to expand it, see 13.1):

In view of the position Gonzalez takes on amnesty, education, and other issues concerning illegal immigrants, it would be natural to expect that he would favor, or at least not oppose, English-only legislation. But in fact, his fifth chapter not only criticizes English-only movements but makes a strong case for a multilingual society. In this paper, I will show . . .

> **WORKING IN GROUPS**
>
> **Bounce Ideas Off Friends Rather Than Sources**
> You can use your classmates for all of the above strategies for finding questions in sources. Ask your writing group, or friends if you don't yet have a group, for their ideas about your topic. They may have ideas that are interesting but in your view wrong, that are in your view right but not properly developed, or that just plain surprise you. If so, plug their ideas into the appropriate formula and you have a candidate for a worthy research question.

2.5 Evaluate Your Questions

Finally, evaluate your questions and scrap those unlikely to yield interesting answers. What follows are some signs of a question you can't use.

You don't have a good question if no one would disagree with your answer: proving it is pointless.

1. You can answer the question too easily.

   - You can just look it up: *What masks are used in Navajo dances?*
   - You can just quote a source: *What does Fisher say about masks and fears?*

2. No one could plausibly *disprove* the answer, because it seems self-evident. *How important are masks in Hopi rituals?* The answer is obvious: *Very.*

   You cannot make a good argument if you cannot identify the best evidence for it.

3. You can't find factual evidence to support the answer.

   - No relevant facts exist: *Are Mayan masks modeled on space aliens?*
   - It's a matter of taste: *Are Balinese or Mayan masks more beautiful?*

4. You would find so many sources that you cannot look at most of them: *How are masks made?* (This usually results from a question that's too broad).

> **QUICK TIP**
> Don't reject a question because you think someone must already have asked it. Most interesting questions have more than one good answer. Don't reject a question because you think your teacher already knows the answer. You should target your paper not at an expert like your teacher but at someone whose knowledge is more like yours.

The crucial point is to find a question that *you* really want to answer. Too many students, even advanced ones, think that education means memorizing the right answers to questions someone else has asked and answered. It is not. Among your most important goals for your education should be to learn to ask your own questions and find your own answers.

3: Planning for an Answer

3.1   Propose Some Working Answers

Before you get far into your project, try one more preliminary step. It's one that many beginners resist but that experienced researchers rely on, so start practicing it now. As soon as you have a question, imagine some plausible answers, no matter how sketchy or speculative. At this stage, don't worry whether they're right. That comes later.

For example, suppose you ask, *Why do some religions use masks in ceremonies while others don't?* You might speculate:

- Maybe cultures with many spirits need masks to distinguish them.
- Maybe masks are common in cultures that mix religion and medicine.
- Maybe religions originating in the Middle East were influenced by the Jewish prohibition against idolatry.

You can look for evidence with only a question to guide you, if you stay on the alert for those data that suggest an answer. But it is more useful to research guided by possible answers. You will then see more readily which data might support (or contradict) a possible answer, helping you focus your reading even more.

> **QUICK TIP**
>
> **Write, Don't Just Think**
> Even early in your project, write out your answers as fully as you can. It is easy to think that you have a clear idea when you don't. Putting a foggy idea into words is the best way to clarify it, or to discover that you can't.

3.1.1   Decide on a Working Hypothesis

If one answer seems most promising, call it your *working hypothesis*. Even the most tentative working hypothesis helps you to think ahead, especially about the *kind* of evidence that you'll need to support it. For example, will you need numbers? Quotations? Observations? Images? Historical facts? If you can imagine the kind of evidence you'll need before you start looking for it, you'll recognize the data you need when you see them.

Some new researchers are afraid to consider *any* working hypothesis early in their project, because they fear it might bias their thinking. There is a risk, if that hypothesis blinds you to a better idea or keeps you from giving it up when the evidence says you should. As in all relationships, don't fall too hard for your first hypothesis: the more you like it, the less easily you'll see its flaws. Even so, it's better to start with a flawed hypothesis than with none at all.

If you can't imagine any working hypothesis, consider changing your question. That might cost time in the short run, but it may save you from a failed project. Under no circumstances put off thinking about a working hypothesis until you begin drafting your report or, worse, until you've almost finished it. Drafting and revising can be acts of discovery, and as you develop your report, you may discover a better answer to your question. Just don't wait until the last page to make that discovery.

3.1.2   If You Can't Find an Answer, Argue for Your Question

We have focused on answering questions so much that you might think that your project fails if you can't answer yours. In fact, many important researchers have argued that a question no one has asked should be, even though the researcher can't answer it. You can write a good paper explaining why your question is important and what it would take to find a good answer.

3.2   Build a Storyboard to Plan and Guide Your Work

For a two- or three-page paper, you might not need much of a plan—a sketch of an outline might do. But for a longer project, you'll need more. The first plan that comes to mind is usually a formal outline, with its *I*'s and *II*'s and *A*'s and *B*'s and so on. An outline is better than no plan, but the problem with an outline is that it can force you to lock down your paper before you've done your best thinking. So if your teacher requires an outline, be ready to change it at the first sign that you can do better.

Many researchers, especially those outside the academic world, plan long reports on what is called a *storyboard*. A storyboard is like an outline broken into pieces and spread over several pages, with lots of space for adding data and ideas as you go. Storyboards are more flexible than outlines. You can leave storyboard pages unfinished until you are ready to fill them, and you can move pages around without reprinting every time you try out a new organization. Storyboards also help you think about organization. You can spread pages across a wall, group related pages, and put minor sections below major ones to create a "picture" of your project that shows at a glance the design of the whole and your progress through it.

3.2.1 State Your Question and Working Hypotheses

To start a storyboard, write at the top of its first page your question and work-ing hypothesis as exactly as you can. At the bottom, add alternative answers so that you can see more clearly the limits and strengths of your favored one. Add new hypotheses as you think of them, and cross off those you prove wrong. But save them all, because you might be able to use a rejected one in your introduction (see *I used to think . . . , but . . .* in 7.2.2).

3.2.2 State Your Reasons

Imagine explaining your project to a friend. You say, *I want to show that Alamo stories helped develop a unique Texan identity,* and your friend asks, *Why do you think so?* Your reasons are the sentences that back up your answer: *Well, first, the stories distorted facts to emphasize what became central to Texan identity. Sec-ond, the stories were first used to show that Texas (and the Wild West) was a new kind of frontier. Third, . . .* and so on. List each of the reasons that might support your hypothesis at the top of a page, one reason per page.

If you have only one or two reasons, you'll probably need more. Make your best guess about possible reasons, and put them at the tops of separate pages: *Reason 3: Something about Alamo stories making Texans feel special??* If you know only *how* you want a reason to support your answer, state that: *Reason 4: Something about Alamo stories being more than just myth.* Each reason, of course, needs support, so for each reason, ask: *Why do I think that? What evidence will I need to prove it?* That will help you focus your search for evidence.

If you're new to your topic or early in your project, *all* of your reasons may be only educated guesses that you will have to change as you learn more. In fact, if you don't change any of your reasons, you might not be self-critical enough. But a list of reasons, no matter how speculative, is the best frame-work to guide your research and focus your thinking, and certainly better than no reasons at all.

QUICK TIP

Try Out Several Orders

When you plan a first draft, you will have to decide what is the best order for its parts, so you might as well try to find a good one now. Lay out your story-board pages on a table or tape them to a wall. Then step back and look at their order. Can you see a logic in that order? Try out different ones—chronology, cause and effect, relative importance, complexity, length, and so on. (For more principles of order, see 7.2.5.) Don't be afraid to play around with this story-board: it's not your final plan, just a way to guide your thinking, plan your research, and organize what you find.

3.2.3   **Sketch in the Kind of Evidence You Should Look For**

Every field likes to see its own kinds of evidence. Psychologists, economists, and sociologists look for numbers. Literary scholars want quotations. Field biologists like to see observations, pictures, and diagrams. So for each reason, sketch the *kind* of evidence that you think you'll need to support it.

Although you may be used to finding all of your evidence in the form of quotations from secondary sources, focus here on *primary* evidence from primary sources (see 4.1.1). Don't read *about* the Gettysburg Address; get a copy. And don't neglect quantitative data. You have more access to good data than ever before, and it is not acceptable to offer as evidence your mere observation that more women are attending college when with one quick search you can find U.S. census data showing that from 1994 to 2004 the number of women with a college degree increased by 7 percent.

If you can't imagine the kind of evidence you'll need, leave that part of the page blank.

WORKING IN GROUPS

Tell and Retell Your Elevator Story

As soon as you have a working hypothesis and a few reasons, create an elevator story. Imagine that you step in an elevator and find your teacher, who asks, "So, how's the paper going? What do you expect to say?" You have only a couple of floors to sum up where you are. Early on, you can use this plan:

I am working on the problem of [*state your question*].

I think I can show that [*state your hypothesis*] because [*state your reasons*].

My best evidence is [*summarize your evidence*].

If you have a writing group, have everyone tell their elevator story at the start of every meeting. If not, tell yours to anyone who will listen—even your dog will do. As you learn more and your argument develops, refine your elevator story and tell it again. The more often you encapsulate your argument in an elevator story, the sooner your paper will come together.

4: Finding Useful Sources

You are ready for the main thrust of your research only after you have at least a research question and a tentative guess at an answer. Better would be a storyboard with an answer you trust enough to be a working hypothesis and a few supporting reasons. With that, you are prepared to look for data to back up your reasons and test your answer. In this chapter, we show you how to locate sources that will provide those data; in the next, we show you how to work with them. But don't think that those are separate steps: first you find all your sources, and then you read them and take notes. Once you find one good source, it will lead you to others. As you fill your storyboard with notes, you'll think of new questions that will send you looking for new sources. So while we discuss finding and using sources as two steps, you'll more often do them together.

Plan to do your reading in three phases. First, read just to learn enough to know what to look for. This phase won't be very systematic; for most of you, it will depend on what online search engines turn up. Second, read to get an overview of your topic and question. This reading will be mostly in reference works like encyclopedias. Third, search out the specific sources that you will use in developing your argument. For this phase, you'll need a careful plan.

4.1   Knowing What Kinds of Sources You Need

The first thought of beginning researchers is often not *What am I looking for?* but *Where do I look?* And what they mean is *Which websites should I check?* So they fire up a search engine and get started. But that only makes sense if you believe that all you have to do is find information to fill pages—which is, of course, the wrong picture of research. It's better to think that your goal is to find just that factual information that you can use as evidence to support your reasons, which support your claim, which in turn answers a research question. If that's what you are doing, then you have to start not with the *where* but the *what*.

In fact, one of the most common complaints about new researchers is that they offer up as evidence the first (and only) bit of relevant data they find. They assume that all evidence is the same, no matter its source, and that one bit of evidence is enough. But every researcher—including students—is expected to consider not only relevant evidence, but the *best available* evidence, and in some cases *all* the available evidence. But to know what evidence you need, you must first know what counts as "available evidence"—which has two factors.

1. You need the appropriate *kind* of evidence: *primary, secondary,* or *tertiary.*

    Think of the distinction in terms of how far you are from the first observation of the facts themselves. Primary sources offer firsthand evidence, reported by whoever first produced or collected the data. Secondary sources offer secondhand reports of what someone else reported in a primary source. Tertiary sources offer thirdhand reports of what others reported in secondary reports. (These aren't sharply defined categories, but they do characterize how researchers think about sources.)

    In general, you are expected to get as close as you can to primary sources. Academic researchers, who have long deadlines, must use *only* primary sources unless a primary source is lost or completely unavailable. In business, where deadlines are often short, researchers are expected to use primary sources whenever they can and only the most reliable of secondary sources if they must.

2. You need the appropriate *amount* of evidence.

    Academic researchers are expected to consider all the evidence that might be relevant to their claim—not just one letter in which Jefferson offers his opinion of Washington's character but *all* the available letters in which he even mentions him. Business researchers are expected to consider all the evidence that might change their claim significantly—interviews not just with one customer but with several of the most important ones.

    Students, however, can't be held to the same standards as professionals. Students don't have as much time or resources for gathering data, and few students have ready access to a top-quality library. So find out your teacher's ground rules for evidence before you start. You, too, should get as close to the primary evidence as you can, but ask what you can do when primary evidence is hard to obtain. On which matters must you use primary evidence? When can you substitute secondhand reports from secondary sources? Will a tertiary source be acceptable if its author is a respected scholar?

Remember that evidence is not inert stuff you pour into your paper. It is part of the act of explaining to readers why they should accept your claim. Plan your search to find the kind and amount of evidence you will need to convince amiable but skeptical readers.

4.1.1 Consult Primary Sources for Evidence

In fields such as literary studies, the arts, and history, primary sources are original works: diaries, letters, manuscripts, images, films, film scripts, recordings, musical scores, and so on. They provide data in the form of words, images, and sounds that you use as evidence to support your reasons. In these fields, your teachers will usually expect you to work with primary sources. If, for example, you were writing on Alamo stories, you'd look for documents written at the time—letters, diaries, eyewitness reports, and so on.

In fields such as economics, psychology, sociology, and so on, most researchers collect their data through observation and experiment. The primary sources are the publications that first report those data, ranging from academic journals to government and commercial databases. You can find journal articles in your library's online catalog, but don't ignore databases, which you can access through search engines like Google's "U.S. Government Search" or Wolfram Alpha. If, for example, you want to support a claim about schools with what you think is the "fact" that dropout rates are higher in city schools than in suburban ones, a quick search would yield the actual numbers, which careful readers would expect you to cite.

4.1.2 Read Secondary Sources to Learn about Your Topic

Secondary sources are scholarly books and articles written by and for other researchers. They use data from primary sources as evidence to support a claim about them. A report analyzing Alamo stories, for example, would be a secondary source. Secondary sources also include specialized encyclopedias and dictionaries that offer essays written by scholars in a field. These sources are usually available only in college and university libraries.

You can use secondary sources in four ways:

1. To substitute for unavailable primary sources.

Secondary sources report data they found in primary sources. For example, a book on global warming will reproduce climate data from primary sources. To use those data, an advanced researcher would be required to find the primary source. If you can obtain the primary source easily, then you too should use it. If you cannot, your teacher will probably allow you to report the data from a secondary source. Be sure to ask.

CAUTION

Always Cite the Source You Consult

Some students think that when they use data reported in a secondary source they should cite the original, primary source. But they are only half right. If you cite just the primary source, you imply that you consulted that source yourself. If you cite just the secondary source, you imply that it is the ultimate source of your data. Both mislead readers. Instead, you should cite *both* sources. For example, if you use a secondary source written by Anderson for primary data in an article by Wong, your citation would look like this:

(Wong 1966, p. 45; quoted in Anderson 2005, p. 19)

---

2. To learn what others have written about your topic.

   Secondary sources are the best way to learn what other researchers have said about your topic. By studying their arguments, you can add to your argument in two ways:

   - You can learn the kinds of questions experts in the field think are important, not only from their research question but from any additional questions they mention at the end of articles. You may be able to model your question on theirs or even to use a question they mention but do not address.
   - You can learn the standard views accepted by most people in the field. These can be useful for setting the context of your argument and for positions you can question.

3. To find models for your own writing and argument.

   Use secondary sources to find out not just *what* others have written about your topic, but *how* they've written about it. You can then model your way of writing on theirs. If most of your sources use headings, charts, and lots of bullet points, then you might consider doing the same; if your sources never use them, you probably shouldn't. Notice things like the language (technical or ordinary?), paragraphs (long or short?), and how they use other sources (quotation or paraphrase?). Pay special attention to the kinds of evidence most of them use and the kinds of evidence they rarely or never use.

   You can also use a secondary source as a model for your argument. For a paper on Alamo stories, you might find out how a source treats stories about

Custer's Last Stand. Is its approach psychological, historical, political? Where does it find evidence? You cannot reuse its particular reasons or evidence, but you might support your answer with the same *kinds* of data and reasoning, perhaps even following the same organization. So if you come across a source that's not right on your topic but treats one like it, skim it to see what you can learn about *how* to argue your case. (You don't have to cite that source if you use only its logic, but you may cite it to give your own more authority.)

QUICK TIP

You may find secondary sources hard to read, because they are intended for advanced researchers. They assume a lot of background knowledge, and many aren't clearly written in the first place. If you're working on a topic new to you, don't start with secondary sources. Begin with an overview in a specialized encyclopedia or reliable tertiary source; then use what you learn there to tackle the secondary sources.

---

4. To find opposing points of view.

Your paper will be complete only when you imagine and respond to your readers' predictable questions and disagreements. You can find those views in secondary sources. What alternatives to your ideas do they offer? What evidence do they cite that you must acknowledge? Don't think that you weaken your case if you mention ideas contradicting your own. The truth is actually the opposite: When you acknowledge views that contradict yours, you show readers that you not only know and have considered those views but can respond to them (see 6.4).

More important, you can use those views to improve your own. You cannot understand what you think until you know why a rational person might think differently. So as you search for sources, look hard for those that support your views, but also be alert for those that contradict them.

4.1.3 Read Tertiary Sources for Introductory Overviews

Tertiary sources are based on secondary sources, usually written for non-specialists. These include general encyclopedias and dictionaries, as well as newspapers and magazines like *Time* and the *Atlantic Monthly* and commercial books written for a general audience. Well-edited general encyclopedias can give you a quick overview of many topics.

Be cautious about using data you find in magazine and newspaper articles and especially cautious about tertiary sources on the web. Some describe the research in secondary sources reliably, but most oversimplify or, worse, misreport it.

4.2 **Record Citation Information Fully and Accurately**

Your readers will trust your report only if they trust your evidence, and they won't trust your evidence if you don't cite your sources fully, accurately, and appropriately.

We have to be candid: Citations are the most boring and nitpicky part of reporting research. It's the one task that no one enjoys. But it is nevertheless important. It helps readers understand your work by seeing whose work you have relied upon. It helps readers find your sources (just as you will use the citations in your sources to find more sources you can use). And it helps readers decide whether you are a careful researcher whose work they can trust.

So we urge you to be doggedly systematic in creating your citations; if you get the information down right the first time, you won't have to go back to do it again.

4.2.1 **Determine Your Citation Style**

Most fields require a specific citation style. You are likely to use one of the three styles that are described in part 2:

- Chicago style (also known as Turabian style), from the University of Chicago Press. This style is widely used in the humanities and qualitative social sciences.
- MLA style, from the Modern Language Association. This style is widely used in literary studies.
- APA style, from the American Psychological Association. This style is widely used in the quantitative social sciences.

If you are uncertain which style to use, consult your instructor. Before compiling your list of sources, read the general introduction to citations in chapter 17.

4.2.2 **Record Bibliographic Data**

You don't need to memorize the details of citation formats, but you do need to know what information to save. Copy this checklist or use it to create a template for recording the data as you go.

For books, record	For articles, record
☐ author(s)	☐ author(s)
☐ title (including subtitle)	☐ title (including subtitle)
☐ title of series (if any)	☐ title of journal, magazine, etc.
☐ edition or volume number (if any)	☐ volume and issue number
☐ city and publisher	☐ database (if any)
☐ year published	☐ date published
☐ title and pages for chapter (if relevant)	☐ pages for article

For some online sources, the information you need is less predictable. Record as much of the above as applies, along with anything else that might help readers locate the source. You will also need at least these:

- URL
- date posted or last modified
- date of access
- sponsoring organization

You might also record the Library of Congress call number. You won't include it in bibliographic citations, but you'll need it if you have to find the source again.

> **QUICK TIP**
>
> You'll be tempted to take shortcuts, because citations are boring and no one can remember all the rules about periods, commas, parentheses, capitalization, and on and on. But nothing labels you as an untrustworthy researcher faster than citations that are incomplete, inaccurate, or inappropriate. You may have software that automatically formats citations for you (Word includes it); if not, there are websites you can use. You enter the data, and they do the rest of the work. These are useful aids, but they cannot substitute for your own care, and not all of their software works perfectly.

4.3 Search for Sources Systematically

Before college, many students do all of their research on the web, because their school libraries are small and they need few sources. In college, you can do much of your research online, starting with your library's online catalog. But if you search just the Internet, you can miss important sources that you'll find only by poking around in your library.

4.3.1 Talk to Reference Librarians

Most college libraries offer tours and short seminars on how to search the catalog, databases, and other sources of information. If you're a new researcher, seize every opportunity to learn the online search techniques in your field.

You can also talk to librarians who specialize in the general area of your topic. They won't find sources for you, but they'll help you look for them. If you have a research question, share it:

I'm looking for data on _____ because I want to find out _____.

If you have a working hypothesis and reasons, share them too:

I'm looking for data to show _[your reason]_ because I want to claim _[your hypothesis]_.

If you've done some research but can't find the evidence you need, bring copies of what you have found and pose your question as a challenge:

I'm looking for data to show __[your reason]__ because I want to claim __[your hypothesis]__. I've found A, B, and C, but they aren't what I need. Can you show me how to find something better?

Reference librarians love a challenge, and they respond well to students who see research as a hunt. Rehearse your questions to avoid wasting your time and theirs.

4.3.2 Skim Specialized Reference Works

Look up your topic in a specialized encyclopedia or dictionary such as the *Encyclopedia of Philosophy* or the *Concise Oxford Dictionary of Literary Terms,* where you may find an overview of your topic. You will also usually find a list of standard primary and secondary sources.

4.3.3 Search Your Library Catalog

Search your online catalog using keywords from your question or working hypothesis—*Alamo, Texas independence, James Bowie.* If you find too many titles, limit your search to those published in the last ten years. If you find too few, search a catalog service like WorldCat (if your library supports it) or go to the Library of Congress catalog at http://www.loc.gov. It has links to large university catalogs. Start early if you expect to get books from interlibrary loan.

ARTICLES. If most sources on your topic are articles, locate a recent one in your library's online databases. Its database entry will include a list of keywords. Use them to find more articles on your topic. In most cases, you can just click on them. Some databases provide abstracts of journal articles. Use these keywords to search the library catalog as well.

BOOKS. Once you find one book relevant to your topic, look it up in your library's online catalog to find its Library of Congress subject headings (at the bottom of the entry). Click on the subject headings to find other books on the same topics. Many of those sources will have more subject headings that can lead you to still more sources. It can turn into an endless trail.

4.3.4 Search Guides to Periodical Literature

If you've done any research before, you probably know how to use ProQuest or a similar online database of periodical literature. You can also find print guides such as the *Readers' Guide to Periodical Literature.* Most specialized fields also have yearly guides to secondary sources, such as *Art Abstracts, Historical Abstracts,* and *Abstracts in Anthropology.* Most are available online or on CDs.

4.3.5 Follow Bibliographical Trails

Every secondary source you find will include a bibliography. If a source looks useful, scan its bibliography for promising titles. Once you locate them, scan their bibliographies. One good source can set you on a trail to all the sources you'll need.

4.3.6 Browse the Shelves

You might think that online research is always faster than walking around your library. It often is, but it can also be slower; and if you work only online, you may miss sources that you'll find only in the library. More important, you'll miss the benefits of serendipity—a chance encounter with a source that you find only in person.

If you can get into the stacks (where the books that you can check out are shelved), find the shelf with books on your topic. Then scan the titles on that shelf and the ones above, below, and on either side. (Then skim titles behind you; you never know.) When you spot a book with a new binding published by a university press, skim its table of contents, then its index. Then skim its bibliography for relevant titles. You can do all that faster with books on a shelf than you can online.

Now do the same for any journal articles you've found. Most volumes include a yearly table of contents; skim them for the prior ten years. Then take a quick look at the journals shelved nearby. Skim their most recent tables of contents.

If a book or article looks promising, skim its preface or introduction. Even if it doesn't seem relevant, record its call number and bibliographic data, and in a few words summarize what it seems to be about. A week later, you might realize that it's more useful than you thought.

> **QUICK TIP**
>
> If you are new to a field, you can get a rough idea of a journal's quality by its look. If it's on glossy paper with lots of illustrations, even advertisements, it might be more journalistic than scholarly.

4.4 Evaluate Sources for Relevance and Reliability

You will probably find more sources than you can use. If so, skim them to evaluate their relevance and reliability.

4.4.1 Evaluate the Relevance of Sources

Once you decide that a source might be relevant, skim it systematically. Look for signs that it includes (1) data you can use as evidence, (2) discussions of matters you plan to discuss, (3) arguments that show you how others are thinking about your question. If your source is an article, do this:

- Read its abstract, if any.
- Skim the last two or three paragraphs of the introduction (or other opening section). If a section is called "Conclusion," skim all of it; if not, skim the last three paragraphs.
- Skim the first paragraph or two after each subhead, if any.

If your source is a book, do this:

- Skim its index for names or keywords related to your question or its answers; then skim those pages.
- Skim its introduction and last chapter, especially their last page or two.
- If the source is a collection of articles, skim the editor's introduction.
- Do the same for chapters that look relevant.

If your source is online, do this:

- If it looks like a printed article, evaluate it as you would a journal article.
- Skim any section labeled "Introduction," "Overview," "Summary," or the like. If there is none, look for a link labeled "About the Site" or something similar.
- If the site has a site map or index, skim it for keywords.
- If the site has a "search" resource, type in keywords.

4.4.2 Evaluate the Reliability of Your Sources

Your evidence will not be persuasive if it comes from a source your readers don't trust. You can't judge a source until you read it, but there are signs of reliability.

4.4.2.1 *Library-Quality Sources*

The first question is whether a source is *library quality*. For a source to be library quality, you do not have to find it in an actual library. But it does have to be provided by someone who subjects it to the same kind of screening that libraries give to their materials. Libraries are so important to researchers not just because they will lend you books and other sources, but because those materials are chosen by trained librarians who are specialists in judging their value and quality. You cannot be certain that everything in a library is a reliable source, but that is a good start.

To determine whether a source is of library quality because it has been screened by experts, look for these signs:

- It is part of a library's collection of physical books, articles, recordings, and other materials.
- It is provided as part of a library's online resources, including article databases, electronic books, electronic archives, and so on.

- It is provided by an online scholarly journal associated with a university or academic publisher.
- It is provided online by a reputable scholarly organization, such as the Rhetoric Society of America (research and other sources on rhetoric), the ARTFL Project (works by French authors), or the Pew Forum on Religion & Public Life (religion and social issues).

For advanced researchers, checking for library quality is just a first step in evaluating sources (see 4.4.2.3). But for your purposes, it is probably enough. Ask your teacher whether you have to screen library-quality sources for additional signs of reliability.

4.4.2.2   *Evaluate the Reliability of Other Online Sources*
When you search online, you will encounter hundreds of sites whose material does not appear to be of library quality. Evaluate each one carefully. The number of reliable online sources grows every day, but they are still islands in a swamp of misinformation.

Before you use online data that is not from a library-quality source, look for these signs of reliability:

1. The site is sponsored by a reputable organization. Some sites supported by individuals are reliable; most are not.
2. It is related to a reliable publisher or professional journal.
3. It is not an advocacy site. It is not sponsored by an organization with a political or commercial agenda, and it avoids one-sided advocacy on a contested social issue.
4. It does not make wild claims, attack other researchers, use abusive language, or make errors of spelling, punctuation, or grammar.
5. It says who is responsible for the site and when it was updated. If it has no date, be cautious.
6. It is not too glossy. When a site has more decorative graphics than words, its designers may care more about drawing you in than about presenting reliable information. If a site has almost no graphics, that may be a sign of neglect, but it might also indicate that its creator cares more about the quality of the words than the look of the page.

Trust a site only if careful readers would trust those who maintain it. If you don't know who maintains it, be skeptical.

4.4.2.3   *Evaluate the Reliability of Library-Quality Sources*
In most cases, beginning researchers are not expected to screen their sources as carefully as a professional must: library quality is usually enough. But when you do have to be more demanding, look for these additional signs of reliability:

1. **The author is a reputable scholar.** Most publications cite an author's academic credentials; you can find more with a search engine.
2. **The source is current.** How quickly a source goes out-of-date varies by subject, so check with someone who knows the field. For articles in the social sciences, more than ten years pushes the limit. For books, figure fifteen or so. Publications in the humanities have a longer shelf life.
3. **The source is published by a reputable press.** You can trust most university presses, especially at well-known schools. You can trust some commercial presses in some fields, such as Norton in literature, Ablex in sciences, or West in the law. Be skeptical of a commercial book that makes sensational claims, even if its author has a PhD.
4. **The article was peer-reviewed.** Most scholarly journals, both print and online, publish an article only after it has been peer-reviewed by experts. Few popular magazines do that. If an article hasn't been peer-reviewed, use it cautiously.

Those signs don't guarantee that a source is reliable, but they should give you some confidence in it. If you can't find reliable sources, admit the limits of the ones you have.

5: Engaging Sources

Once you find a source worth a close look, don't read it mechanically, recording only what it says. Note-taking is not clerical work. You must record the words of a source accurately, but you have to go further to engage its ideas: *Why does she use those words? How is this section connected to the next? Are these ideas consistent with earlier ones?*

But you must take yet another step, from its words and ideas to their implications, shortcomings, and unspoken possibilities. Talk back to your source as if its writer were sitting with you, eager to hear what you have to say (imagine your readers engaging you in the same way). If you passively absorb your research and then pass it on untouched by your own ideas, your report will be no more than a summary.

5.1   Read Generously to Understand, Then Critically to Evaluate

If you can, read promising sources twice, first quickly to understand them on their own terms. Read as if your job was to believe everything the author says. If you disagree too quickly, you're likely to misunderstand and miss useful ideas.

Then reread slowly and critically, as if you were amiably but pointedly questioning a friend; imagine the writer's answers, then question them. You probably won't be able to engage any source that fully until you've read enough to develop a few ideas of your own. But from the outset, be alert for ways to read sources not passively, as a mere transcriber, but actively and creatively, as an engaged partner.

5.2   Use Templates to Take Notes Systematically

There are two ways to record the information in sources: some researchers photocopy or download everything that might be useful; others do that only for very long passages and write or type out the rest.

If you just copy everything, you'll save some trouble and reduce your chance of misquoting. But many researchers find that they do not read as carefully or engage a source as fully when they rely only on copies. So if you copy or download, be sure to add to your photocopy all the other kinds of notes we recommend: keywords, summaries, responses, questions, how it supports or complicates your argument, and so on.

If you write out most of your notes, you'll force yourself to engage your sources more carefully, and you'll often get ideas while writing that would not come to you just by reading. But you'll risk mechanical errors in transcribing a quotation. So if you write out notes, create a template that helps you record information accurately, that clearly distinguishes your words from those of the source, and that encourages you to analyze and organize your notes into useful categories.

Some instructors still suggest taking notes in longhand on 3 × 5 cards, as in figure 5.1. That may seem old-fashioned, but it is a template for efficient note-taking, even if you take notes on a laptop.

Sharman, <u>Swearing</u>, p. 133.   HISTORY/ECONOMICS (GENDER?)

CLAIM: Swearing became economic issue in 18th c.

DATA: Cites <u>Gentleman's Magazine</u>, July 1751 (no page reference) woman sentenced to ten days' hard labor because couldn't pay one-shilling fine for profanity.

"... one rigid economist entertained the notion of adding to the national resources by preaching a crusade against the opulent class of swearers."

SUPPORT: As much about class and money as about morality. Legal treatment the same as for social rather than religious transgressions.

COMPLICATION: ——

Qs: Were men fined as often as women? Not economic earlier?

Figure 5.1

Here is a plan for a template on your laptop (start a new page for each general idea or claim that you record from a source).

- At the top of each page, create slots for author, short title, page number.
- Make another space at the top for keywords (see upper right above). Those words let you sort and re-sort your notes by content (see 5.3.3).

- Create two boxes with labels for different kinds of notes: one for summary and paraphrase and one for exact quotations. (For more on summary, paraphrase, and quotation, see chapter 9.)
- Create a third space for your reactions, questions, and further ideas. Have a section headed "How this supports my argument" and another "How this complicates my argument." This space will encourage you to do more than simply record what you read.
- This is important: When you quote a source, record its words in a distinctive color or font so that you can recognize quotations at a glance; enclose them in large quotation marks as well. If you mistake the words of others for your own, you invite a charge of plagiarism.
- This is also important: When you paraphrase a passage, record the paraphrase in a distinctive color or font so that you cannot mistake it for a quotation or for your own ideas; enclose it in curly brackets. If you mistake the ideas of others for your own, you invite a charge of plagiarism.

Finally, *never* assume that you can use what you find online without citing its source, even if it's free and publicly available. *Nothing* releases you from the duty to acknowledge your use of *anything* you did not personally create yourself. (For more on plagiarism, see chapter 10.)

> **CAUTION**
>
> **Quote Freely in Your Notes**
> If you don't record important words now, you can't quote them later. When in doubt, copy or photocopy passages so that you'll have what you need if you decide to quote them in your paper. You should have many more quotations in your notes than in your paper.

5.3 Take Useful Notes

Readers will judge your paper not just by the quality of your sources and how accurately you report them, but also by how deeply you engage them. To do that, you must take notes in a way that not only reflects but encourages a deeper understanding of your project.

5.3.1 Take Notes to Advance Your Thinking

Many inexperienced researchers think that note-taking is just a matter of recording data. Once they find a source, they photocopy pages or write down exactly what's on them. If that's all you do, if you don't *talk back* to your sources actively, you will simply accumulate a lot of inert information that will be equally inert in your report.

If you photocopy sources, annotate the copied pages to encourage your critical thinking. Pick out sentences that express crucial elements in its argument (its claim, major reasons, and so on). Label them in the margin. Then mark information that you might use as evidence in your report. (If you use a highlighter, use different colors to indicate these different elements.)

Summarize what you've highlighted or sketch a response to it on the back of the page, or make notes in the margin to help you interpret the highlighting. Be sure to indicate how you think the source supports or complicates your argument. The more you write about a source now, the better you will understand and remember it later.

5.3.2 Record Relevant Context for Each Key Point

Those who deliberately misreport sources are dishonest, but an honest researcher can mislead inadvertently if she merely records words and ignores their qualifications, complications, or role in a larger argument. To guard against misusing a source, follow these guidelines:

1. Record the context of a quotation. When you note an important conclusion, record the author's line of reasoning:

   > Not: Bartolli (p. 123): The war was caused . . . by Z.
   > But: Bartolli: The war was caused by Y and Z (p. 123), but the most important was Z (p. 123), for two reasons: First, . . . (pp. 124–26); Second, . . . (p. 126).

   Even if you care only about a conclusion, you'll use it more accurately if you record how a writer reached it.

2. Record the scope and confidence of a statement. Don't make a claim seem more certain or far-reaching than it is. The second sentence below doesn't report the first fairly or accurately:

   > **Original:** One study on the perception of risk (Wilson 1988) suggests a correlation between high-stakes gambling and single-parent families.
   > **Misleading report:** Wilson (1988) says single-parent families cause high-stakes gambling.

3. Record how a source uses a statement. Is it an important claim, a minor point, a qualification or concession, and so on? Such distinctions help avoid mistakes like this:

   > **Original by Jones:** We cannot conclude that one event causes another because the second follows the first. Nor can statistical correlation prove causation. But no one who has studied the data doubts that smoking is a causal factor in lung cancer.
   > **Misleading report:** Jones claims "we cannot conclude that one event causes another because the second follows the first. Nor can statistical correlation prove causation." Therefore, statistical evidence is not a reliable indicator that smoking causes lung cancer.

5.3.3 Record Keywords That Categorize Your Notes for Sorting

Finally, a conceptually challenging task: as you take notes, categorize each one under two or more keywords (see the upper right corner of fig. 5.1). Don't mechanically use words from the source: categorize the note by what it implies for your question, by a general idea larger than its specific content. Use the same keywords for related notes: don't create a new one for every new note.

This step is crucial because it forces you to find the central ideas in a note. If you take notes on a computer, the keywords let you instantly group related notes with a single Find command. If you use more than one keyword, you can recombine your notes in different ways to discover new relationships (especially important when you feel you are spinning your wheels).

5.3.4 Record How You Think the Note Is Relevant to Your Argument

If you let your question and hypothesis guide your research, you will choose to record information not just because it is on topic, but because it is relevant to the argument you think you can make. Record that information in your notes. Say why you think a source might support or, just as importantly, complicate your argument. At this point, guesses or hunches are OK: you'll have time to reconsider later. But you can't reconsider what you cannot remember. So don't rely on your memory to reconstruct what you were thinking when you decided to make a note.

5.4 Write as You Read

We've said this before (and will again): Writing forces you to think hard, so don't wait to nail down a budding idea before you write it out. Experienced researchers know that the more they write, the sooner and better they understand their project. There is good evidence that successful researchers set a fixed time to write every day—from fifteen minutes to more than an hour. They might write only a paragraph, but they write *something,* not to start a first draft of their report, but to sort out their ideas and maybe discover new ones.

If you write something that seems promising, add it to your storyboard. You will probably revise it for your final draft, maybe even discard it. But no matter how sketchy or rough this early writing might be, it will help you draft more easily later.

> **CAUTION**
>
> **Don't Expect Too Much of Your Early Writings**
>
> If you're new to a topic, much of your early writing may be just summary and paraphrase. If you see too few of your own ideas, don't feel discouraged at your lack of original thinking. Summarizing and paraphrasing are how we all gain

control over new ideas and learn new ways of thinking. Rehashing what we want to understand is a typical, probably even necessary, stage in just about everyone's learning curve.

5.5 Review Your Progress

Regularly review your notes and storyboard to see where you are and where you have to go. Full storyboard pages indicate reasons with support; empty ones indicate research still to do. Is your working hypothesis still plausible? Do you have good reasons supporting it? Good evidence to support those reasons? Can you add new reasons or evidence?

5.6 How and When to Start Over

We have urged you to create a storyboard with a working hypothesis and a few reasons to guide your research. But some writers start with an idea so vague that it evaporates as they chase it. If that happens to you, search your notes for a generalization that might serve as a working hypothesis, then work backward to find the question it answers.

5.6.1 Search Your Notes for a Better Answer

Use the strategies described in 2.4 to look for questions, disagreements, or puzzles in your sources and in your reaction to them. What surprises you might surprise others. Try to state it in writing:

I expected the first mythic stories of the Alamo to originate in Texas, but they didn't. They originated in . . .

That surprise suggests a potential claim: the Alamo myth began not as a regional story adopted for national purposes but as a national story from the start. Now you have a promising start.

5.6.2 Invent the Question

Now comes a tricky part. It's like reverse engineering: you've found the answer to a question that you haven't yet asked, so you have to reason backward to invent the question that it answers. In this case, it might be *Was the Alamo myth developed primarily to suit national needs, or was it developed for regional purposes that were then adapted to the national context?* It may seem paradoxical, but experienced researchers often discover their question only after they answer it.

5.6.3 Re-categorize and Re-sort Your Notes

If none of that helps, try re-sorting your notes. When you first chose keywords for your notes, you identified general ideas that could organize not just your evidence but your thinking. Now re-sort your notes in different ways to get a new slant on your material. If your keywords no longer seem relevant, review your notes to create new keywords and reshuffle again.

| 5.7 | **Manage Moments of Normal Panic** |

This might be a good time to address a problem that afflicts even experienced researchers and at some point will probably afflict you. As you shuffle through hundreds of notes and a dozen lines of thought, you start feeling that you're not just spinning your wheels but spiraling down into a black hole of confusion, paralyzed by what seems to be an increasingly complex and unmanageable task.

The bad news is that there's no sure way to avoid such moments. The good news is that most of us have them and they pass. Yours will pass too if you keep moving along, following your plan, taking on small and manageable tasks instead of trying to get your head around the whole project. It's another reason to start early, to break a big project into its smallest steps, and to set achievable deadlines, such as a daily page quota when you draft.

6: Planning Your Argument

Most of us would rather read sources than start to write a draft. But well before you've done all the research you'd like to do, you have to start thinking about the first draft of your paper. You might be ready when your storyboard is full and you're satisfied with how it looks. But you can't be certain until you start planning that first draft. Do that in two steps:

- Sort your notes into the elements of a research argument.
- Organize those elements into a coherent form.

In this chapter, we explain how to assemble the elements of your argument; in the next, how to organize them. As you gain experience, you'll learn to combine those two steps into one process.

6.1   What a Research Argument Is and Is Not

The word *argument* has bad associations these days, partly because radio and TV stage so many nasty ones. But the argument in a research paper is not the verbal combat we so often get from politicians and pundits. It doesn't try to intimidate an opponent into silence or submission. In fact, there's rarely an "opponent" at all. A research argument is like an amiable conversation in which you and your readers reason together to solve a problem. But those readers won't accept that solution until they hear a case for it: good reasons, reliable evidence that grounds those reasons, and your responses to their reasonable questions and reservations.

It is challenging enough to maintain a sense of amiable cooperation with others who do not share your views when you can talk face-to-face. But it is doubly difficult when you write, because you usually write alone. You have to imagine your readers' role in that conversation: not only do you have to hold up your end, but your imagination has to hold up theirs. Your argument can answer your readers' questions only if you can first imagine those readers asking those questions for you to answer.

When readers hear traces of their questions in your written report, they recognize that you've thought not just about your views but about theirs as well. Remember this core principle of argument: Each of us can believe what we want, for whatever reason we want, but we have no right to ask others to believe it unless we can give them good reasons to do so, reasons that make sense *from their point of view.*

When you make a research argument, you must lay out your reasons and evidence so that your readers can see how you reasoned your way to a conclusion; then you must imagine their questions and answer them. That sounds challenging—and for a complex argument it can be. But it's more familiar than you may think, because in fact you have that kind of conversation every day.

6.2   Build Your Argument Around Answers to Readers' Questions

6.2.1   Identify (or Invent) Target Readers Interested in Your Question

You cannot anticipate your readers' questions unless you have a good idea of who they are and what they know. That's a problem for many class papers, since you have no obvious readers but your teacher—who isn't reading as herself (see the Caution below). That's why teachers often set up research papers so that your target readers are your classmates. If not, you have to select at least one target reader for yourself. Your best choice is someone you know who would be interested in your question and who knows as much about it as you did before you started your research. (Even better if you know two or more such people.) Have them in mind when you imagine your readers' questions. If you don't know such a person, invent one. The more you can imagine specific, familiar people asking you questions, the better your argument will be.

CAUTION

Write for Target Readers, Not Your Teacher

Your teacher may be your only reader, but don't write with only your teacher in mind. First of all, teachers generally judge papers not as themselves but from the point of view of your target readers, who know less than they do. Second, you risk making unconscious assumptions that distort your argument: you will fail to explain matters your teacher already understands but readers don't, fail to anticipate questions that readers might have but your teacher won't, and generally produce a paper that is fully suited neither to your teacher nor to your target readers. Once you identify your target readers, write only for them.

6.2.2   **How Arguments Grow from Questions**

You already know about asking the kinds of questions whose answers will compose your argument because you ask and answer them every day. Consider this exchange:

A: I hear you had a hard time last semester. How do you think this one will go? [*A poses a problem in the form of a question.*]

B: Better, I hope. [*B answers the question.*]

A: Why so? [*A asks for a reason to believe B's answer.*]

B: I'm taking courses in my major. [*B offers a reason.*]

A: Like what? [*A asks for evidence to back up B's reason.*]

B: History of Art, Intro to Design. [*B offers evidence to back up his reason.*]

A: Why will taking courses in your major make a difference? [*A doesn't see the relevance of B's reason to his claim that he will do better.*]

B: When I take courses I'm interested in, I work harder. [*B offers a general principle that relates his reason to his claim that he will do better.*]

A: What about that math course you have to take? [*A objects to B's reason.*]

B: I know I had to drop it last time I took it, but I found a good tutor. [*B acknowledges A's objection and responds to it.*]

If you can see yourself as *A* or *B,* you'll find nothing new in the argument of a research report, because you build its argument out of the answers to those same five questions.

· What is your claim?
· What reasons support it?
· What evidence supports those reasons?
· How do you respond to objections and alternative views?
· How are your reasons relevant to your claim?

If you ask and answer those five questions, you can't guarantee that your readers will accept your claim, but you make it more likely that they'll treat it—and you—with respect.

6.3   **Assemble the Core of Your Argument**

At the core of your argument is your claim, supported by your reasons for believing it and the evidence that grounds those reasons. To that core you will add at least one more element: you must acknowledge and respond to your readers' questions, objections, and alternative points of view. Most students find these elements easy to understand when they think of them in light of the predictable questions they answer:

What do you want me to believe?
Why should I believe that?
How do you know that's true?
What about my ideas on this matter?

The fifth element, a warrant, is less common and more difficult to understand and use; you can build perfectly adequate arguments without them. So if you struggle with them, focus on the four elements that your readers will always expect to see.

Before you address the views and concerns of your readers, you have to be clear about your own. So your first step is to assemble the claim, reasons, and evidence that make up the core of your argument.

6.3.1 Turn Your Working Hypothesis into a Claim

In the early stages of your research, your job was to find a question and imagine a tentative answer. We called that answer your *working hypothesis*—the most promising answer to your research question that you would keep around, but only on probation. Now that you think you can build a case to support that hypothesis, it's time to take it off probation and think of it as your main *claim*. That main claim is the center of your argument, the answer to your question, the point of your report (some teachers call it a *thesis*).

> **SOME TERMINOLOGY**
>
> **Your Claim's Many Names**
>
> Every good research paper is built around a main idea, a most important result, a conceptual head honcho that dominates all the rest. It has many names because you have to think about it from many points of view. From the point of view of your problem statement, it is your *main result*, the *answer* to your question. Doing your research, call it your *working hypothesis*. Making your argument, call it your *main claim*. Organizing your paper, call it your *main point*. You need so many names for this one idea because it plays so many roles in your paper.

6.3.2 Evaluate Your Claim

Start a new first page of your storyboard (if you already have one, replace it). At the bottom, state your claim in a sentence or two. Be specific, because the words in this claim will help you plan and execute your draft. Avoid vague value words like *important, interesting, significant,* and the like. Compare the following two claims:

Masks play a big role in many religious ceremonies.

In cultures from pre-Columbian America to Africa and Asia, masks allow religious celebrants to bring deities to life so that worshippers experience them directly.

Now judge the *significance* of your claim (*So what?* again). A significant claim doesn't make a reader think, *I know that,* but rather, *Really? What makes you think so?* (Review 1.2.) These next claims are too trivial to justify writing a report on them:

This report discusses teaching popular legends such as the Battle of the Alamo to elementary school students. (*So what if it does?*)

Teaching our national history through popular legends such as the Battle of the Alamo is common in elementary education. (*So what if it is?*)

Of course, what your readers will count as interesting depends on what they know. But that's hard to predict when you're early in your research career. So don't think you've failed if you can't find a convincing answer to *So what?* If you're writing one of your first reports, assume that the most important judge of the significance of your argument is you. It is enough if *you alone* think your answer is significant, if it makes you think, *Well, I didn't understand that when I started.*

But if *you* think your claim is vague or trivial, don't try to build an argument to support it. If you can find no reason to make a case for your claim, neither will your readers. Find a new claim.

6.3.3 Support Your Claim with Reasons and Evidence

It may seem obvious that you must back up a claim with reasons and evidence. But it's easy to confuse those two words because we often use them as if they mean the same thing:

What reasons do you base your claim on?
What evidence do you base your claim on?

But they mean different things:

- We *think up logical* reasons, but we *collect factual* evidence; we don't *collect factual* reasons and *think up logical* evidence.
- We base reasons on evidence; we don't base evidence on reasons.
- A reason is an idea, and you don't have to cite its source (if you thought of it yourself). In contrast, evidence usually comes from outside your mind, so you must always cite a reliable source for it. Even if you found your evidence through your own observation or experiment, you must show what you did to find it.

In short: *Reasons are your ideas that need the support of evidence; evidence is composed of facts that need no support beyond a reference to a reliable source.*

The problem is that what you think is a true fact and therefore hard evidence, your readers might not. For example, suppose a researcher offers the following claim and reason, backed up by this "hard" evidence:

Early Alamo stories reflected values already in the American character.*claim* The story almost instantly became a legend of American heroic sacrifice.*reason* Jones reports that soon after the battle, many newspapers used the story to celebrate our heroic national character.*evidence*

If readers accept that statement as an unquestioned fact, they may accept it as evidence. But a skeptical reader, the kind you should expect (even hope for), is likely to ask: *How many is "many"? Which newspapers? In news stories or editorials? What exactly did they say? How many papers didn't mention it?* Even if they think Jones is a reliable source, they expect the researcher to offer more specific facts: the numbers behind "many," the specific forms of "celebration," perhaps even quotes from news stories.

To be sure, we sometimes accept a claim based only on a reason, if that reason seems self-evidently true or is from a trusted authority:

We are all created equal,*reason* so no one has a natural right to oppress us.*claim*

Instructors in introductory courses often let students support reasons with no more than the reports of an authoritative source: *Wilson says X about religious masks, Yang says Y, Schmidt says Z.* Find out from your teacher if you can use the claims of authorities as evidence. But when you do more advanced work, you have to look for harder evidence than the word of an authority. Readers want evidence drawn not from a secondary source but from primary sources or your own observation (see 4.1).

Review your storyboard: Can you back up each reason with what your readers will think is evidence of the right kind, quantity, and quality? Might your readers think that what you offer as evidence needs more support? Or a better source? If so, you must find more data or acknowledge the limits of what you have.

Your claim, reasons, and evidence make up the core of your argument, but it needs at least one more element, maybe two.

6.4   Acknowledge and Respond to Readers' Points of View

Recall that we said a written argument is not a one-sided lecture to passive listeners but a two-sided conversation in which you speak with and for your readers. No argument is complete that fails to bring in your readers' points of view. You must acknowledge your readers by *imagining* questions and objections on their behalf, then by answering them.

6.4.1   Imagining Readers' Views

Readers raise two kinds of questions; try to imagine and respond to both.

1. The first kind of question points to problems *inside* your argument, usually its evidence.

    Imagine a reader making any of these criticisms of your evidence. If one of them might be reasonable, construct a mini-argument in response:

    - Your evidence is from an unreliable or out-of-date source.
    - Your evidence is inaccurate.
    - You don't have enough evidence.
    - What you report doesn't fairly represent all the evidence available.
    - You have the wrong kind of evidence for our field.

    Then imagine these kinds of objections to your reasons. If one of them might be reasonable, construct a mini-argument in response:

    - Your reasons are inconsistent or contradictory.
    - You don't have enough reasons.
    - They are too weak to support your claim.
    - They are irrelevant to your claim and so do not *count* as reasons (see 6.5).

2. The second kind of question points to problems *outside* your argument. Those who see the world differently are likely to define words differently, reason differently, even offer evidence that you think is irrelevant.

    Don't treat these differing points of view simply as objections. You'll lose readers if you insist that your view is right and theirs is wrong. Instead, acknowledge the differences, then compare them so that readers can understand your argument on its own terms. They might not agree, but you'll show them that you understand and respect their views. They are then more likely to respect and try to understand yours.

    If you're a new researcher, you'll find these questions hard to imagine because you might not know how in fact your readers' views differ from your own. Even so, try to think of some plausible questions and objections and then respond to them. It's important to get into the habit of asking yourself, *What could cast doubt on my claim?*

    But when you do more advanced work, you will be expected to know the issues that others in your field are likely to raise. So practice imagining and responding to disagreements. Even if you just go through the motions, you'll cultivate a habit of mind that your readers will respect and that may keep you from jumping to questionable conclusions.

    Add those acknowledgments and responses to your storyboard where you think readers will raise them.

WORKING IN GROUPS

Ask Friends to Object

If you cannot imagine objections or alternatives to your argument, enlist help from your writing group. Ask them to read your draft and make the longest list they can of objections, alternative conclusions, different interpretations of evidence, and so on. Ask them not to censor themselves—you want even their nuttiest ideas. You may find in their views a question to acknowledge and respond to; and if not, their list might give you an idea of your own.

6.4.2   Acknowledging and Responding

When you acknowledge an anticipated question or objection, you can give it more or less weight. You can mention and dismiss it, summarize it quickly, or address it at length. Do not dismiss a position that your readers take seriously; do not address at length one for which you have no good response.

Standard Forms for Acknowledging

We order these expressions from most dismissive to most respectful. (Brackets and slashes indicate choices.)

1. You can downplay an alternative by summarizing it in a short phrase introduced with *despite, regardless of,* or *notwithstanding:*

   [**Despite / Regardless of / Notwithstanding**] Congress's claims that it wants to cut taxes,*acknowledgment* the public believes that . . .*response*

   You can use *although, while,* and *even though* in the same way:

   [**Although / While / Even though**] Congress claims it wants to cut taxes,*acknowledgment* the public believes that . . .*response*

2. You can signal an alternative with *seem* or *appear,* or with a qualifying adverb, such as *plausibly, reasonably, understandably, surprisingly, foolishly,* or even *certainly.*

   In his letters, Lincoln expresses what [**seems / appears**] to be depression.*acknowledgment* But those who observed him . . .*response*
   Liberals [**plausibly / reasonably / foolishly** / etc.] argue that the arts ought to be supported by taxes.*acknowledgment* But we all know . . .*response*

3. You can acknowledge an alternative without naming its source. This gives it just a little weight.

   It is easy to [**think / imagine / say / claim / argue**] that taxes should . . .
   There is [**another / alternative / possible / standard**] [**explanation / argument / possibility**] . . .

> Some evidence [**might** / **can** / **could** / **would** / **does**] [**suggest** / **indicate** / **lead some to think**] that we should . . .

4. You can acknowledge an alternative by attributing it to a more or less specific source. This construction gives it more weight.

> There are [**some** / **many** / **few**] who [**might** / **could** / **would**] [**say** / **think** / **claim** / **charge** / **object**] that Cuba is not . . .
> [**Most** / **Many** / **Some** / **A few**] administrators [**say** / **think** / **claim** / **charge** / **object**] that researchers . . .
> Jones [**says** / **thinks** / **claims** / **charges** / **objects**] that students . . .

5. You can acknowledge an alternative in your own voice or with concessive adverbs such as *admittedly, granted, to be sure,* and so on. This construction concedes that the alternative has some validity, but by changing the words, you can qualify how much validity you acknowledge.

> I [**understand** / **know** / **realize** / **appreciate**] that liberals believe in . . .
> It is [**true** / **possible** / **likely** / **certain** / **must be admitted**] that no good evidence proves that coffee causes cancer . . .
> [**Granted** / **Admittedly** / **True** / **To be sure** / **Certainly** / **Of course**], Adams stated . . .
> We [**could** / **can** / **might** / **would**] [**say** / **argue** / **claim** / **think**] that spending on the arts supports pornographic . . .
> We have to [**consider** / **raise**] the [**question** / **possibility** / **probability**] that further study [**could** / **might** / **will**] show crime has not . . .
> We cannot [**overlook** / **ignore** / **dismiss** / **reject**] the fact that Cuba was . . .

Readers use the words of your acknowledgment to judge how seriously you take an objection or alternative. But they will base that judgment even more on the nature of your response. If your readers think an alternative is a serious one, they expect you to respond to it in some detail, including reasons and evidence to support that response. Do not dismiss or attack a position that your readers believe strongly: if you cannot make a convincing argument against it, simply show how it differs from yours and explain why you believe as you do.

Standard Forms for Introducing Responses

You can respond in ways that range from tactfully indirect to blunt.

1. You can state that you don't entirely understand:

> But I do not quite understand . . . / I find it difficult to see how . . . / It is not clear to me that . . .

2. Or you can state that there are unsettled issues:

    But there are other issues . . . / There remains the problem of . . .

3. You can respond more bluntly by claiming the acknowledged position is irrelevant or unreliable:

    But as insightful as that point may be, it [**ignores / is irrelevant to**] the issue at hand.
    But the evidence is [**unreliable / shaky / thin / not the best available**].
    But the argument is [**untenable / wrong / weak / confused / simplistic**].
    But that view [**overlooks / ignores / misses**] key factors.
    But that position is based on [**unreliable / faulty / weak / confused**] [**reasoning / evidence**].

6.5 Use Warrants if Readers Question the Relevance of Your Reasons

Sometimes readers question an argument not because they object to its evidence or see an alternative interpretation of events, but because they cannot see its logic. Consider this argument, made by the ex-basketball star and TV commentator Charles Barkley:

I should not be held to a higher standard in my behavior,$_{claim}$ because I never put myself forward as a role model for kids.$_{reason}$

He was immediately criticized. His critics agreed that his reason was true: In fact, Barkley never claimed to be a role model. But, they said, that reason was irrelevant: He was a role model to be held to a higher standard, whether he asked for it or not.

Barkley and his critics did not disagree about evidence or reasons: all agreed that Barkley had never asked to be a role model. What they disagreed about was the underlying principle of reasoning that should apply to that fact. For Barkley, the principle was something like this:

Whenever someone does not ask to be a role model, he is not responsible to meet the standard of behavior applied to role models.

But the critics applied a different principle:

Whenever someone willingly engages in an activity that makes him famous and admired, he is a role model whether he asked for it or not.

If we think Barkley's principle is the right one, then we must accept his claim; if we think the critics have the right principle, then we must reject his and accept theirs.

A warrant is a general principle that if one thing is true, then something else must also be true. It answers those who believe that your reasons are true but still don't see why they should accept your claim: they think your reasons are *irrelevant* to believing your claim because they do not know (or accept) the principle of reasoning that connects them.

As we said, warrants are less common than the other parts of argument. They are used most often when an argument is about politics and morality (where people hold many contradictory principles) or when an expert makes an argument for lay readers (because experts know lots of principles that lay readers may not).

CAUTION

Don't Let Warrants Intimidate You

If warrants still seem confusing, don't be dismayed. Warrants are most important when you write for readers who think in ways very different from you. They are least important when your readers are a lot like you. Since you're likely to have target readers who do think more or less as you do, you may not need warrants at all. So if one comes to mind as you draft, include it. But don't try to force yourself to include warrants. As you become more experienced and tackle more advanced research projects, you can revisit the issue of warrants and their uses.

6.6   An Argument Assembled

Here is a small argument that pulls together all five parts:

TV aimed at children can aid their intellectual development, but that contribution has been offset by a factor that could damage their emotional development—too much violence.*claim* Parents agree that example is an important influence on a child's development. That's why parents tell their children stories about heroes. It seems plausible, then, that when children see degrading behavior, they will be affected by it as well.*warrant* In a single day, children see countless examples of violence.*reason* Every day the average child watches almost four hours of TV and sees about twelve acts of violence (Smith 1992).*evidence* Tarnov has shown that children don't confuse cartoon violence with real life (2003).*acknowledgment of alternative point of view* But that may make children more vulnerable to violence in other shows. If they only distinguish between cartoons and people, they may think real actors engaged in graphic violence represent real life.*response* We cannot ignore the possibility that TV violence encourages the development of violent adults.*claim restated*

Most of those elements could be expanded to many paragraphs.

Arguments in different fields look different, but they all consist of answers to just these five questions:

- What are you claiming?
- What are your reasons?
- What evidence supports your reasons?
- But what about other points of view?
- How are your reasons relevant to your claim?

Your storyboard should answer those questions many times. If it doesn't, your paper will seem thin and unconvincing.

7: Planning a First Draft

Once you assemble your argument, you might be ready to write your draft. But experienced writers know that the time they invest in planning a draft more than pays off when they write it. Some plans, however, are better than others.

WORKING IN GROUPS

Organize a Writing Group

If you haven't done it yet, now is the time to organize a writing group of three to five classmates (no more). If you already have a group, now is the time to get to work seriously. Plan to meet once or, if your deadline is near, twice a week. Have an agenda that reflects your stage in the process of research and writing. Start every meeting with elevator stories (see 3.2.3). If your storyboard Is starting to fill up, bring it to the meeting. Although your colleagues' suggestions are always welcome, your goal early on is to have someone willing to listen and respond to your ideas. The sooner you get those ideas out of your mind and into the light of day, the better you will know how well you really understand them.

7.1   Unhelpful Plans to Avoid

Do not organize your report in any of these three ways:

1. Do not organize it as a story of your research, especially not as a mystery, with your claim revealed at the end. Readers care about what you found, not every step it took you to get there. You see signs of that in language like *The first issue was . . . Then I compared . . . Finally I conclude . . .*

2. Do not patch together quotations, summaries of sources, or downloads from the web. Teachers want to see *your* thinking, not that of others. They *really* dislike reports that read like a collage of web screens. Do that, and you'll seem not only an amateur but, worse, a plagiarist (see 10.3).

3. Do not mechanically organize your paper around the terms of your assignment or the most obvious elements of your topic.

- If your assignment lists issues to cover, don't think you must address them in the order given.
- If you decide to compare and contrast Freud's and Jung's analyses of the imagination, avoid organizing your report in the two most obvious parts, the first on Freud, the second on Jung. Break those two big topics into their parts, then organize your report around them.

7.2 Create a Plan That Meets Your Readers' Needs

Some fields require a preset plan for a report. Readers in the experimental sciences, for example, expect reports to follow some version of this:

Introduction—Methods and Materials—Results—Discussion—Conclusion

If you must follow a preset plan, ask your instructor for a model. But if you are left to create one on your own, it must not only make sense to readers; it must be *visible* to them. To create a visible form, go back to your storyboard or outline.

7.2.1 Converting a Storyboard into an Outline

Your best tool for planning a draft is your storyboard. But if you prefer to work from an outline, you can turn your storyboard into one:

- Start with a sentence numbered *I* that states your claim.
- Add full sentences under it numbered *II, III* . . . , each of which states a reason from the top of a reason page in your storyboard.
- Under each reason, use capital letters to list sentences summarizing your evidence; then list by numbers the evidence itself. For example (the data are invented for the illustration):

I. Introduction: Value of classroom computers for writing is uncertain.
II. Different uses have different effects.
    A. All uses increase number of words produced.
        1. Study 1: 950 vs. 780
        2. Study 2: 1,103 vs. 922
    B. Labs allow students to interact.
III. Studies show limited benefit on revision.
    A. Study A: writers on computers are more wordy.
        1. Average of 2.3 more words per sentence
        2. Average of 20% more words per essay
    B. Study B: writers need hard copy to revise effectively.
        1. 22% fewer typos when done on hard copy vs. computer screen
        2. 2.26% fewer spelling errors

IV. Conclusion: Too soon to tell how much computers improve learning.
    A. Few reliable empirical studies
    B. Little history because many programs are in transition

7.2.2   Sketch a Working Introduction

Write your introduction twice: write a sketchy one now for yourself and a final one for your readers after you've revised your draft and know what you have written. That final introduction usually has four parts, so you might as well build your working introduction to anticipate them.

> **Create a Four-Part Scheme for Your Introduction**
>
> For now, think of your introduction as having these parts:
>
> 1. Current Situation (what your readers now think or do)
> 2. Research Question (what your readers need to know but don't)
> 3. Significance of the Question (your answer to *So what?*)
> 4. Answer (what your readers should know)
>
> (We explain these parts more fully in 13.1.) In this section we explain how to sketch them in your storyboard.

If you followed our earlier suggestion, you have written your main claim at the bottom of the first page of your storyboard. Now fill in the page above it with what leads up to that claim.

1. At the top of the page state the **Current Situation** that your question will disrupt.

Since the centerpiece of your introduction is your disruptive research question, you first have to offer readers something for your question to disrupt. Briefly state what your readers (or others) believe that you will challenge with your question (you might review the examples in 2.4). Think of this as the first half of a contradiction:

> I used to think . . . , but . . .
> Most people think . . . , but . . .
> What events seem to show is . . . , but . . .
> Researchers have shown . . . , but . . .

For example, you might set up a question about the Alamo by asking readers to think about its status as a national legend. You can state that in terms of

- what you believed before you began your research (*I used to think . . .*)

    > I always thought of the Battle of the Alamo as a major event in our nation's history.

- what others believe (*Most people think . . .*)

  The Battle of the Alamo has always been treated as a major historical event, not only in history textbooks but in popular culture as well.

- an event or situation (*What events seem to show is . . .*)

  In 2004 the blockbuster film *The Alamo* was nominated for the Harry Award for promoting the public understanding of a historical event. That film was a remake of a 1960 film by the same name, which was nominated for seven Oscars and won one.

- what other researchers have found (*Researchers have shown . . .*)

  What really happened at the Alamo is well known. Historians have uncovered almost every detail relevant to understanding the true Alamo story.

  If you are ambitious, you can make this part of your introduction a *literature review* in which you summarize the major research leading up to your paper. If so, do *not* cover all the sources you find. Instead, summarize only those whose findings you intend to extend, modify, or correct.

2. Under that, rephrase your **Research Question** as a statement about what we don't know or understand in light of the Current Situation. Since this is the second half of the contradiction, it should start with *but* or *however.*

   Research Question:
   Why has the story of the minor regional battle at the Alamo become a national legend?
   Problem Statements:
   I always thought of the Battle of the Alamo as a major event in our nation's history. **But** the Alamo was a minor regional battle that somehow became a national legend.

   What really happened at the Alamo is well known. Historians have uncovered almost every detail relevant to understanding the true Alamo story. **But** few historians have tried to explain why this minor regional battle has become so important in our national mythology.

   Writers do this in many ways, so as you read, note how your sources do it, then use them as models.

3. Next, if you can, explain the **Significance** of your question by answering *So what if we don't find out?*

   If we can explain how the Alamo became a national legend, we can better understand how American culture has fostered a feeling of national unity in a diverse population that shares relatively little history.

At this point in your career, you may find any larger significance to your answer hard to imagine. If so, you can state the significance in terms of the themes of your class:

> If we can explain how the Alamo became a national legend, we can better understand the issues of American identity and diversity.

If that doesn't work for you yet, don't dwell on it. We'll return to it in 13.1.3.

4. Revise your claim as the **Answer** to the question, in terms that match those of the first three parts:

> The Alamo became a national legend not because it was important to the history of the United States or even to the history of Texas, but because it reflected both the traditional virtue of heroic self-sacrifice and the frontier virtue of self-reliance.

For now, you should leave that answer at the bottom of the introduction page of your storyboard. Later you might decide to move it from the end of the introduction to the conclusion so that your paper can build up to it as a climax. That's generally a bad idea, but you can confront that issue later.

CAUTION

Don't Fear Giving Away Your Answer
Some new researchers fear that if they reveal their claim early, in their introduction, readers will be bored and stop reading. Others worry about repeating themselves. Both fears are baseless. If you ask an interesting question, readers will want to see how well you can support its answer.

7.2.3 Identify Key Terms That Unite Your Paper

Readers will feel that your paper is coherent only if you repeat a few key concepts that run through all of its parts. But readers may not recognize that you have repeated those concepts if you use lots of different words to name them.

Suppose, for example, you were writing a paper about white artists "covering" African American music in the '50s and '60s. Your paper would have as one organizing theme the concept of fairness. But readers might miss the connection if you use too many different words and phrases to name it: *fair use, reasonable economic benefits of their work, social equity, similar access to radio play, exclusive concert venues, recording contracts that are unfavorable to artists, unequal economic power*. Although these all relate to your theme of fairness, readers might not make that connection in each case. You would help them if more of those references included your key term *fair*: not *economic benefits of their* work, but *fair economic return for their work; not similar access to radio play,* but *fair and equal access to radio play.*

Your readers need to see one specific term that repeatedly refers to each concept that serves as an organizing theme for your paper, not every time you mention the concept, but often enough that readers can't miss the connection.

Before you start drafting, identify the key concepts that you intend to run through your whole report. For each concept, select one term that you will use most often. As you draft, you may find new themes and drop some old ones, but you'll write more coherently if you keep your most important terms and concepts in the front of your mind.

How to Identify Global Concepts to Unite the Whole Paper

1. On the introduction and conclusion pages of your storyboard, circle four or five words that name your key concepts. You should find those words in your claim.

   - Ignore words obviously connected to your topic: *Alamo, battle, defeat.*
   - Focus on concepts that *you* bring to the argument and intend to develop: *frontier self-reliance, triumph in loss, heroic sacrifice, national spirit,* and so on.

2. For each concept, select one key term that you can run through the body of your paper. It can be one of your circled words or a new one. If you find few words that can serve as key terms, your claim may be too general (review 6.3.2).

As you draft, keep a list of those terms in front of you. They will help you keep yourself—and therefore your readers—on track. If you find yourself drafting two or more pages without those terms, don't just wrench yourself back to using them. You might be discovering a new trail that's worth following.

7.2.4 Find the Key Terms Distinctive to Each Section

Now do the same thing for each section: Find the key terms that unify the section and distinguish it from the others. Circle the important words in the reason at the top of each reason page. Some of them should be related to the words circled in the introduction and conclusion. The rest should identify concepts that distinguish that section from all the others. If you cannot find key terms to distinguish a section, think hard about what that section contributes to the whole. Readers may think it repetitive or irrelevant.

Even if papers in your field don't use subheads, we recommend that you use them in your drafts. Create a subhead for each section out of the key terms you identified in that section. If your field dislikes subheads, use them to keep yourself on track, then delete them from your last draft.

7.2.5   Order Your Sections by Ordering Your Reasons

When you first assemble your argument, you don't have to put your reasons in any special order (one benefit of a storyboard). But when you plan a draft, you must choose an order that meets your readers' needs.

Some Standard Principles of Order

When you're not sure how best to order your reasons, consider these options. You can choose orders that reflect what's "out there":

- **Chronological.** This is the easiest, from earlier to later, or vice versa.
- **Part by part.** If you analyze your topic by its parts, order them by their relationship to one another.

Other orders reflect the needs of your readers:

- **Short to long, simple to complex.** Most readers prefer to deal with simpler issues before they work through more complex ones.
- **More familiar to less familiar.** Most readers prefer to read what they know about before they read what's new.
- **Most acceptable to most contestable.** Most readers move more easily from what they agree with to what they don't.
- **Less important to more important (or vice versa).** Most readers prefer to cover more important reasons first (but those reasons may have more impact when they come last).
- **Step-by-step understanding.** Readers may need you to explain some events, principles, definitions, and so on before they are ready to understand what's most important.

To test an order, create *one* paragraph that includes just your reasons in the order you want to test. If that paragraph reads like a convincing elevator story (test it on your writing group or a friend), then you have found a usable order.

Often the principles cooperate: what readers agree with and most easily understand might also be shortest and most familiar. But they may also conflict: reasons that readers understand most easily might be the ones they reject most quickly; what you think is your most decisive reason might to readers seem least familiar. No rules here, only principles of choice. Whatever order you choose, it should be one that meets your readers' needs, not the order in which ideas occurred to you.

7.2.6   ## Sketch a Brief Introduction to Each Section and Subsection

Just as your paper needs an introduction that frames what follows, so does each section. This introductory segment should end with a sentence expressing the point of that section (usually a reason). That sentence should also mention the key concepts for that section.

7.2.7   ## Sketch in Evidence and Acknowledgments

Flesh out the parts of each section by filling in the storybook page for each major reason. Remember that a section may include sub-points that must be supported by mini sub-arguments.

EVIDENCE.   Most sections consist primarily of evidence supporting reasons, so sketch the supporting evidence at the bottom of each reason page. If you have different kinds of evidence supporting the same reason, group and order them in a way that makes sense to your readers.

EXPLANATIONS OF EVIDENCE.   You may have to explain your evidence—where it came from, why it's reliable, how it supports a reason. Usually, these explanations follow the evidence, but you can sketch them before, if that seems more logical.

ACKNOWLEDGMENTS AND RESPONSES.   Imagine what readers might object to and where, then sketch a response. Responses are typically sub-arguments with at least a claim and reasons (*Some researchers have said . . . , but I believe* _____ *because . . .*); they often include evidence and maybe even a second response to an imagined objection to your first response.

Writers in different fields arrange these elements in slightly different ways, but the elements themselves and their principles of organization are the same in just about every field or profession. And in every research report, regardless of field, you must order the parts of your argument not just to reflect your own thinking, but to help your readers understand it.

QUICK TIP

Save the Leftovers

Once you have a plan, you should discover that you have material that doesn't fit into it. That's a good thing: research is like diamond mining—you have to dig up a lot of dirt to find a few gems. So be glad about your leftovers. If you don't have any, you haven't done enough research.

Resist the temptation to shoehorn the leftovers into your report, thinking that if you found it, your readers should read it. File them away for future use. They may contain the seeds of another project.

8: Drafting Your Paper

Many inexperienced writers think that once they have an outline or storyboard, they can just write it up, grinding out sentences for a draft. And if you've followed our advice to write as you gather evidence, you may think that you can plug that exploratory writing into your draft. Experienced writers know better. They know that thoughtful drafting is an act of discovery that an outline or storyboard may prepare them for, but can never replace. So they don't expect to reuse their early writing without change or to follow their storyboard mindlessly.

In fact, most writers don't know what they *can* think until they see it appear on the page before them. You'll experience one of the most exciting moments in research when you discover yourself writing out ideas that you did not know you had. So don't look at drafting as just translating your storyboard into words. Think of it as an opportunity to discover what your storyboard has missed.

8.1   Draft in a Way That Feels Comfortable

Experienced writers draft in different ways. Some are slow and careful: they have to get every paragraph right before they start the next one. But to do that, they need a specific, complete plan. So if you draft slowly, plan carefully. Other writers let the words flow, skipping ahead when they get stuck, omitting quotations, statistics, and so on that they know they can plug in later. If they are stopped by a trivial stylistic issue like whether to write out a number in words or numerals, they insert a [?] and keep going until they run out of gas, then go back and fix it. But quick drafters need time to revise. So if you draft quickly, start early.

Most experienced writers draft quickly, then revise extensively. If you don't yet know which is your best method, start with that. But you should draft in whatever way works for you, so go slow if you feel you must. What you can't do is wait until the day before your paper is due: If you draft slowly, you won't finish; if you draft quickly, you'll turn in a half-baked mess.

8.2 Picture Your Readers Asking Friendly Questions

We said this before, but it's important enough to say again: You will write better and more easily if you picture yourself talking with a group of friendly readers who have lots of questions. Before you start drafting, imagine the specific readers you hope to address (*not* your teacher!). Imagine their questions, and build your draft around your answers. For now, think of those readers as friendly and supportive: *Why do you say that? I think I see where you are going, but I'm not sure: can you explain it a little more? That's interesting: what's your evidence for it?* While you are drafting, imagine readers whose questions help you move along, who *want* to agree with you if only you will give them the information they need.

Especially if you draft quickly, you need to quiet your own internal censor while you draft. Your goal is to get your ideas down as fully and freely as you can. You'll have time and (in chapters 12–14) lots of help to get them right in revision. But if you worry over every little detail, you'll spend more time in responding to that voice in your head than in discovering what you think about what you have learned. So let your imagined friendly readers dominate as you draft.

Later on you'll imagine skeptical, even nasty questions so that you can know where you have to improve your completed draft. But for now, banish the skeptics.

WORKING IN GROUPS

Avoid Negative Responses

There will come a time when you will want your writing group to be as hard on your paper as you can: better to find out what the problems are before you turn it in. But when you are drafting is not that time. When you meet during the drafting stage, make it a rule that everyone will avoid all but the most obvious criticisms and concentrate on positive suggestions. Too many negative thoughts will only stop up the flow of your writing.

8.3 Be Open to Surprises and Changes

If you write as you go and plan your argument before you draft, you're unlikely to be utterly surprised by what you write. Even so, be open to new directions from beginning to end:

- When your drafting heads off on a tangent, go with it for a bit to see whether you're on to something better than you planned.
- When your evidence leads you to think that a reason may not hold up, don't ignore that feeling. Follow it up.
- When you get a feeling that your reasons may be in the wrong order, experiment with new ones, even if you thought you were almost done.

- Even when you reach your final conclusion, you may see how to restate your claim more clearly and pointedly.

If you get better ideas early enough, invest the time to change your plan. It is a cheap price for a big improvement.

8.4 Develop Productive Drafting Habits

Most of us learn to write in the least efficient way—under pressure, rushing to meet a deadline, doing a quick draft the night before, and proofreading maybe a few minutes in the morning. That sometimes works for a short paper. It never works for a long one. You need time and a plan that lets you draft a little at a time, not in marathon sessions that dull your thinking and kill your interest. Give yourself a few days to write, set an achievable page goal for each day, and stick to it.

Always draft in a suitable environment. You may not need a particularly quiet place—in fact, the two of us prefer a little background noise when we write. But you *must* avoid interruptions. Turn off your cell; take your chat program offline; don't let your friends talk to you while you draft. One of the greatest obstacles to successful drafting is *anything* that forces you to pay attention to something other than what you are writing.

When you start a drafting session, review your storyboard to decide what you're ready to draft that day. How will it fit into its section and the whole? What reason does this section support? Where does it fit in the overall logic? Which key terms state the concepts that distinguish this section? If you're blocked, skip to another section.

Before you draft, picture your friendly readers and summarize for them (out loud if possible) what has come before the place you plan to start. Then imagine that what you write next simply continues that conversation.

As you draft, keep in front of you a list of the key terms for the concepts that you'll run through your whole report and another list of the key terms for the section you are working on. From time to time, check how often you've used them.

CAUTION

Avoid Procrastinators' Tricks

Don't play procrastinators' tricks on yourself—something everyone is prone to do, including the two of us. (We have missed more than one deadline in preparing this book.) You cannot do your best work if you waste the time you have available. Here are the top four mistakes to avoid:

- Don't substitute more reading for writing. Start writing as soon as you have enough evidence to go on. You may have to go back for more, but don't fool yourself that the writing will be easier if only you do more reading.

- Don't keep revising the same pages over and over. Focus on getting a complete draft that you can then revise.
- Don't focus on how much more you have to do. You will freeze up if you become intimidated by how much you have left. Set small achievable goals for each day and focus on them.
- Don't allow yourself to do anything else during your writing time. Never spend a few minutes on texting or chatting, and never, never tell yourself that a quick computer game will refresh your mind so you can get back to work.

Writing is hard. But you won't make it any easier by wasting away the time you set aside to write. Put your head down and tell yourself, *Just get it done.*

8.5 Work through Writer's Block

If you can't get started on a first draft or struggle to draft more than a few words, you may have writer's block. Some cases arise from anxieties about school and its pressures; if that sounds like you, see a counselor. But most cases have causes you can address.

- You may be stuck because you have no goals or, conversely, goals that are too high. If so, set goals that are small and achievable. Then create a routine that helps you achieve them. Don't hesitate to use devices to keep yourself moving, such as a progress chart or regular meetings with a writing partner.
- You may feel so overwhelmed by the project that you don't know where to begin. If so, break the process into small achievable tasks; then focus on doing one at a time. Don't dwell on the whole until you've completed several small parts of it.
- You may think that you have to make every sentence or paragraph perfect before you move on to the next one. You don't. Tell yourself you're not writing a final draft but only sketching out some ideas, grit your teeth, then do some quick and dirty writing to get yourself started. If you write along the way, you'll be less obsessed with making your draft perfect. And in any event, we all compromise on perfection to get the job done.

QUICK TIP

Getting Unstuck

If you have problems like these with most of your writing, go to the student learning center. You will find people there who have worked with every kind of procrastinator and blocked writer and can tailor their advice to your problem.

On the other hand, some cases of writer's block are opportunities to let your ideas simmer in your subconscious while they combine and recombine into something new and surprising. If you're stuck *and* have time (another reason to start early), do something else for a day or two. Then return to the task to see if you can get back on track.

8.6 Preparing an Oral Report

It will not be until you are ready to draft that you can even think of giving an oral report to your class. Before then, you will have too little to say and you will be too unsure of what you do have. But you can learn a great deal from giving an oral report as you draft. It cannot be the same kind of report you give after you have completed your paper (see 13.4), but it can be a useful exercise.

At this point, your oral report should have two goals: (1) to force you to formulate a coherent forecast of what you final paper will say, so that you can discover whether it makes as much sense when you say it as when you just think it; and (2) to test your ideas through the responses of your classmates. In particular, a report at this state should do three things:

- Present your research question and answer/claim.
- Outline your reasons and sub-reasons supporting that claim.
- Forecast the kind of evidence you will use to support those reasons.

8.6.1 Prepare Notes, Not a Script

Most of us are at least a little anxious at the idea of speaking before a group, and you're likely to be a tad more anxious at the idea of presenting a paper you have not yet written. Many students think that the cure for that anxiety is to write out a script for their presentation, so that they can just read rather than remember and think. That's generally a bad idea. You don't have the time to do all that extra writing, and no one wants to sit while you read it.

Instead of a script, prepare good notes that include the following:

- a complete introduction and conclusion
- your reasons, in order, in large bold type
- for each reason, a bulleted list of your two or three best bits of evidence, named but not explained

8.6.2 Write Out a Complete Introduction and Conclusion

There are two parts of your presentation that you must get right: your introduction, which prepares listeners for what's coming, and your conclusion, which tells them what to remember. Because they are so important, these are the only two parts for which you should write a script that you rehearse. You don't need to memorize them, but you should rehearse enough that you can deliver them with only a few glances at your notes. That way, you will get off to a confident start, which will improve the rest of your performance, and you will end with a confident close, which will improve how your audience remembers your report (and your performance of it).

If you have been filling your storyboard as you go, you have there a sketch of a working introduction and some notes on a conclusion. Write them out in language *to be spoken*. Except for necessary technical terms, do not use any words that you will feel uncomfortable saying or that make you sound like a textbook. State your research question as clearly as you can. Be sure to end with your answer. In between, do what you can to explain the significance of your research question.

8.6.3 Make the Body of Your Notes an Outline

Concentrate on reasons in the body of your presentation. Use them to organize your notes and put them in big bold type. These are the sentences you must be sure to say. For everything else, adapt to your audience: spend time on what seems to engage them; skip what doesn't. But do cover each reason. And just before you conclude, run through your main reasons in order: this is the best summary of your argument.

If you have time, present some of your best evidence, especially for reasons that your audience is unlikely to accept right off. But at this stage, your report should be focused on your problem, its answer, and your reasons supporting that claim. Communicate them clearly, and you will have done a fine job.

9: Quoting, Paraphrasing, and Summarizing Sources

You should build most of your paper out of your own words that represent your own thinking, but that thinking should be supported by quotations, paraphrases, and summaries of information you found in sources. In fact, new researchers typically find almost all of their evidence in sources. So it is crucial not only that you fully integrate the information from sources into your argument but that you present it in ways that lead your readers to trust it. For that you must know what readers expect, what choices you have, and how those choices lead readers to draw conclusions about your sources and about you.

9.1   When to Quote, Paraphrase, or Summarize

You can present information from a source in the source's words or in your own. Which you choose depends on how you plan to use the information in your argument, but also on the kind of paper you are writing, since different fields use quotation, paraphrase, and summary in different proportions. In general, researchers in the humanities quote most often. Social and natural scientists typically paraphrase and summarize. But you must decide each case for itself.

> **Principles for Choosing Summary, Paraphrase, or Quotation**
>
> **Summarize** when details are irrelevant or a source isn't important enough to warrant the space.
>
> **Paraphrase** when you can state what a source says more clearly or concisely than the source does, or when your argument depends on the details in a source but not on its specific words. (Before you paraphrase, however, read 9.3.)
>
> **Quote** for these purposes:
>
> - The quoted words themselves are your evidence, and you need to deal with them exactly as they appeared in the original.

- The quoted words are strikingly original, well expressed, odd, or otherwise too useful to lose in paraphrase.
- The passage states a view that you disagree with, and to be fair you want to state it exactly.
- The passage is from an authority who backs up your view.
- The passage expresses your key concepts so clearly that the quotation can frame the rest of your discussion.

You must balance quotations, paraphrases, and summaries with your own fresh ideas. Do not merely repeat or, worse, download words and ideas of others that you then stitch together with a few sentences of your own. Teachers grind their teeth over papers that show so little original thinking.

Readers value research only to the degree that they trust its sources. So when you include a summary, paraphrase, or quotation in your first draft, record its bibliographic data in the appropriate citation style right then and there. (See part 2).

9.2 Creating a Fair Summary

Use a summary to report information from a source when only its main points are relevant to your argument. Because a good summary leaves out details, it is shorter than the original. In some cases, readers expect a summary to cover all the main points, but when you summarize for a research paper, you do not have to cover everything in the source or even in the part you summarize. You can and usually should include only those points relevant to your argument, as long as you do not leave out crucial points that might change how readers understand what the source says.

Suppose, for example, that you were writing a paper on the role of creativity in research. For that paper, the following paragraph would fairly summarize the previous chapter on drafting:

Colomb and Williams (2010) emphasize that drafting is a process of discovery that can fuel a writer's creative thinking. They acknowledge that some writers have to draft carefully and stick close to their outlines, but they advise writers to draft as freely and as openly as they can. They encourage even slow and careful drafters to be open to new ideas and surprises and not to be limited by what they do before drafting. They still stress the value of steady work that follows a plan—for example, writing a little bit every day rather than all at once in a fit of desperate inspiration. But they show writers how to make the best of a plan while hoping that a better idea will come along.

This summary does not cover the entire chapter: for instance, it ignores the information on oral reports and on procrastination and writer's block. But that's OK, since that information is less relevant to issues of creativity and leaving it out does not distort what the chapter says. The following leaves out so much that it would not be a fair summary:

Colomb and Williams (2010) emphasize that drafting is a process of discovery that can fuel a writer's creative thinking. They advise writers to draft as freely as they can in order to be open to new ideas and surprises and not to be limited by the plans they make before drafting. They show writers how to go beyond their plans, hoping that a better idea will come along.

Here the writer gives a false impression of what the chapter says by leaving out something that the chapter emphasizes: the tension between our need to make and follow plans and to free our minds to make the most of new ideas.

When you summarize information for a research paper, you should give the summary a slant by focusing on that part of the information most relevant to your argument. But you cannot slant it so much that you misrepresent what the source actually says—which means that you'll have to be sure that *you* understand what the source says. It's another case where you'll have to exercise some judgment.

> **How to Create a Fair and Relevant Summary**
> To be sure that your summary is concise, relevant, and fair, do this:
>
> 1. Summarize only if readers can understand without knowing details. If readers may need more than just the gist of what a source says, don't summarize: quote or paraphrase.
> 2. Decide why the information from the source is relevant to your argument. What reason does it support? What does it add to that support?
> 3. Pick out the most important sentences in the source that are most relevant to a specific part of your argument. In most cases, focus on reasons. But if you will use the summary as evidence, pick out the most important reports of evidence.
> 4. Paraphrase those sentences; list the paraphrases in the order they occur in the original.
> 5. Add any other information that readers might need to understand accurately what the source says.
> 6. Revise to turn the list into a passage that flows.

9.3 Creating a Fair Paraphrase

As with a summary, when you paraphrase you report what a source says in your own words. But you don't leave out important details. Don't worry about length: your paraphrase may be a little shorter or longer than the original. What's important is that you convey all of the important information from the original.

Some new researchers wonder why they should bother to paraphrase: If a paraphrase has to contain everything important in the original, why not just quote it? That's easier, not to mention safer. Quoting may be easier, but quotations are not always the best way to approach readers. First, when readers see too many quotations, they may suspect that you have just quilted together the ideas of others, with no contribution of your own. Second, when you use your own words, you show readers not only that you understand the source but how you understand it. Finally, many sources use language that you would never use. For example, how many students would use a phrase like this one from the quote below: "technology begets more technology"? Your paper will seem more unified and more a product of your own understanding if it sounds more like you than like your sources.

When you paraphrase, read the passage until you think you understand not just its main idea but its details and complications. Then, without looking back at the source, say out loud what you understand as though you were explaining it to a classmate. (If you stumble, try it again.) When you are happy with an oral version, write it in your draft. Be sure that your paraphrase sounds more like you than like the source:

Original:
According to Jared Diamond, "Because technology begets more technology, the importance of an invention's diffusion potentially exceeds the importance of the original invention. Technology's history exemplifies what is termed an autocatalytic process: that is, one that speeds up at a rate that increases with time, because the process catalyzes itself" (301).

Paraphrase:
According to Jared Diamond, technology feeds on itself. One invention leads to another, and then to still more at a rate that increases with time. So what is most important about an invention may not be the invention itself but how quickly it spreads (301).

In most cases, writers introduce a paraphrase in the same way that they introduce a stand-alone quotation, with a phrase or clause that names the source:

According to Jared Diamond, technology feeds on itself. . . .

Jared Diamond argues that technology feeds on itself. . . .

QUICK TIP

How to Name Your Sources
When you refer to a source the first time, use his or her full name. Do not precede it with *Mr.*, *Ms.*, *Professor*, or *Doctor*; you can use titles like *Mayor, Sena-*

tor, President, Reverend, or *Bishop.* If you mention the source again, use just the last name:

According to Steven Pinker, "Claims about a language instinct . . . have virtually nothing to do with possible genetic differences between people." Pinker goes on to argue that "language is not . . ."

9.4   Adding Quotations to Your Text

You can insert quotations into your text in two ways:

- For four or fewer lines, use a *run-in quotation* by putting the quoted words on the same line as your text.
- For five or more lines, use a *block quotation* set off as a separate, indented unit.

You can integrate both run-in and block quotations into your text in two ways:

1. Include the quotation as an independent clause, sentence, or passage:

    Jared Diamond reminds us that "circumstances change, and past primacy is no guarantee of future primacy" (417).

    Jared Diamond says, "The histories of the Fertile Crescent and China . . . hold a salutary lesson for the modern world: circumstances change, and past primacy is no guarantee of future primacy" (417).

    According to Jared Diamond,

    > Because technology begets more technology, the importance of an invention's diffusion potentially exceeds the importance of the original invention. Technology's history exemplifies what is termed an autocatalytic process: that is, one that speeds up at a rate that increases with time, because the process catalyzes itself. (301)

2. Weave the quotation into the grammar of your own sentence:

    As Diamond points out, the "lesson for the modern world" in the history of the Fertile Crescent and China is that you can't count on history to repeat itself because "circumstances change, and past primacy is no guarantee of future primacy" (417).

To make a quotation grammatically mesh with your own sentence, you can modify it, so long as you don't change its meaning and you clearly indicate added or changed words with square brackets and deletions with three dots (called *ellipses*). This sentence quotes the original intact:

Posner focuses on religion not for its spirituality, but for its social functions: "A notable feature of American society is religious pluralism, and we should consider how this relates to the efficacy of governance by social norms in view of the historical importance of religion as both a source and enforcer of such norms" (299).

This version modifies the quotation to fit the grammar of the writer's sentence:

> In his discussion of religion, Posner says of American society that "a notable feature . . . is [its] religious pluralism." He argues that to understand how well social norms control what we do, we should consider "the historical importance of religion as both a source and enforcer of such norms" (299).

9.5 Introducing Quotations and Paraphrases

You can introduce an independent quotation or paraphrase with a phrase, clause, or sentence *before* the quotation:

In Diamond's view, . . .
Diamond says, . . . *or* Diamond says that . . .
Diamond shows that no society can expect to thrive forever: "The histories . . ." (417).

That introductory part usually names the source, but it does not have to:

As a recent study has shown, "The histories . . ." (Diamond, 417).
If there is one thing that America should learn from the past, it's that nothing lasts forever: "The histories . . ." (Diamond, 417).

You can also identify a quotation at its middle or end, although that may feel backward to readers.

"The histories of the Fertile Crescent and China . . . hold a salutary lesson for the modern world," according to Jared Diamond, because "circumstances change, and past primacy is no guarantee of future primacy" (417).
"The histories . . . future primacy," according to Diamond (417).
"The histories . . . future primacy," argues Diamond (417).

Most of those introductory clauses take the form of *Source says*:

Diamond says, "The histories of . . ." (417).
Diamond says that there is a lesson in "the histories of . . ." (417).

Experienced writers use many verbs in place of *says* because the verb that introduces a quotation or paraphrase tells readers how you want them to think about that information and its source. For example, you can indicate whether you think the information is reliable: "Diamond wants to think that" vs. "Diamond proves that." Or you can indicate whether the information is factual or contested: "Diamond reports that" vs. "Diamond maintains that." So think carefully about what readers will infer from the verb you use to introduce information from a source.

Verbs for Introducing a Quotation or Paraphrase
We can't give you a complete guide to the shades of meaning in the verbs that introduce quotations and paraphrases, but we can give you some ways to use them:

All-Purpose Verbs
Use these verbs for claims, facts, opinions, inferences, guesses, or any other kind of information in a source.

These are **neutral**:

Source says that . . .
Also: writes, adds, notes, comments

These indicate **how strongly the source feels** about the information:

Source emphasizes that . . .
Also: affirms, asserts, explains, suggests, hints

These indicate that the information is **a problem for the source**:

Source admits that . . .
Also: acknowledges, grants, allows

Verbs for Argued Claims

These are **neutral**:

Source claims that . . .
Also: argues, reasons, contends, maintains, holds

These indicate that you find the claim **convincing**:

Source proves that . . .
Also: shows, demonstrates, determines

Verbs for Opinions

These are **neutral**:

Source thinks that . . .
Also: believes, assumes, insists, declares

These indicate that you find the opinion **weak** or **irresponsible**:

Source wants to think that . . .
Also: wants to believe, just assumes, merely takes for granted

Verbs for Matters of Judgment

Source judges that . . .
Also: concludes, infers

9.6   **Mixing Quotation with Summary and Paraphrase**

Although we have explained summary, paraphrase, and quotation as though they were entirely distinct, experienced writers often incorporate quotations into the other two. For example, when you weave a quotation into your own sentence, that sentence usually includes some paraphrase (the paraphrase is underlined):

As Diamond points out, the "lesson for the modern world" in the history of the Fertile Crescent and China is that you can't count on history to repeat itself because "circumstances change, and past primacy is no guarantee of future primacy" (417).

In his discussion of religion, Posner says of American society that "a notable feature . . . is [its] religious pluralism." He argues that to understand how well social norms control what we do, we should consider "the historical importance of religion as both a source and enforcer of such norms" (299).

Similarly, you can include quotations in a summary:

Colomb and Williams (2010) emphasize that drafting is "an act of discovery" (83) that can fuel a writer's creative thinking. They acknowledge that some writers have to draft carefully and stick close to their outlines, but they advise writers to draft as freely and as openly as they can. They encourage even slow and careful drafters to be open to new ideas and surprises and not to be limited by what they do before drafting. They still stress the value of steady work that follows a plan—for example, writing a little bit every day rather than all at once in a fit of desperate inspiration. But they show writers how to make the best of a plan while hoping that you will "discover what your storyboard has missed" (83).

When you mix a few quotations into your summaries and paraphrases, you seem a more sophisticated writer. You give readers a better sense of the source without quoting so much that your paper seems a cut-and-paste job. You can also take advantage of those places where your source offers an especially interesting or memorable phrase. If you find that you have drafted a couple of pages that are all summary and paraphrase, go back to your notes to find notable phrases or sentences that you can add to liven up your prose.

9.7 Interpret Complex Quotations Before You Offer Them

By the time you add a quotation to your draft, you may have studied it so much that you think readers can't miss its relevance. But complex evidence never speaks for itself, especially not a long quotation, image, table or chart, and so on. So when you quote a passage that is long, difficult to understand, or written in complex language, you must speak for it by adding a sentence stating what you want your readers to get out of it.

You have already seen examples of quotations introduced by an introductory sentence:

If there is one thing that America should learn from the past, it's that nothing lasts forever: "The histories of the Fertile Crescent and China . . . hold a salutary lesson for the modern world: circumstances change, and past primacy is no guarantee of future primacy" (Diamond, 417).

Such introductory sentences tell readers how the writer wants them to understand the quotation that follows.

You may need even longer introductions when the relationship between the quotation and the claim it supports is not obvious. For example, it's hard to see how the quoted lines in this next passage support the claim:

When Hamlet comes upon his stepfather Claudius at prayer, he coolly and logically thinks about whether to kill him on the spot._claim_

> Now might I do it [kill him] pat, now [while] he is praying:
> And now I'll do't; and so he goes to heaven;
> And so am I reveng'd . . .
> [But this] villain kills my father; and for that,
> I, his sole son, do this same villain send to heaven.
> Why, this is hire and salary, not revenge._evidence_

Nothing in those lines specifically refers to Hamlet's cool logic. Compare this:

When Hamlet comes upon his stepfather Claudius at prayer, he logically analyzes whether to kill him on the spot._claim_ First he wants to kill Claudius immediately, but then he pauses to think: If he kills Claudius while he is praying, he sends his soul to heaven. But he wants Claudius damned to hell, so he coolly decides to kill him later:_interpretive introduction_

> Now might I do it [kill him] pat, now he is praying:
> And now I'll do't; and so he goes to heaven;

And so am I reveng'd . . .
[But this] villain kills my father; and for that,
I, his sole son, do this same villain send to heaven.
Why, this is hire and salary, not revenge._{evidence}

That kind of explanatory introduction is even more important when you present quantitative evidence in a table or figure (see 11.3.1).

10: Preventing Plagiarism

10.1   Guard against Inadvertent Plagiarism

It will be as you draft that you risk making one of the worst mistakes you can make: you lead readers to think that you're trying to pass off the work of another writer as your own. Do that and you risk an accusation of plagiarism, a charge so serious that, if sustained, could mean a failing grade or, if you're in a college class, expulsion.

These days teachers are intensely concerned about plagiarism, because they believe the Internet makes it easier for students to cheat. So they are especially vigilant for signs of plagiarism. Even if you don't mean to cheat, you may still have a problem if you fail to follow the rules for using and citing material from sources, because many teachers won't accept ignorance as an excuse. In any case, you do not help readers trust you or your argument if you fail on something as basic as properly citing everything you have used from a source.

Many instructors punish students for plagiarism but don't explain it, because they think it needs no explanation. And in some cases they are right: students don't need to be told that they cheat when they put their name on a paper they didn't write. Most also know they cheat when they pass off as their own work page after page downloaded from the web. But many students fail to realize that they risk a charge of plagiarism even when they are not intentionally dishonest, but only ignorant or careless.

> **Three Principles for Citing Sources**
>
> When you use any source in any way, readers expect you to follow three principles. You risk a charge of plagiarism if you ignore any one of them.
>
> 1. You must cite the source for any words, ideas, or methods that are not your own.
>
>   Writers can avoid paraphrasing too closely if they focus on remembering what they understand from the original, not its actual words. One way

to do this is simply to put the original aside as you write the paraphrase (Colomb and Williams, 92). But a better way is to imagine that you are explaining the idea to someone who hasn't read the original.

2. When you quote the exact words of a source, you must put those words in quotation marks or a block quotation, *even if you cite the source in your own text*. This would be plagiarism:

According to Colomb and Williams, when you quote the exact words of a source, you must put those words in quotation marks or a block quotation, *even if you cite the source in your own text* (100).

3 When you paraphrase the words of a source, you must use your own sentences, not sentences so similar to the original that they are almost a quotation. This would be considered plagiarism by many teachers:

According to Colomb and Williams, you risk being charged with plagiarism when you paraphrase a passage from a source not in your own words but in sentences so similar to it that you almost quote them, regardless of whether your own text cites the source (100).

Some students think that they don't have to cite all of the material freely circulated online. Not so. These principles apply to sources of any kind—printed, recorded, oral, *and* online—but teachers are most on the lookout for plagiarism of online sources. You risk a charge of plagiarism if you fail to cite *anything* you get from a source, *especially* if it's from a website, a database, a podcast, or other online source. A source is a source, and you must cite them all.

10.2 Take Good Notes

We warned you about this earlier, in 4.2, but it is so important to take good notes that we will repeat ourselves. You cannot follow the rules in using and citing information from a source if you don't have the right information in your notes. So, long before you draft, you have to make sure that your notes do the following:

- Record all bibliographic data for each source.
- Clearly distinguish between your words and those of the source.
- Correctly transcribe each quotation, including punctuation.
- Record page numbers for each quotation and paraphrase in your notes.

10.3 Signal Every Quotation, Even When You Cite Its Source

Even if you cite your source, readers must know unambiguously which words are yours and which you quote. You risk a charge of plagiarism if you fail to use quotation marks to signal that you have copied as little as a single line.

It gets complicated, however, when you copy just a few words. Suppose you were writing about this passage from Jared Diamond:

Because technology begets more technology, the importance of an invention's diffusion potentially exceeds the importance of the original invention. Technology's history exemplifies what is termed an autocatalytic process: that is, one that speeds up at a rate that increases with time, because the process catalyzes itself (Diamond, 301).

To write about Diamond's ideas, you would probably use some of his words, such as *the importance of an invention*. But you wouldn't put that short phrase in quotation marks, because it shows no originality of thought or expression. Two of his phrases, however, are so striking that they do need quotation marks: *technology begets more technology* and *autocatalytic process*. For example:

The power of technology goes beyond individual inventions because technology "begets more technology." It is, as Diamond puts it, an "autocatalytic process" (301).

Once you cite those words, you can use them again without quotation marks or citation:

So as one invention begets another to spark a self-sustaining catalysis, the effect spreads exponentially across all national boundaries.

This is a gray area: words that seem striking to some are commonplace to others. If you use quotation marks around too many common phrases, readers may think you're naive or insecure. But if you fail to use them when readers think you should, they may suspect you of plagiarism. It's better to seem naive than dishonest, especially early in your research career, so use quotation marks freely.

10.4   Don't Paraphrase Too Closely

You paraphrase appropriately when you represent an idea in your own words more clearly or pointedly than the source does. But readers will think that you cross the line from fair paraphrase to plagiarism if they can match most of your words with those of your source. For example, unlike the paraphrase in 10.3, this one plagiarizes the original:

Original:
Because technology begets more technology, the importance of an invention's diffusion potentially exceeds the importance of the original invention. Technology's history exemplifies what is termed an autocatalytic process: that is, one that speeds up at a rate that increases with time, because the process catalyzes itself (Diamond, 301).

Paraphrase:

According to Diamond, technology gives birth to more technology. As a result, the importance of the spread of an invention may exceed the importance of the invention itself. The history of technology shows what is called an autocatalytic process through which the invention of new technologies speeds up at an increasing rate because the process of change catalyzes itself (301).

The writer of this version may think that she has used her own words: she changes some of Diamond's complex phrases into simpler ones: *begets → gives birth, diffusion → spread, exemplifies → shows.* But the paraphrase follows the original step-by-step, word by word. That, for most readers, is plagiarism.

> **QUICK TIP**
>
> **Safe Paraphrasing**
> To avoid unintentionally seeming to be guilty of plagiarism by paraphrase, don't read your source as you paraphrase it. Read the passage, look away, think about it for a moment. *Then still looking away,* restate it in your own words. Then check whether you can run your finger along your sentence and find the same ideas in the same order as in your source. If you can, so can your readers. Try again.

10.5 (Almost Always) Cite a Source for Ideas Not Your Own

The basic principle is simple: Cite a source for a borrowed idea whenever your readers might think you are claiming that you are its original source. But when you try to apply it, the rule becomes more complicated, because most of our own ideas come from some identifiable sources somewhere in history. Readers don't expect you to find and cite every distant source for every familiar idea. But they do expect you to cite the source for an idea when (1) the idea is associated with a specific person *and* (2) it's new enough not to be part of a field's common knowledge.

For example, psychologists claim that we think and feel in different parts of our brains. But no one would expect you to cite the source of that idea, because it's so familiar to psychologists that no reader would think you were taking credit for originating that idea. On the other hand, some psychologists argue that emotions are crucial to rational decision making. You would have to cite the source of that idea because it is so new and so closely tied to particular researchers.

> **QUICK TIP**
>
> **When to Cite Ideas**
> If you are a new researcher, you have a problem: You can't cite every borrowed idea, but how are you supposed to know which ideas are too familiar to cite? Here are some signs to look for:

- If an idea is a main claim in the source, you should cite it.
- If the source spends time showing how the idea differs from the ideas of others, you should cite it.
- If the source cites an idea, you should too.
- If more than one source uses the idea without citing it, then you don't have to cite it either.

10.6 Don't Plead Ignorance, Misunderstanding, or Innocent Intentions

To be sure, what looks like plagiarism is often just honest ignorance of how to use and cite sources. In those cases, students defend themselves by claiming they didn't *intend* to mislead. The problem is, we read words, not minds. So think of plagiarism not as an act you intend but as one that others *perceive*. Avoid any sign that might give your readers a reason to suspect you of it. Whenever you put your name on a paper, you implicitly promise that you wrote every word that you don't clearly and specifically attribute to someone else.

Here is how to think about this: If someone read your paper immediately after reading your source written by Johnson. Would she think, *This sounds just like Johnson* or *I remember these words* or *This idea must have come from Johnson*. If so, you must cite Johnson and set off any sequence of his exact words in quotation marks or a block quotation.

10.7 Guard against Inappropriate Assistance

Before experienced writers turn in their work, they often show drafts to others for criticism and suggestions, and you should too. But teachers differ on how much help is appropriate and what help you should acknowledge. Most instructors encourage students to get general criticism and minor editing, but not detailed rewriting or substantive suggestions. You usually aren't required to acknowledge general criticism, minor editing, or help from a school writing tutor, but you must acknowledge help that's special or extensive. Your instructor, however, sets the rules, so ask.

11: Presenting Evidence in Tables and Figures

At an early stage in your development as a researcher, you are unlikely to have assignments that require you to collect and report large sets of numerical data. But if you do, your readers will grasp those complex numbers most easily if you present them graphically rather than in words. You can present the same numerical data in different graphic forms, but some forms will suit your data and message better than others. In this chapter, we show you how to choose the right graphic form and to design it so that readers can see both what your data are and how they support your argument.

A NOTE ON TERMINOLOGY

We use the term *graphics* to name all visual images offered as evidence. Traditionally, graphics are divided into *tables* and *figures*.

- A table is a grid with columns and rows that present data in numbers or words organized by categories.
- Figures are all other graphic forms, including graphs, charts, photographs, drawings, and diagrams.

Figures that present quantitative data are divided into two kinds:

- Charts typically consist of bars, circles, points, or other shapes.
- Graphs typically consist of continuous lines.

11.1 Choosing Verbal or Visual Representations

Few new researchers work with the kinds of data that are best presented graphically. So chances are that you can present your data in sentences rather than in tables or charts. Readers can understand numbers like these without the help of graphics:

In 1996, on average, men earned $32,144 a year, women, $23,710—a difference of $8,434.

You need graphics only when readers have to deal with more than five or six numbers, particularly if they have to compare them. For example, most readers would struggle to see the important relationships among the numbers in a passage like this:

Between 1970 and 2000, the structure of families changed in two ways. In 1970, 85 percent of families had two parents, but in 1980 that number declined to 77 percent, then to 73 percent in 1990, and to 68 percent in 2000. The number of one-parent families rose, particularly families headed by a mother. In 1970, 11 percent of families were headed by a single mother. In 1980, that number rose to 18 percent, in 1990 to 22 percent, and to 23 percent in 2000. Single fathers headed 1 percent of the families in 1970, 2 percent in 1980, 3 percent in 1990, and 4 percent in 2000. Families with no adult in the home have remained stable at 3–4 percent.

Such data are best presented graphically.

For most of you, our advice is to avoid graphics and stick to words, at least at first. You have enough to keep in mind in learning how to get the words right. But if you do have to present data too complex for words, this chapter will show you how.

11.2 Choosing the Graphical Form That Best Achieves Your Intention

When you graphically present data as complex as that paragraph above, you can choose a table, a bar chart, or a line graph. Each communicates something different to readers.

A **table** seems precise and objective. It emphasizes individual numbers and forces readers to figure out relationships or trends (unless you state them in an introductory sentence):

Table 11.1: Changes in family structure, 1970–2000

	Percentage of total families			
Family type	1970	1980	1990	2000
2 parents	85	77	73	68
mother	11	18	22	23
father	1	2	3	4
no adult	3	4	3	4

Charts and **line graphs** communicate specific values less precisely than a table, but their images communicate their message quickly and with greater impact. They also have different effects:

- A bar chart emphasizes comparisons among discrete items that can be seen at a glance.

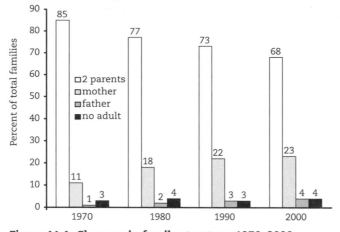

Figure 11.1: Changes in family structure, 1970–2000

- A line graph emphasizes the story of trends over time:

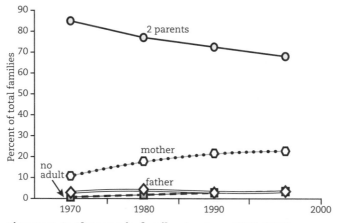

Figure 11.2: Changes in family structure, 1970–2000

Decide on the effect you want, then choose the graphic that fits. Do not choose the first form that comes to mind or the one you found in your source.

CAUTION

Your Software Likes Your Graphics Fancy, Your Readers Like Them Simple

Your computer software will encourage you to use many more graphics than we cover here, but stick to the basics. Unless you have lots of experience creating graphics, limit your choices to tables, bar charts, and line graphs. Even if you have experience, avoid most of the choices your software allows: no merely decorative colors, no 3-D graphics, no fancy graphics when a simple one will do. You don't improve your report with graphics that look dazzling but confuse or distract readers.

11.3 Designing Tables and Figures

You use graphics to present quantitative data that serve as evidence in support of your reasons. So you must design them to communicate two things: what the data are and how they support your reason.

11.3.1 Tell Readers What Your Graphic Shows

A graphic representing complex numbers rarely speaks for itself. You must introduce and label it so that readers know both what to see in it and how it is relevant to your argument.

For example, readers have to study table 11.2 closely to see how it supports its claim:

Most predictions about gasoline consumption have proved wrong.*claim*

Table 11.2: Gasoline consumption

	1970	1980	1990	2000
Annual miles (000)	9.5	10.3	10.5	11.7
Annual consumption (gal.)	760.0	760.0	520.0	533.0

To see the connection, we need a more specific claim, a table title that better identifies what the numbers represent, highlighting that draws our eye to the most important data, *and* another sentence that explains how the numbers relate to the claim:

Gasoline consumption did not grow as many had predicted.*claim* **Even though Americans drove 23 percent more miles in 2000 than in 1970, they used 32 percent less fuel.**

Table 11.3: Per capita mileage and gasoline consumption, 1970–2000

	1970	1980	1990	2000
Annual miles (000)	9.5	10.3	10.5	11.7
(% change vs. 1970)		8.4%	10.5%	23.1%
Annual consumption (gal.)	760.0	760.0	520.0	533.0
(% change vs. 1970)			(31.5%)	(31.6%)

That added information tells readers how to interpret the key data in table 11.3.

How to Set Up a Graphic

1. Introduce each table or figure with a sentence that states how the data support your point. Include in that sentence any specific number that you want readers to focus on. (That number must also appear in the table or figure, visually highlighted if possible.)
2. Label every table and figure in a way that describes its data.

   - For a table, the label is called a *title* and is set flush left above.
   - For a figure, the label is called a *caption* (or *legend*) and is set flush left below.

   Keep titles and captions short but descriptive enough to indicate exactly what the data represent and to differentiate each graphic from every other one. Do not use the label or caption to imply a claim about the figure:

   Not: Weaker effects of counseling on depressed children before profes-sionalization of staff, 1995–2004
   But: Effect of counseling on depressed children, 1995–2004

3. Put into a table or figure information that helps readers see how the data support your point. For example, if numbers in a table show a trend and the size of the change matters, add the change to the final column. Or if a line on a graph changes in response to an influence not mentioned on the graph, add text to the image to explain it.

All of the framing elements work to make figure 11.3 easy to understand: (1) The introductory sentence explains what the graph shows and points out not only the trend but what readers should see in it; (2) the label tells readers what the data represent; and (3) the inserted callouts explain the important changes in the data.

Although reading and math scores initially declined by almost 100 points fol-lowing redistricting, that trend was substantially reversed by the introduction of supplemental math and reading programs.

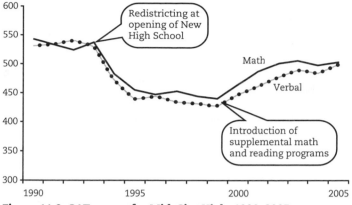

Figure 11.3: SAT scores for Mid-City High, 1990–2005

11.3.2 **Keep the Image as Simple and Informative as Its Content Allows**
Some guides encourage you to put as much data as you can in every graphic, and most software encourages you to make them visually complex. But readers want to see only the data relevant to your claim, presented in an image free of distractions. As a new researcher, you can let your software take care of most of the effort in designing your graphics, but you'll have to change several default settings. Follow these guidelines.

For all graphics:

· Don't put a box around a graphic unless you group two or more figures.
· Never color or shade the background.
· Plot data on three dimensions only when you cannot display the data in any other way and your readers are familiar with such graphs.

For tables:

· Never divide columns and rows with both horizontal and vertical lines. Use light gray lines in one direction only if a table is complex.
· For tables with many rows, lightly shade every fifth row.
· Clearly label rows and columns.
· Order rows and columns by a principle that lets readers quickly find what you want them to see. Do not automatically choose alphabetic order.
· Sum totals at the bottom of a column or at the end of a row, not at the top or left.

Compare tables 11.4 and 11.5. Table 11.4 looks cluttered and its items aren't helpfully organized:

Table 11.4: Unemployment in major industrial nations, 1990–2000

	1990	2001	*Change*
Australia	6.7	6.5	(.2)
Canada	7.7	5.9	(1.8)
France	9.1	8.8	(.3)
Germany	5.0	8.1	3.1
Italy	7.0	9.9	2.9
Japan	2.1	4.8	2.7
Sweden	1.8	5.1	3.3
UK	6.9	5.1	(1.8)
USA	5.6	4.2	(1.6)

In contrast, table 11.5 is clearer because its title is more informative, the table has less distracting visual clutter, and its items are organized to let us see patterns more easily.

Table 11.5: Changes in unemployment rates of industrial nations, 1990–2000
English-speaking vs. non-English speaking nations

	1990	2001	*Change*
Australia	6.7	6.5	(0.2)
USA	5.6	4.2	(1.6)
Canada	7.7	5.9	(1.8)
UK	6.9	5.1	(1.8)
France	9.1	8.8	(.3)
Japan	2.1	4.8	2.7
Italy	7.0	9.9	2.9
Germany	5.0	8.1	3.1
Sweden	1.8	5.1	3.3

For bar charts:

- Do not use grid lines unless the graphic is complex. Make all grid lines light gray.
- When specific numbers matter, add them to bars or segments.
- Clearly label both axes.
- Color or shade bars only to show a contrast.
- Never use three-dimensional or iconic bars (for example, images of cars to represent automobile production). They add nothing, distort how readers judge values, and look amateurish.
- Group and arrange bars to give readers an image of an order that matches your point.

For example, look at figure 11.4 in the context of the explanatory sentence before it. The items are listed alphabetically, an order that doesn't help readers see the point.

Most of the desert area in the world is concentrated in North Africa and the Middle East:

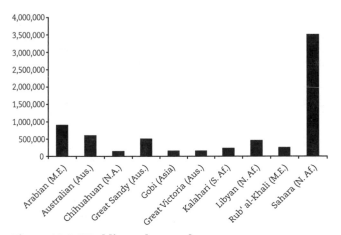

Figure 11.4: World's ten largest deserts

In contrast, figure 11.5 supports the claim with a coherent image.

Most of the desert area in the world is concentrated in North Africa and the Middle East:

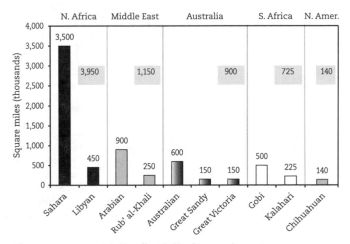

Figure 11.5: World distribution of large deserts

Table 11.6: Common graphic forms and their uses

	Data	Rhetorical Uses
Bar Chart	Compares the value of one variable across a series of items called *cases* (e.g., average salaries for service workers$_{variable}$ in six companies$_{cases}$).	Creates strong visual contrasts among individual cases, emphasizing individual comparisons. For specific values, add numbers to bars. Can show ranks or trends. Vertical bars (called *columns*) are most common, but can be horizontal if cases are numerous or have complex labels.
Bar Chart, Grouped or Split	Compares the value of one variable, divided into subsets, across a series of cases (e.g., average salaries$_{variable}$ for men and women service workers$_{subsets}$ in six companies$_{cases}$).	Contrasts subsets within and across individual cases; not useful for comparing total values for cases. For specific values, add numbers to bars. Grouped bars show ranking or trends poorly; useful for time series only if trends are unimportant.
Bar Chart, Stacked	Compares the value of one variable, divided into two or more subsets, across a series of cases (e.g., harassment complaints$_{variable}$ segmented by region$_{subsets}$ in six industries$_{cases}$).	Best for comparing totals across cases and subsets *within* cases; difficult to compare subsets *across* cases (use grouped bars). For specific values, add numbers to bars and segments. Useful for time series. Can show ranks or trends for total values only.
Histogram	Compares two variables, with one segmented into ranges that function like the cases in a bar graph (e.g., service workers$_{continuous\ variable}$ whose salary is $0–5,000, $5–10,000, $10–15,000, etc.$_{segmented\ variable}$).	Best for comparing segments within continuous data sets. Shows trends, but emphasizes segments (e.g., a sudden spike at $5–10,000 representing part-time workers). For specific values, add numbers to bars.
Image Chart	Shows value of one or more variable for cases displayed on a map, diagram, or other image (e.g., states$_{cases}$ colored red or blue to show voting patterns$_{variable}$).	Shows the distribution of the data in relation to preexisting categories; de-emphasizes specific values. Best when the image is familiar, as in a map or diagram of a process.
Pie Chart	Shows the proportion of a single variable for a series of cases (e.g., the budget share$_{variable}$ of U.S. cabinet departments$_{cases}$).	Best for comparing one segment to the whole. Useful only with few segments or segments that are very different in size; otherwise comparisons among segments are difficult. For specific values, add numbers to segments. Common in popular venues, frowned on by professionals.

Table 11.6 (*continued*)

	Data	Rhetorical Uses
Line Graph		
	Compares continuous variables for one or more cases (e.g., temperature$_{variable}$ and viscosity$_{variable}$ in two fluids$_{cases}$).	Best for showing trends; deemphasizes specific values. Useful for time series. To show specific values, add numbers to data points. To show the significance of a trend, segment the grid (e.g., below- or above-average performance).
Area Chart		
	Compares two continuous variables for one or more cases (e.g., reading test scores$_{variable}$ over time$_{variable}$ in a school district$_{case}$).	Shows trends; deemphasizes specific values. Can be used for time series. To show specific values, add numbers to data points. Areas below the lines add no information, but will lead some readers to misjudge values. Confusing with multiple lines/areas.
Area Chart, Stacked		
	Compares two continuous variables for two or more cases (e.g., profit$_{variable}$ over time$_{variable}$ for several products$_{cases}$).	Shows the trend for the total of all cases, plus how much each case contributes to that total. Likely to mislead readers on the value or the trend for any individual case.
Scatter Plot		
	Compares two variables at multiple data points for a single case (e.g., housing sales$_{variable}$ and distance from downtown$_{variable}$ in one city$_{case}$) or at one data point for multiple cases (e.g., brand loyalty$_{variable}$ and repair frequency$_{variable}$ for ten manufacturers$_{cases}$).	Best for showing the distribution of data, especially when there is no clear trend or when the focus is on outlying data points. If only a few data points are plotted, it allows a focus on individual values.
Bubble Chart		
	Compares three variables at multiple data points for a single case (e.g., housing sales,$_{variable}$ distance from downtown,$_{variable}$ and prices$_{variable}$ in one city$_{case}$) or at one data point for multiple cases (e.g., image advertising,$_{variable}$ repair frequency,$_{variable}$ and brand loyalty$_{variable}$ for ten manufacturers$_{cases}$).	Emphasizes the relationship between the third variable (bubbles) and the first two; most useful when the question is whether the third variable is a product of the others. Readers easily misjudge relative values shown by bubbles; adding numbers mitigates that problem.

CAUTION

Avoid Pie Charts

Most data that fit a bar chart can also be represented in a pie chart. It is a popular choice in magazines, tabloids, and annual reports, but it's harder to read than a bar chart, and it invites misinterpretation because readers must mentally compare proportions of segments whose size is hard to judge accurately. Most researchers consider them amateurish. Use bar charts instead.

For line graphs:

- Use grid lines only if the graphic is complex. Make all grid lines light gray.
- If you have fewer than ten data points, indicate them with dots. If only a few are relevant, add numbers to show their value.
- Choose the variable that makes the line go in the direction, up or down, that supports your point. If the good news is a reduction (down) in high school dropouts, you can more effectively represent the same data as an increase (up) in retention.
- Do not plot more than six lines on one graph unless you cannot make your point in any other way.

QUICK TIP

Try Out Different Graphics

If you are new to using graphics, all of these rules and principles can make your choice of graphics confusing. You can cut through that confusion if you try out several ways to represent the same data (your computer program will usually let you do that quickly). Then ask someone unfamiliar with the data to tell you what they see in each graphic. You might also ask them to judge the alternatives for impact and clarity.

12: Revising Your Draft

Some students think that once they have a draft, they're done. Thoughtful writers know better. They write a first draft to see whether they can make a case to support their answer. Then they revise their draft until they think they've presented that case in a way that meets the needs and expectations of their readers.

That's hard, because we all know our own work too well to read it as others will. To revise effectively, you cannot simply read a draft to see whether it satisfies you. You must know what readers look for and whether your draft helps them find it. To that end, we will give you advice that may seem mechanical. But only when you can analyze your draft objectively can you avoid reading into it what you want your readers to get out of it.

We suggest revising top down: first check the shape of the outer frame (you'll write the last draft of your introduction and conclusion later). Then look at the overall organization, then sections, paragraphs, sentences, finally grammar, spelling, and punctuation (for guidance on these issues, see part 3). Of course, no one revises so neatly. We all fiddle with words as we revise paragraphs and revise sentences as we reorganize sections. But you're likely to make the best revisions if you revise from whole to part, even if at the moment you're revising, a part is the only whole you have.

> **QUICK TIP**
>
> **Revise on Hard Copy**
> One secret to successful revising is to get a fresh look at your work. You can do that if you revise on hard copy, especially when you want to catch the small details. So edit early drafts on-screen, if you prefer. But you will catch more errors and get a better sense of the structure of your report if you read at least one version of it on paper, as your readers will.

12.1   Check Your Introduction, Conclusion, and Claim

Your readers must see three things quickly and unambiguously:

- where your introduction ends
- where your conclusion begins
- what sentences in one or both state your main claim

To make the first two clearly visible, insert a subhead or extra space between your introduction and body and another between the body and conclusion. To make your main claim clear, underline it. We'll come back to it in chapter 13.

WORKING IN GROUPS

Trading Papers

One of your greatest obstacles to revising well is your memory. By the time you are ready to revise, you know your paper so well that you can't really read it; you can only remember what you meant when you wrote it. That's why our suggestions for revision are so mechanical: they help you by-step your too-good memory of your paper.

But your group provides an even better way to by-step your memory. For the revision steps here and in chapter 14, trade papers with a colleague. Each of you should mark up and diagnose the other's paper. We guarantee that you'll be far better at finding what needs improvement in your colleague's paper than in your own.

But don't just read and make suggestions. Suggestions are welcome, but what is far more valuable is for each of you to go through each diagnostic step with the other's paper. You can't fix a problem you can't find.

12.2   Make Sure the Body of Your Report Is Coherent

Once you frame your report clearly, check its body. Readers will think your report is coherent when they see the following:

- the key terms that run through your whole report
- where each section ends and the next begins
- how each section relates to the one before it
- what role each section plays in the whole
- what sentence in each section and subsection states its point
- what distinctive key terms run through each section

To be sure that your readers see those features, check for the following:

1. Did you repeat key terms through your whole report?

    If readers don't see key terms on each page, they may think your report wanders. If you can't find them, neither will your readers.

    - Circle the key terms in the claim in your introduction and in your conclusion (review 7.2.3).
    - Circle those same terms in the body of your report.
    - Underline other words related to the ideas named by those circled terms.

Revise by working those terms into parts that lack them. If you underlined many more words than you circled, change some of them to the circled key terms. If you don't find on every page three or four terms either underlined or circled, you may have strayed too far from your line of reasoning. If so, you have more extensive revising to do.

2. Did you clearly signal the beginning of each section and subsection?

If your paper is longer than three or four pages, it will have distinct sections. Even if each section is only two or three paragraphs long, readers must clearly see where one ends and the next begins. For a longer paper, you can use subheads or an extra space to signal new sections.

3. Did you begin each major section with words that signal how that section relates to the one before it?

Readers must not only recognize where a section begins and ends, but understand why it is where it is (see 7.2.5–7.2.6). Be sure that you signaled the logic of your order with words such as *First, Second, More important, The next issue, Some have objected that,* and so on.

4. Did you make clear how each section is relevant to the whole?

For each section, ask: *What question does this section answer?* If a section doesn't help answer one of the questions of argument (review 6.2), ask whether it is relevant. Does it create a context, explain a background concept or issue, or help readers in some other way? If you can't explain how a section relates to your claim, cut it.

5. Did you state the point of each section at the end of a brief opening (or at the end of the section)?

If you have a choice, state the point of a section at the end of its opening. Under no circumstances bury the point of a section in its middle. If a section is longer than three or four pages, you might restate the point at its end.

6. Did you distinguish each section by running key terms through it?

Just as some key terms unify your whole report, other key terms unify its sections. To find those terms, repeat step 1 for each section. Find the sentence that expresses its point and identify the key terms that distinguish that section from the others. Then check whether those terms run through that section. If you find none, then your readers might not see what distinct ideas that section contributes to the whole. (You can use those key terms in headings.)

12.3   **Check Your Paragraphs**

Each paragraph should be relevant to the point of its section. And like sections, each paragraph should have a sentence or two introducing it, usually stating its point and including the key concepts that the rest of the paragraph develops. If the opening sentence or sentences of a paragraph do not state its point, then its last one must. Order your sentences by some principle and make them relevant to the point of the paragraph.

> **QUICK TIP**
>
> Avoid strings of short paragraphs (fewer than five lines) or very long ones (for most fields, more than half a page). Reserve the use of two- or three-sentence paragraphs for lists, transitions, introductions and conclusions to sections, and statements that you want to emphasize. (We use short paragraphs here because our readers sometime need to skim sections, not a consideration in research writing.)

12.4   **Let Your Draft Cool, Then Paraphrase It**

If you start your project early, you'll have time to let your revised draft cool. What seems good one day often looks different the next. When you return to your draft, don't read it straight through; skim its top-level parts: its introduction, the first paragraph of each major section, and conclusion. Then based on what you have read, paraphrase it for someone who hasn't read it. Does the paraphrase hang together? Does it fairly sum up your argument? Even better, ask someone else to read and summarize it: how well that person summarizes your report will predict how well your readers will understand it.

> **QUICK TIP**
>
> **Don't Ignore Your Teacher's Comments**
>
> If your teacher comments on your draft, always revise in light of that advice. Otherwise, you will miss an opportunity to improve your paper. And you will annoy someone who took time to read your work to help you, only to see you ignore their efforts. You don't have to follow all or even most of the suggestions, but your revision should show that you considered each one seriously.
>
> Almost as irritating as students who ignore a teacher's suggestions are those who follow the minor editorial suggestions (grammar, spelling, etc.) but ignore all comments that ask them to rethink larger issues. No teacher wants to be treated as a proofreader.

13: Writing Your Final Introduction and Conclusion

Once you have a complete draft and can see what you have in fact written, you can write your final introduction and conclusion. These two parts of your paper strongly influence how readers read and remember the rest, so it's worth your time to make them as clear as you can.

Your introduction has three goals. It should

- put your research in context;
- make your readers think they should read your paper;
- give them a framework for understanding it.

Your conclusion has two goals. It should

- leave readers with a clear idea of your claim;
- reinforce its importance.

13.1 Draft Your Final Introduction

In chapter 7, we suggested that you sketch a working introduction with four steps:

1. **Current situation or background.** When this summarizes research, it's called a *literature review.* It puts your project in the context of what is known and thought about your topic and sets up the next step.
2. **A statement of your research question.** This states what isn't known or understood that your paper will answer. It typically begins with a *but, however,* or other word signaling a qualification.

3. **The significance of your question.** This answers *So what?* It is key to motivating your readers.
4. **Your claim as an answer.** This answers your research question.

As a way to prepare readers for the rest of your paper, these steps follow a seemingly natural progression:

Here's what we think we know.
Here's what we don't know.
Here's why we need an answer.
Here's the answer.

But those steps follow another pattern, one that is common not just in research papers but in all types of writing—term papers, essays, business documents, and many others. In most academic and professional writing, the pattern that introductions follow is a familiar dramatic one: stability—disruption and danger—resolution. It's a pattern we learned as toddlers, in the form of fairy tales:

Once upon a time . . . Fairy tales begin by "defining a world" so that we know what to expect. When we see Little Red Riding Hood walking through the forest, we know not to expect dragons and we are not surprised when a woodsman shows up. When we learn in another tale that a wise old king has a beautiful daughter but no sons, we don't look for a fairy godmother, but do expect to see knights (and maybe a dragon).

But then . . . Once we learn about that stable world, the next step is always trouble—a wolf, a talking fish, an evil stepmother, or one of those dragons.

And now the dragon's fire . . . The main body of a fairly tale is, of course, a story of peril for the main character. Here is where the wolf bares his teeth or the dragon shows his fire. It's the dragon's fire that makes him a problem that must be solved.

And they lived happily ever after. In the end, all is well. But that happy ending is brought about not through the efforts of the main character but through the work of a helper with special powers: the burly woodsman, a fairy godmother, the valiant knight.

Each move in the fairy tale has a corresponding part in the basic pattern of introductions, and so does each character: The main character is your reader. The dragon is your research question: it disrupts the stable world you describe in the opening. The dragon's fire is the significance of your question: it shows why that question is a problem by showing readers what they lose by not knowing its answer. The helper with special powers? That's you. Once you show readers that they need an answer to your question, you save the day by offering one.

The Dramatic Pattern of Introductions and Fairy Tales

The typical introduction to a research paper draws some of its ability to motivate readers from the dramatic pattern it shares with fairy tales:

Current Situation / *Once upon a time . . .*

The fairy tale defines a stable world that it will disrupt; the research paper defines a current way of thinking that it will show to be wrong, or at least inadequate.

Research Question / *But then, the dragon . . .*

The fairy tale disrupts its world with a problem creature; the research paper disrupts the current way of thinking with a problem question.

Significance of the Question / *And now the dragon's fire . . .*

The fairy tale puts its main character in danger; the research paper shows its readers what they will lose without an answer to its question.

Answer / *And they lived happily ever after.*

In the fairy tale, a helper with special powers steps in to remove the danger, thereby saving the day; in the research paper, the writer with special knowledge (learned from research) steps in to answer the question, thereby saving the day.

You can see how the pattern works in this abbreviated introduction (each sentence could be expanded to a paragraph or more):

Colleges report that binge drinking is increasing. We have long known its practical risks—death, injury, property damage. We also know that bingers ignore those risks, even after they have been told about them.*situation* But no one has yet determined what causes bingers to ignore those known risks: social influences, a personality attracted to risk, or a failure to understand the nature of the risks.*question* If we can determine why bingers ignore the risks of their actions, we can better understand not only the causes of this dangerous behavior but also the nature of risk-taking behavior in general.*significance* This study reports on our analysis of the beliefs of 300 first-year college students. We found that students more likely to binge knew more stories of other student's bingeing, so that they believed that bingeing is far more common than it actually is.*answer*

Whether they are conscious of it or not, readers look for those four elements, so you should understand them in some detail.

13.1.1 Describe the Current Situation

As a rule, writers begin with the ideas that their own work will extend, modify, or correct. For the kind of projects most beginners undertake, the current situation can be described in a few sentences:

Drinking has been a part of college life for centuries. From football weekends to fraternity parties, college students drink and often drink hard. For the most part, we have always thought of this drinking as harmless, part of college high jinks. But colleges are increasingly concerned about the kind of hard drinking called binge drinking. Colleges report that bingeing is on the rise, despite their efforts to teach students about the known risks— death, injury, property damage. Recently Smith (2008) has shown that bingers ignore those risks, even after they have been told about them.

When advanced students write a report for other researchers, this opening describes more fully a line of research studies that the report will extend or modify.

Ever since the first studies by Weber (1982) and Claus and Stiglitz (1982, 1985), colleges have known about the dangers and prevalence of binge drinking. The earliest research determined the prevalence of bingeing (Wang and Olefson 1988; James 1988; Geoffrey 1989), the gender mix of bingers (Wang 1990; Osborne 1992), and the risks (for a summary, see Mateland 2005). The latest research has focused on the causes and ways to prevent bingeing. Recently Smith (2008) has shown that bingers ignore those risks, even after they have been told about them.

Some advanced researchers go on like that for pages, citing scores of books and articles.

QUICK TIP

Two Alternatives to the Literature Review

Early in your career, you may not feel confident writing a review of the prior research on your topic. But you have two easy alternatives.

1. Use one source as your prior research.

   If you have found one source that can set up your research question, use it as your current situation. You might copy one of the patterns in section 2.4.

2. Use *your* prior understanding.

   Imagine your reader as someone like yourself *before* you started your research. Make your current situation what you thought then. This is where you can use a working hypothesis that you rejected: *It might seem that X is so, but . . .*

No one expects a beginner to provide an extensive review of the prior research. But you do have to define *some* stable context, a way of thinking about your issue that your research question will disrupt, improve, or amplify. The four most common sources of this context are these:

- What you believed before you began your research (*I used to think . . .*).
- What others believe (*Most people think . . .*).
- An event or situation (*What events seem to show is . . .*).
- What other researchers have found (*Researchers have shown . . .*).

You have other options. If you find a good one in your reading, use it. But these four are reliable ways to get your paper started.

WRITING IN GROUPS

Use Your Colleagues' Misunderstandings

If you cannot think of any reasonable stable context to state as your Current Situation, turn to your writing group. Ask them what they think of your topic: *Why do you think students get involved in binge drinking?* If their answer is wrong or misleading, that is the current thinking your paper will correct: "Many students think that . . . , but . . ."

13.1.2 Restate Your Question as Something Not Known or Fully Understood

After the opening context, state what is wrong or missing in that current way of thinking. Introduce this step with *but, however,* or some other term indicating that you're about to modify the received knowledge and understanding that you just described:

Drinking has been a part of college. . . . [B]ingers ignore those risks, even after they have been told about them.*situation* **But** no one has yet determined what causes bingers to ignore the known risks: social influences, a personality attracted to risk, or a failure to understand the nature of the risks.*question restated as what we don't know*

Note: Although you must build you paper around a research *question*, you should state it in your introduction not as a direct question—*What causes bingeing?*—but as an assertion that we don't know something: *We don't know what causes bingeing.*

13.1.3 State the Significance of Your Question

Now you must show your readers the *significance* of answering your research question. Imagine a reader asking that vexing question, *So what?*, then answer it. Frame your response as a larger cost of not knowing the answer to your research question:

Drinking has been a part of college. . . . [B]ingers ignore those risks, even after they have been told about them.*situation* But no one has . . . or a failure to understand the nature of the risks.*question* [*So what?*] Until we can determine why bingers ignore known risks of their actions, we will not be able to identify the causes of this dangerous behavior, which is essential if we are to find a way to control it._{significance}

Alternatively, you can phrase the cost as a benefit:

Drinking has been a part of college. . . . [B]ingers ignore those risks, even after they have been told about them._{situation} But no one has . . . or a failure to understand the nature of the risks._{question} [So *what?*] If we can determine why bingers ignore known risks of their actions, we can better understand not only the causes of this dangerous behavior but also the nature of risk-taking behavior in general._{significance}

You may struggle to answer that *So what?* because you don't know enough about the larger context of your research question. If nothing better comes to mind, state its significance in terms of what your class has studied:

Drinking has been a part of college. . . . [B]ingers ignore those risks, even after they have been told about them._{situation} But no one has . . . or a failure to understand the nature of the risks._{question} [So *what?*] If we can determine why bingers ignore known risks of their actions, we can better understand the psychology of pleasure and happiness that has been a major topic in our class._{significance}

13.1.4   State Your Claim

Once you state what isn't known or understood and why readers need to know it, readers want an answer:

Drinking has been a part of college. . . . [B]ingers ignore those risks, even after they have been told about them._{situation} But no one has . . . or a failure to understand the nature of the risks._{question} [So *what?*] If we can determine . . . the nature of risk-taking behavior in general._{significance} This study reports on our analysis of the beliefs of 300 first-year college students. We found that students more likely to binge knew more stories of other student's bingeing, so that they believed that bingeing is far more common than it actually is._{claim/answer}

If you have reason to hold your claim until the end of your paper, write a sentence to end your introduction that uses the key terms from that claim and that frames what follows but without completely revealing your claim.

Recent research suggests the key to this behavior lies not in bingers' knowledge of risk but in their beliefs about the prevalence of bingeing._{promise of claim}

Those four steps may seem mechanical, but they constitute the introductions to most research reports in every field, both inside the academic world and out.

QUICK TIP

Model Your Work on What You Read
As you read your sources, especially journal articles, watch for that four-part framework. You will not only learn a range of strategies for writing your own introductions but better understand the ones you read.

13.1.5 Write a New First Sentence

Some writers find it so hard to write the first sentence of a paper that they fall into clichés. Avoid these:

- Do not repeat the language of your assignment.
- Do not quote a dictionary definition: Webster's *defines risk as . . .*
- Do not try to be grand: *For centuries philosophers have debated the burning question of . . .* (Good questions speak their own importance.)

If you want to begin with something livelier than prior research, try one or more of these openers (but note the warning that follows):

1. A striking quotation:

   "If you're old enough to fight for your country, you're old enough to drink to it."

2. A striking fact:

   A recent study reports that at most colleges three out of four students "binged" at least once in the previous thirty days, consuming more than seven drinks at a sitting. Almost half binge once a week, and those who binge most are not just members of fraternities, but their officers.

3. A relevant anecdote:

   When Jim S., president of Omega Alpha, joined his fourth-year fraternity brothers in the State U tradition of "a fifth in your fourth," by downing most of a fifth of whiskey in less than an hour, he didn't plan to become this year's eighth college fatality from alcohol poisoning.

You can combine all three:

   It is often said that "if you're old enough to fight for your country, you're old enough to drink to it."*quotation* Tragically, Jim S., president of Omega Alpha, no longer has a chance to do either. When he joined his fourth-year fraternity brothers in the State U tradition of "a fifth in your fourth," by downing most of a fifth of whiskey in less than an hour, he didn't expect to become this year's eighth college fatality from alcohol poisoning.*anecdote* According to a recent study, at most colleges three out of four students have, like Jim S., drunk seven drinks at a sitting in the last thirty days. And those who drink the most are not just members of fraternities, but, like Jim S., officers.*striking fact*

Be sure to include in these openers terms that anticipate the key concepts you'll use when you write the rest of the introduction (and the rest of the paper). In this case, they include *old enough, tradition, didn't expect, fatality, alcohol poisoning, three out of four.*

13.2 Draft Your Final Conclusion

If you have no better plan, build your conclusion around the elements of your introduction, in reverse order.

13.2.1 Restate Your Claim

Restate your claim early in your conclusion, more fully than in your introduction:

Bingeing college students may be irrational when they ignore risks that they know well, but they are not acting without *some* reason. Our survey shows that students more likely to binge hear and remember more stories of bingeing among their peers than do students less likely to binge. As a consequence, bingers believe that bingeing is far more prevalent than it is. And since they are unlikely to know anyone who has suffered direct harm from bingeing, they believe that their chances of being harmed are quite low.

Take this last chance to make your claim as specific and complete as you can.

13.2.2 Point Out a New Significance, a Practical Application, or New Research

After stating your claim, remind readers of its significance or, better, state a new significance or a practical application:

These findings suggest bingeing may be less irrational, less a matter of uncontrollable impulses than at first it might seem. If one cause of bingeing is the common practice of bragging about one's exploits at parties and bars, it may be possible to counter the effects of those stories with simple facts. If students know that bingeing is not the norm among students, they may think more carefully when they assess its risks.

Finally, suggest other questions that your results might raise. This gesture suggests how other researchers can continue the conversation. It mirrors the opening context:

Although these results improve our understanding of the causes of bingeing, they do not tell us how to counter the effects of overestimating the prevalence of bingeing. There is no evidence to show that we can counter the effects of vivid and exciting stories told by peers with dry facts recited by college administrators. There is more research to do before we can know how to use these results effectively.

13.3   Write Your Title Last

Your title is the first thing your readers read; it should be the last thing you write. It should both announce the topic of your paper and signal its important concepts, so build it out of the key terms that you earlier circled and underlined. Compare these three titles:

Bingeing

Ignoring the Risks of Bingeing

A Story is Worth a Thousand Facts:
Why Binge Drinkers Overestimate Its Prevalence and Underestimate Its Risks

The first title is accurate but too general to help us through what is to come. The second is more specific, but the third uses both a title and subtitle to give us advance notice about the keywords that will appear in what follows. When we see the keywords in a title turn up again in an introduction and then again throughout the paper, we're more likely to feel that its parts hang together. Two-part titles are most useful: they give you an opportunity to use your keywords to announce your key concepts.

13.4   Preparing an Oral Report

You may be asked to present the final results of your research. If so, review our advice for a preliminary presentation in section 8.6. Most of that advice still applies:

- Prepare notes, not a script.
- Prepare and rehearse an introduction and conclusion. Don't just read them from your final paper: rewrite them to sound like something you would say, not something you would only write.
- Organize your notes around your main reasons, which you should put in big, bold type.

There are two relevant differences between a preliminary and a final oral report: Before you were guessing what your argument might be; now you know. That should make your report more confident, but not different in structure. Also, you now know how your evidence supports each reason. Accordingly, you should give more attention to evidence in a final report than in a preliminary one. *Do not try to walk readers through every scrap of evidence.* Do that and you'll be sure to run out of time (which might not matter since everyone will be asleep). Instead, present one best bit of evidence for each reason. This will assure your audience that you have good backup without forcing them to listen to all of it.

If your evidence is suitable for it, prepare a handout: create a list of quotations, reproduce graphics or tables, create illustrations, and so on. (You can do this in PowerPoint rather than a handout, if you have the skills.)

14: Revising Sentences

Your last big task is to make your sentences as clear as your ideas allow. On some occasions, you may know your writing is awkward, especially if you're writing about an unfamiliar and complex topic. But too often you won't recognize when your sentences need help. You need a plan to revise sentences that you know are a problem, but even more, you need a way to identify those that you think are fine, but that readers will think are not.

We can't tell you how to fix every problem in every sentence, but we can tell you how to deal with those that most often afflict a writer struggling to sound like a "serious scholar," a style that most experienced readers think is just pretentious. Here is a short example:

1a. An understanding of terrorist thinking could achieve improvements in the protection of the public.

However impressive that sounds, the student who wrote it meant only this:

1b. If we understood how terrorists think, we could protect the public better.

To diagnose (1a) and revise it into (1b), however, you must know a few grammatical terms: *noun, verb, active verb, passive verb, whole subject, simple subject, main clause, subordinate clause.* If they're a dim memory, skim a grammar guide before you go on.

14.1 Focus on the First Seven or Eight Words of a Sentence

Just as the key to a clearly written report is in its first few paragraphs, so the key to a clearly written sentence is in its first few words. When readers grasp those first seven or eight words easily, they read what follows faster, understand it better, and remember it longer. It is the difference between these two sentences:

2a. The Federalists' argument in regard to the destabilization of government by popular democracy arose from their belief in the tendency of factions to further their self-interest at the expense of the common good.

2b. The Federalists argued that popular democracy destabilized government, because they believed that factions tended to further their self-interest at the expense of the common good.

In this section we will show you how to write a sentence like (2b)—or to revise one like (2a) into (2b).

Five Principles for Clear Sentences

To draft clear sentences or revise unclear ones, follow these five principles:

1. Make subjects short and concrete, ideally naming the character that performs the action expressed by the verb that follows.
2. Avoid interrupting the subject and verb with more than a word or two.
3. Put key actions in verbs, not in nouns.
4. Put information familiar to readers at the beginning of a sentence, new information at the end.
5. Avoid long introductory phrases: get to a short, familiar subject quickly.

Those principles add up to this: Readers want to get past a short, concrete, familiar subject quickly and easily to a verb expressing a specific action. When you do that, the rest of your sentence will usually take care of itself. To diagnose your own writing, look for those characteristics in it. Skim the first seven or eight words of every sentence. Look closely at sentences that don't meet those criteria, then revise them as follows.

14.1.1   Make Subjects Short and Concrete

Readers must grasp the subject of a sentence easily, but can't when the subject is long, complex, and abstract. Compare these two sentences (the whole subjects in each are underlined; the one-word simple subject is boldfaced):

3a. A school system's successful **adoption** of a new reading curriculum for its elementary schools depends on the demonstration in each school of the commitment of its principal and the cooperation of teachers in setting reasonable goals.

3b. A school **system** will successfully adopt a new reading curriculum for elementary schools only when each **principal** demonstrates that **she** is committed to it and **teachers** cooperate to set reasonable goals.

In (3a) the whole subject is fourteen words long, and its simple subject is an abstraction—*adoption*. In (3b), the clearer version, the whole subject of every verb is short, and each simple subject is relatively concrete: *school system, each principal, she, teachers*. Moreover, each of those subjects performs the action in its verb: **system** *will adopt,* **principal** *demonstrates,* **she** *is committed,* **teachers** *cooperate.*

The principle is this: Readers tend to judge a sentence to be readable when the subject of its verb names the main character in a few concrete words, ideally a character that is also the "doer" of the action expressed by the verb that follows.

But there's a complication: You can often tell clear stories with characters that are not people. Those characters can be entities such as "school system" in (3b) or "athletics" in (4):

4. <u>Athletics</u> debases a college's educational mission only when <u>it</u> overstimulates the passions of alumni and others <u>who</u> no longer need an education but do need a source of meaning in their lives.

Or they can be purely abstract characters:

5. <u>No skill</u> is more valued in the professional world than problem solving. <u>The ability to solve problems quickly</u> requires us to frame situations in different ways and to find more than one solution. In fact, <u>effective problem solving</u> may define general intelligence.

Few readers have trouble with those abstract subjects, because they're short and familiar: *no skill, the ability to solve problems quickly,* and *effective problem solving.* What gives readers trouble is an abstract subject that is long and unfamiliar.

To fix sentences with long, abstract subjects, revise in three steps:

- Identify the main character in the sentence.
- Find its key action, and if it is buried in an abstract noun, make it a verb.
- Make the main character the subject of that new verb.

For example, compare (6a) and (6b) (actions are boldfaced; verbs are capitalized):

6a. Without a means for **analyzing interactions** between social class and education in regard to the **creation** of more job opportunities, success in **understanding** economic mobility will REMAIN limited.

6b. Economists do not entirely UNDERSTAND economic mobility, because they cannot ANALYZE how social class and education INTERACT to CREATE more job opportunities.

In both sentences, the main character is *economists,* but in (6a) that character isn't the subject of any verb; in fact, it's not in the sentence at all: we must infer it from actions buried in nouns: *analyzing* and *understanding* (what economists do). We revise (6a) into (6b) by making the main characters (*economists, social class,* and *education*) subjects of action verbs (*understand, analyze, interact,* and *create*).

Readers want subjects to name the main characters in your story, ideally flesh-and-blood characters, and verbs to name their key actions.

14.1.2 Avoid Interrupting Subjects and Verbs with More than a Word or Two

Once past a short subject, readers want to get to a verb quickly, so avoid splitting a verb from its subject with long phrases and clauses:

7a. Some economists, because they write in a style that is impersonal and objective, do not communicate with laypeople easily.

In (7a), the *because* clause separates the subject *some economists* from the verb *do not communicate,* forcing us to suspend our mental breath. To revise, move the interrupting clause to the beginning or end of its sentence, depending on whether it connects more closely to the sentence before or after. When in doubt, put it at the end (for more on this see 14.1.4).

7b. Because some economists write in a style that is impersonal and objective, they do not communicate with laypeople easily. This inability to communicate . . .
7c. Some economists do not communicate with laypeople easily because they write in a style that is impersonal and objective. They use passive verbs and . . .

Readers manage short interruptions more easily:

8. Few economists deliberately write in a style that is impersonal and objective.

14.1.3 Put Key Actions in Verbs, Not in Nouns

Readers want to get to a verb quickly, but they also want that verb to express a key action. So avoid using an empty verb such as *have, do, make,* or *be* to introduce an action buried in an abstract noun. Make the noun a verb.

Compare these sentences (action nouns are boldfaced; action verbs are capitalized; verbs with little action are underlined):

9a. During the early years of the Civil War, the South's **attempt** at **enlisting** Great Britain on its side <u>was met</u> with **failure**.
9b. During the early years of the Civil War, the South ATTEMPTED to ENLIST Great Britain on its side, but it FAILED.

In (9a) three important actions aren't verbs, but nouns: *attempt, enlisting, failure.* Sentence (9b) seems more direct because it expresses those actions in verbs: *attempted, enlist, failed.*

14.1.4 Put Familiar Information at the Beginning of a Sentence, New at the End

Readers understand a sentence most readily when they grasp its subject easily, and the easiest subject to grasp is not just short and concrete, but *familiar.* Compare how the second sentence in each of the following passages does or doesn't "flow":

10a. New questions about the nature of the universe have been raised by scientists studying black holes in space. The collapse of a dead star into a point perhaps no larger than a marble creates a black hole. So much matter squeezed into so little volume changes the fabric of space around it in odd ways.

10b. New questions about the nature of the universe have been raised by scientists studying black holes in space. A black hole is created by the collapse of a dead star into a point no larger than a marble. So much matter squeezed into so little volume changes the fabric of space around it in odd ways.

Most readers think (10b) flows better than (10a), partly because the subject of the second sentence, *A black hole,* is shorter and more concrete than in (10a): *The collapse of a dead star into a point perhaps no larger than a marble.* But (10b) also flows better because the order of its ideas is different.

In (10a) the first words of the second sentence express information that is new to this passage:

10a. ... black holes in space. The collapse of a dead star into a point perhaps no larger than a marble creates ...

Those words about collapsing stars seem to come out of nowhere. But in (10b), the first words echo the end of the previous sentence:

10b. ... black holes in space. A black hole is created by ...

Moreover, once we make that change, the end of that second sentence introduces the third more cohesively:

10b. ... the collapse of a dead star into a point no larger than a marble. So much matter compressed into so little volume changes ...

That is why readers think passage (10a) feels choppier than (10b): the end of one sentence does not flow smoothly into the beginning of the next.

No principle of writing is more important than this: old before new, familiar information introduces unfamiliar information.

14.1.5 Avoid Long Introductory Phrases

Compare these two sentences (introductory phrases are boldfaced; whole subjects underlined):

11a. **In view of claims by researchers on higher education indicating at least one change by most undergraduate students of their major field of study,** <u>first-year students</u> seem not well informed about choosing a major field of study.

11b. <u>Researchers on higher education</u> claim that <u>most students</u> change their major field of study at least once during their undergraduate careers. **If that is so,** then <u>first-year students</u> seem not well informed when they choose a major.

Most readers find (11a) harder to read than (11b), because it makes them work through a twenty-four-word phrase before they reach its subject (*first-year students*). In the two sentences in (11b), readers start with a subject either immediately, *Researchers . . .* , or after a very short delay, *If that is so, . . .*

The principle is this: Start most of your sentences directly with their subjects. Begin only a few sentences with introductory phrases longer than ten or so words. You can usually revise long introductory phrases and subordinate clauses into their own independent sentences as in (11b).

14.1.6 Choose Active or Passive Verbs to Reflect the Previous Principles

You may recall advice to avoid passive verbs—good advice, when a passive verb forces you to write a sentence that contradicts the principles we have discussed, as here:

12a. Global warming may have many catastrophic effects. Tropical diseases and destructive insect life even north of the Canadian border could be increased*passive verb* by this climatic change.

That second sentence opens with a twelve-word subject conveying new information: *Tropical diseases . . . Canadian border.* It is the subject of a passive verb, *be increased,* and that verb is followed by a short, familiar bit of information from the sentence before: *by this climatic change.* That sentence would be clearer if its verb were active:

12b. Global warming may have many catastrophic effects. This climatic change could increase*active verb* tropical diseases and destructive insect life even north of the Canadian border.

Now the subject is familiar, and the new information in the longer phrase is at the end. In this case, the active verb is the right choice.

But if you never make a verb passive, you'll write sentences that contradict the old-new principle. We saw an example in (10a):

10a. New questions about the nature of the universe have been raised by scientists studying black holes in space. The collapse of a dead star into a point perhaps no larger than a marble creates$_{active\ verb}$ a black hole. So much matter squeezed into so little volume changes the fabric of space around it in odd ways.

The verb in the second sentence of (10a) is active, but the passage flows better when it's passive:

10b. New questions about the nature of the universe have been raised by scientists studying black holes in space. A black hole is created$_{passive\ verb}$ by the collapse of a dead star into a point no larger than a marble. . . .

Readers prefer a subject that is short, concrete, and familiar, even if you must use a passive verb. So *choose* active *or* passive, depending on which gives you the right kind of subject: short, concrete, and familiar.

14.1.7 Use First-Person Pronouns Appropriately

Almost everyone has heard the advice to avoid using *I* or *we* in academic writing. In fact, opinions differ on this. Some teachers tell students never to use *I*, because it makes their writing "subjective." Others encourage using *I* as a way to make writing more lively and personal.

Most instructors and editors do agree that two uses of *I* should be avoided in two specific situations:

· Insecure writers begin too many sentences with *I think* or *I believe* (or their equivalent, *In my opinion*). Readers assume that you think and believe what you write, so you don't have to say so.
· Inexperienced writers too often narrate their research: *First, I consulted . . .* , *Then I examined . . .* , and so on. Readers care less about the story of your research than about its results.

But we believe, and most professionals agree, that the first person is appropriate on two occasions. That last sentence illustrates one of them: *we believe . . . that the first person . . .*

· An occasional introductory *I* (or *we*) *believe* can soften the dogmatic edge of a statement. Compare this blunter, less qualified version:

13. But ~~we believe, and most professionals agree, that~~ the first person is appropriate on two occasions.

The trick is not to hedge so often that you sound uncertain or so rarely that you sound smug. The second occasion depends on the action in the verb:

· A first-person *I* or *we* is also appropriate as the subject of a verb naming an action unique to you as the writer of your argument:

14. In this report, I will show that social distinctions at this university are . . .

Verbs referring to such actions typically appear in introductions: *I will show/ argue/prove/claim that X*, and in conclusions: *I have demonstrated/concluded/* . . . Since only you can show, prove, or claim what's in your argument, only you can say so with *I*.

On the other hand, researchers rarely use the first person for an action that others must repeat to replicate the reported research. Those words include *divide, measure, weigh, examine,* and so on. Researchers rarely write sentences with active verbs like this:

15a. I *calculated* the coefficient of X.

Instead, they're likely to write in the passive, because anyone can repeat this calculation:

15b. The coefficient of X *was calculated*.

Those same principles apply to *we,* if you're one of two or more authors. But many instructors and editors do object to two other uses of *we:*

· the royal *we* used to refer reflexively to the writer
· the all-purpose *we* that refers to people in general

Not this:

16. We must be careful to cite sources when we use data from them. When we read writers who fail to do that, we tend to distrust them.

Finally, though, your instructor decides. If he flatly forbids *I* or *we,* then so be it.

QUICK TIP

Read Drafts Aloud
You can best judge how your readers will respond to your writing if you read it aloud—or better, have someone read it back to you. If that person stumbles or seems to drone, you can bet your readers will like your prose less than you do.

14.2 **Diagnose What You Read**

Once you understand how readers judge what they read, you also know why so much of what you must read seems so dense. Sometimes you struggle to understand academic writing because its content is difficult. But sometimes you struggle because the writer didn't write clearly. This next passage, for example, is the sort that might be found in any textbook:

15: Learning from Your Returned Paper

15.1 Find General Principles in Specific Comments
15.2 Visit Your Instructor

Teachers are baffled and annoyed when a student looks only at the grade on a paper and ignores substantive comments or, worse, can't be bothered to pick up the paper at all. Since you'll write many research papers in your academic and professional life, it's smart to understand how your teachers make their judgments and how you can use them to do better next time. For that, you need one more plan.

15.1   Find General Principles in Specific Comments

When you read your teacher's comments, focus on those that you can apply to your next project:

- Look for a pattern of errors in spelling, punctuation, and grammar. If you see one, make a list so that you know what to work on next time.
- If your teacher says you made factual errors, check your notes to see why: Did you misreport them? Were you misled by an unreliable source? Whatever you find, you know what to do in your next project.
- If your teacher says your writing is choppy, dense, or awkward (indicated by AWK or K), check your sentences using the steps in chapter 14.
- If he says your report is disorganized, check it against chapter 12. You won't always find what caused the complaints, but when you do you'll know what to work on next time.

15.2   Visit Your Instructor

If your teacher's comments are mostly impressionistic words like *disorganized, illogical,* or *unsupported* and you can't see anything in your paper that earned that criticism, make an appointment to ask. As with every other step in your project, that visit will go better if you plan and even rehearse it. Do this *before* you talk to your teacher:

- If your teacher marked up spelling, punctuation, and grammar, correct those errors. The corrections will show that you took his comments seriously.
- Jot down your own responses after any comments about your argument to show that you've read them closely.

In the office:

- Don't whine about your grade. Be clear that you want only to understand the comments so that you can do better next time.
- Focus on the most important comments. Rehearse your questions so that they'll seem amiable: not "You say this is disorganized but you don't say why," but rather "Can you help me see where I went wrong with my organization so I can do better next time?"
- Do not ask "What didn't you like?" but rather "Where did I go wrong and how would I fix it?"
- If your teacher can't clearly explain his judgment, he may have graded your paper impressionistically. If so, bad news: you may learn little from your visit.

16: On the Spirit of Research

As we've said, we can reach good conclusions in many ways other than re-search: we can rely on intuition, emotion, even spiritual insight. But the truths we reach in those ways are personal. When we ask others to accept and act on them, we can't present our feelings as evidence for them to agree; we can ask only that they take our report of our inner experience—and our claims—on faith.

The truths of research, however, and how we reached them must be available for public study. We base research claims on evidence available to every-one and on principles of reasoning that, we hope, our readers accept as sound and relevant. And then we test all of that in every way that we and others can imagine. That may be a high standard, but it must be if we expect others to base their understanding and actions, even their lives, on what we ask them to believe.

When you accept the principles that shape public, evidence-based belief, you accept two more that can be hard to live by. One concerns our relation-ship to authority. No more than five centuries ago, the search for better un-derstanding based on *evidence* was typically regarded as a threat. Among the powerful, many believed that the important truths were known and that the scholar's job was to preserve and transmit them, certainly not to challenge them. If new facts cast doubt on an old belief, the belief usually trumped the facts. Many who dared to follow evidence to conclusions that challenged authority were banished, imprisoned, and on occasion killed.

Even today, those who reason from evidence can anger those who hold a cherished belief. For example, some historians claim that, based on the sum of the evidence, Thomas Jefferson probably fathered at least one child by his slave Sally Hemings. Others disagree, not because they have better counter-evidence, but because of a fiercely held belief: *A person of Jefferson's stature couldn't do such a thing.* But in the world of research, both academic and pro-fessional, good evidence and sound reasoning trump belief every time, or at least they should.

In some parts of the world, it's still considered more important to guard settled beliefs than to test them. But in those places informed by the values of research, we think differently: we believe not only that we *may* question settled beliefs, but that we *must,* no matter how much authority cherishes them—so long as we base our answers on sound reasons based on reliable evidence.

But that principle requires another. When we make a claim, we must ex-pect and even encourage others to question not just our claim but how we reached it, to ask: *Why do you believe that?* It's often hard to welcome such questions, but we're obliged to listen with goodwill to objections, reservations, and qualifications that collectively imply *I don't agree, at least not yet.* And the more we challenge old ideas, the more we must be ready to acknowledge and answer those questions, because we may be asking others to give up something they cherish.

When some students encounter these values, they find it difficult, even painful, to live by them. Some feel that a challenge to what they believe isn't a lively search for truth, but a personal attack on their beliefs, sometimes on their deepest values. Others retreat to a cynical skepticism that doubts everything and believes nothing. Others fall into mindless relativism: *We're all entitled to our own beliefs, and so all beliefs are right for those who hold them!* Many turn away from an active life of the mind, rejecting not only answers that might disturb their settled belief but even the questions that inspired them.

But in our worlds of work, scholarship, civic action, and even politics, we can't replace tested knowledge and hard-won understanding with personal opinion, a relativistic view of truth, or the comfortable settled knowledge of "authority."

That does not mean we reject long-held and time-tested beliefs lightly. We replace them only after we're persuaded by sound arguments backed by good reasons based on the best evidence available, and after an amiable but searching give-and-take that tests those arguments as severely as we can. In short, we become *responsible* believers when we can make our own sound arguments that test and evaluate those of others.

You may find it hard to see all of this at work in a paper written for a class, but despite its cold type, a research report written for any audience is a conversation, imagined to be sure, but still a cooperative yet rigorous inquiry into what we should and should not believe.

PART II
Citing Sources

In part 2, we show you how to create citations that your readers will trust because they are complete, accurate, and in the correct format. Now we know that most of you take no pleasure in this part of your project. Even the most persnickety researchers do not *enjoy* keeping track of their citations: it demands more attention to detail than most of us want to give. And if citations are tedious for experienced researchers who know what to expect, for beginners they can seem like slow torture.

So we understand if you'd rather just skip the citations. But we also know how much citation mistakes can cost you. If you fail to cite what you should, you open yourself to a charge of plagiarism (see chapter 10). If you cite inaccurately, you may lose the trust of readers: *If I can't trust you with the small, easy things, then how can I trust you with the more challenging ones?* Even a tiny slip in the format of your citations can harm you with the pickiest readers. Of course, at this stage in your career as a researcher, you cannot harm anyone with a bad citation: you do not yet have readers who need to trust you because their well-being depends on the results of your research. But you will. And so your teacher will be as demanding now as she knows your most important readers will be then.

Read Me First: How to Use Part 2

Citations are boring but crucial, so you will have to motivate yourself to be extra careful creating them. Because the job can be tedious, we want to help you get through it with ease, if not with pleasure. Because mistakes can be costly, we want to help you make sure you don't slip up. If you follow these steps, you will give yourself the best chance to create accurate, proper citations as painlessly as possible.

Before you start to research:

Read chapter 17: it will help you guide your research and drafting. It will also help you understand the rationale for the standard forms of citations, which will help you make better decisions if your sources do not exactly match the models. If you are interested, you might also read the introductory sections of the chapter that explains the citation style you plan to use. Don't try to study and remember all the models: you will consult them as you create and check individual citations.

As you research:

Record all the bibliographical data on each source as you find it, *before* you do anything else with the source. Be disciplined about this job and you will save much trouble later (see 4.2). You may have access to citation software. If so, record the data directly in the software. If you are working away from your computer, write down the information and enter it as soon as possible.

Before you draft:

Read the section that explains how to cite sources in your text (for Chicago 18.1.1, MLA 19.1, or APA 20.1). If you are using MLA or APA, add the in-text citations as you draft. If you are using Chicago style, do not create full notes as you draft: You will disrupt the flow of your drafting with lots of trips back to check on the proper form. Instead, quickly record the source and page numbers in your draft, so that you can come back later to create proper notes.

If you use citation software, you can let the software create citations as you draft, but only if you have already entered the bibliographic data on your sources. (Do not disrupt your drafting to enter bibliographic data as you go.) If you take advantage of this convenience, *do not think that you can leave it all to the software.* Many systems are outdated and all of them make mistakes, so you must recheck each in-text citation for the correct form and accurate information.

After you draft:

Once you are sure that your in-text citations are correct, create notes and a bibliography for Chicago style (18.1–2), a works cited list for MLA (19.2), or a reference list for APA (20.2). For each source, find the model for that kind of source and create an entry that matches the model exactly. Pay close attention to all the picky details, including capitalization, punctuation, and spacing. You can let your software create a draft of bibliographical entries, but you must check each one against the appropriate model.

The secret to success here is steady, systematic work. Apply yourself for an hour or two, and you'll get it right the first time and be done with this chore.

Go to www.turabian.org to find supplemental materials related to part 2.

17: Citations

In this chapter, we explain what you need to know about citations, no matter which kind of citations you plan to use: why researchers cite sources, the general form of citations, and a plan for collecting information for your citations. You'll find models for your specific citations in chapters 18–20. But first read this chapter for an overview that will help you make better decisions when you use the models.

17.1 Why Cite Sources?

You have two kinds of reasons for doing the work to create citations that are complete, accurate, and in the proper format. First are the reasons that all researchers share: when you cite sources well, you help your readers understand and trust your research. You also help yourself, not only by gaining your readers' trust, but also by protecting yourself from inadvertently cutting corners in your research. But you also have more immediate, more self-interested reasons. We'll get to those in a moment.

As a researcher in your future career, you will cite sources for four reasons:

1. **To be honest about what you did and what you borrowed.** With every citation, you give credit to the person(s) behind a source for the hard work that went into finding and reporting the information you used. You also *avoid* seeming to take credit for work you did not do, which protects you against a charge of plagiarism.

2. **To assure readers that they can trust your evidence.** You can't expect readers to accept evidence simply on your own say-so. They want to know where it came from and why they should trust it. For evidence you gathered yourself, they want to know how and where you found it. For evidence gathered by others, they want to know its source so that they can judge its

reliability, perhaps even check it out for themselves. Readers do not trust a source they do not know and cannot find; if they do not trust your sources, they will not trust your evidence; if they do not trust your evidence, they will not trust your paper—or you. You establish the first link in that chain of trust by citing sources fully and properly.

3. **To tell readers which earlier researchers informed your work.** Researchers cite some sources for the data they use as evidence, but they also cite work whose ideas or methods influenced how they thought about their problem and its solution. When you cite sources that influenced your thinking, you show readers how your work connects to that of others.

4. **To help readers follow or extend your research.** Just as you used the references in your sources to find other useful works on your question (see 4.3.5), so your readers may use your sources to guide their research.

We understand that some of these reasons may seem distant from your immediate situation. But consider them as you work: with these goals in mind, the rules you must follow will make more sense, and you'll make better decisions in following them.

As a student now, you have some more immediate, practical reasons for being careful about citations. Unless your teacher tells you otherwise, assume that every research assignment requires proper citations for all sources. Get your citations wrong and you'll face a double penalty in your grade: not only will you lose what your teacher takes off for poor citations, but everything about your paper will seem suspect if you lose your teacher's trust. Fail to cite sources at all and you'll open yourself to a charge of plagiarism, which can cost you a failed assignment, a failed course, or worse—not to mention giving you the reputation of a cheater. So if you can't think of a better reason, work on citations simply because you have to.

17.2 When You Must Cite a Source

You must include a citation every time you use the words, ideas, or distinctive methods of a source (see 10.3). In particular, include a citation every time you use a source in these three ways:

·   You quote the exact words of a source, including single words or phrases if they are distinctive enough. You must also indicate every quotation with quotation marks or a block indent.
·   You paraphrase the words of a source.
·   You use distinctive ideas or methods you found in a source.

17.3 Three Citation Styles

Researchers have been publishing research reports for more than four centuries. In that long tradition of citing sources, researchers have developed many distinctive citation systems. Here we will cover the three most popular citation styles for academic research:

- Chicago style (also known as Turabian style), from the University of Chicago Press. This style is widely used in the humanities and qualitative social sciences.
- MLA style, from the Modern Language Association. This style is widely used in literary studies.
- APA style, from the American Psychological Association. This style is widely used in the quantitative social sciences.

The distinctive features of each style are described at the beginning of their respective chapters.

In all three styles, you must identify citations in two places: in your text and in a separate list of sources at the end. First, you must indicate in your text where you used a source and what parts of a source you used. For Chicago style, you do that with notes: insert a raised number (superscript) in the text to indicate where you used the source and add a footnote to identify the source and the page(s) you used.

Most Americans think of homelessness as a recent development, but it has always been part of the American heritage. Beggars had long been common in London,[1] which led early Americans to think of homeless beggars as a normal feature of city life. Of course, America's early cities did not have extensive slums, which were the source of most of London's beggars. Nevertheless . . .

---

1. Tim Hitchcock, "Begging on the Streets of Eighteenth-Century London," *Journal of British Studies* 44, no. 3 (July 2005): 489.

For MLA and APA style, you do not use notes but insert a brief parenthetical reference with the page number(s) and just enough information to find the source in your list at the end:

MLA:
Most Americans think of homelessness as a recent development, but it has always been part of the American heritage. Beggars had long been common in London (Hitchcock 489), which led . . .

APA:
Most Americans think of homelessness as a recent development, but it has always been part of the American heritage. Beggars had long been common in London (Hitchcock, 2005, p. 489), which led . . .

Then at the end of your paper, you include an alphabetical list of all your sources, with complete bibliographical information for each.

Don't let yourself become overwhelmed by all the picky details you have to get right. Few researchers try to remember even half of them. Experienced researchers learn the basic form for common citations, let their word processor create a first draft, and then consult a book like this one to check the details.

17.4 What to Include in a Citation

Although the Chicago, MLA, and APA styles format citations differently, they have the same goal: to give readers the information they need to identify and find a source. For most sources, that information must answer three questions:

1. *Who is responsible for the text?*

   This is usually the author, but it might also be an editor, a translator, or an organization.

2. *What's the name of the text?*

   This includes the title and subtitle of the work itself. If the work is part of a series or multivolume collection, it includes that title as well.

3. *Who published it, where, and when?*

   For an article, this includes the title of the journal or magazine as well as a volume number and the page numbers of the article. For a book, it includes the publisher and the place of publication. For a website, it includes the sponsoring organization and the URL. For articles and books, this also includes the date of publication; for websites, it usually includes the date you accessed it.

   With this information, readers can almost always identify and find the specific source in your citation.

17.5 Collect Bibliographical Data as You Research and Draft

As you go through the early stages of your project, you may be tempted to ignore the picky details of citations until you can't put them off any longer. Resist. Not only will you make double work for yourself (you'll have to find each source twice—once to read it and again to get data for a citation), but you won't always be able to find the source again. And if you are like the two of us, you'll have more time for citations at the beginning than at the end, when your deadline is looming. So record *all* of the bibliographical data the first time you locate a source. You'll be glad you did.

17.5.1 What Bibliographical Data You Should Save

You don't need to memorize the details of citation formats, but you do need to know what information to save. If you can't remember it, copy this checklist or put it on your computer desktop.

For books, record	For articles, record
☐ author(s)	☐ author(s)
☐ title (including subtitle)	☐ title (including subtitle)
☐ title of series (if any)	☐ title of journal, magazine, etc.
☐ edition or volume number (if any)	☐ volume and issue number
☐ city and publisher	☐ database (if any)
☐ year published	☐ date published
☐ title and pages for chapter (if relevant)	☐ pages for article

For some online sources, the information you need is less predictable. Record as much of the above as applies, along with anything else that might help readers locate the source. You will also need at least these:

- URL
- date posted or last modified
- date of access
- sponsoring organization

A CAUTIONARY TALE

The Scholar Who Misplaced His Source

Many years ago, a young Professor Williams made an important discovery about the history of the English language because he found some old church records that no one had thought to connect to how people spoke in Shakespeare's time. But when it came time to publish his discovery, he came to an awful realization: he had not recorded all of the bibliographical data on the source, and he could not remember exactly where he had found it. For more than a year, he could not publish his paper, while he searched for that source. Then it came to him one night in his sleep: he had been looking in the wrong library!

Professor Williams was happy to report that he never made that mistake again.

17.5.2 How to Find the Data You Need

For the most part, you will find all of the bibliographic data you need at the beginning of books and journals and on the title page of articles. For websites, you may have to look around. Here are some examples of where to find data for the most common kinds of sources.

The Trial in American Life

Title

ROBERT A. FERGUSON —— Author's name

Publisher's name

City of publication
(cite only the first
city, "Chicago")

The University of Chicago Press   *Chicago & London*

ROBERT A. FERGUSON is the George Edward Woodberry Professor of
Law, Literature, and Criticism at Columbia University. He is the
author of *Law and Letters in American Culture*; *The American
Enlightenment, 1750–1820*; and *Reading the Early Republic.*

The University of Chicago Press, Chicago 60637
The University of Chicago Press, Ltd., London

Year of publication ——— © 2007 by The University of Chicago
All rights reserved. Published 2007
Printed in the United States of America

16 15 14 13 12 11 10 09 08 07   1 2 3 4 5

ISBN-13: 978-0-226-24325-2 (cloth)
ISBN-10: 0-226-24325-7 (cloth)

Library of Congress Cataloging-in-Publication Data
Ferguson, Robert A., 1942–
The trial in American life / Robert A. Ferguson.
p. cm.
Includes bibliographical references and index.
ISBN-13: 978-0-226-24325-2 (cloth: alk. paper)
ISBN-10: 0-226-24325-7 (cloth: alk. paper)
1. Trials—United States. 2. Trials—United States—History. I. Title.
KF220.F37 2007
345.73'07—dc22
2006022239

The University of Chicago Press gratefully acknowledges the generous
support of the John Simon Guggenheim Memorial Foundation
toward the publication of this book.

Edited Book

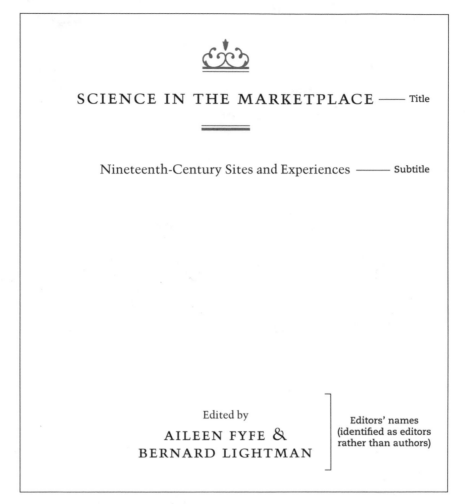

SCIENCE IN THE MARKETPLACE ——— Title

Nineteenth-Century Sites and Experiences ——— Subtitle

Edited by

AILEEN FYFE &
BERNARD LIGHTMAN

Editors' names
(identified as editors
rather than authors)

Revised Edition

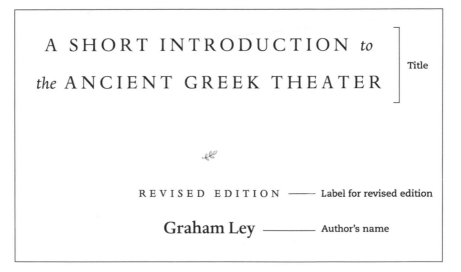

A SHORT INTRODUCTION *to*
the ANCIENT GREEK THEATER ⌉ Title

REVISED EDITION ———— Label for revised edition

Graham Ley ———— Author's name

The University of Chicago Press, Chicago 60637
The University of Chicago Press, Ltd., London
© 1991, 2006 by The University of Chicago
All rights reserved. Originally published in 1991
Revised edition published 2006
Printed in the United States of America

Year of publication
(cite only the year of
the revised edition)

Article title   Article subtitle

Before Democracy: The Production and Uses of Common Sense

Sophia Rosenfeld ——— Author's name
University of Virginia

> And all henceforth, who murder Common-Sense,
> Learn from these Scenes that tho' Success you boast,
> You shall at last be haunted with her Ghost.
> (HENRY FIELDING[1])

Many of the factors that shaped modern political life remain obscure to us. Some of these factors are now imperceptible because they were private, illegal, off-limits, or socially marginal. Others were, in Alain Corbin's elegant phrase, simply too banal ever to have been much remarked upon, even if they made whole categories of thought and experience possible.[2] Corbin was famously talking about what we call sense experiences: smelling, touching, and the like. But what of the historical evolution and significance of our most commonplace and trite assumptions about these banal experiences—or what is best known as common sense?

Common sense is, of course, hardly an unfamiliar notion these days. Talk of it permeates every aspect of contemporary Western democratic political culture. We evoke or appeal to common sense in order to signal that the practical, everyday wisdom of ordinary people in ordinary situations, as opposed to the unrealistic and extremist advice of so-called experts, provides the foundation for our political ideals. We also use the notion of common sense to suggest that bitter, partisan disagreements have been or should be jettisoned in favor of nonideological and therefore consensual solutions to the issues of our times. This is a rhetorical stance with which no one is likely to disagree. Speaking in the name of common

[1] Henry Fielding, *Pasquin. A Dramatick Satire on the Times: Being the Rehearsal of Two Plays, viz., A Comedy call'd The Election; and a Tragedy, call'd The Life and Death of Common Sense. As it is acted at the theatre in the Hay-Market* (London, 1736), act 5, 64.

[2] Alain Corbin, "A History and Anthropology of the Senses," in *Time, Desire, and Horror: Towards a History of the Senses,* trans. Jean Birrell (Cambridge, MA, 1995), 190. On the latent and consequently invisible dimension of history, see also Jacques Rancière, *The Names of History: On the Poetics of Knowledge,* trans. Hassan Melehy, foreword by Hayden White (Minneapolis, 1994).

Journal title —— *The Journal of Modern History* 80 (March 2008): 1–54 —— Pages of article

Volume number   Date of publication

Online Journal Article

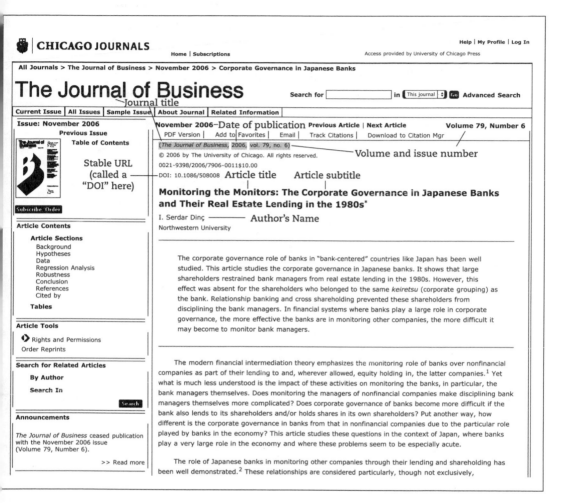

The Journal of Business
—Journal title

Search for ☐ in (This journal ◆) Go Advanced Search

| Current Issue | All Issues | Sample Issue | About Journal | Related Information |

Issue: November 2006

Previous Issue

Table of Contents

Stable URL (called a "DOI" here)

Subscribe/Order

Article Contents

Article Sections
Background
Hypotheses
Data
Regression Analysis
Robustness
Conclusion
References
Cited by

Tables

Article Tools

◆ Rights and Permissions
Order Reprints

Search for Related Articles

By Author

Search In

Search

Announcements

The Journal of Business ceased publication with the November 2006 issue (Volume 79, Number 6).

>> Read more

November 2006—Date of publication Previous Article | Next Article   **Volume 79, Number 6**

PDF Version | Add to Favorites | Email | Track Citations | Download to Citation Mgr

(*The Journal of Business*, 2006, vol. 79, no. 6) —— Volume and issue number

DOI: 10.1086/508008   Article title   Article subtitle

Monitoring the Monitors: The Corporate Governance in Japanese Banks and Their Real Estate Lending in the 1980s[*]

I. Serdar Dinç ———— Author's Name
Northwestern University

The corporate governance role of banks in "bank-centered" countries like Japan has been well studied. This article studies the corporate governance in Japanese banks. It shows that large shareholders restrained bank managers from real estate lending in the 1980s. However, this effect was absent for the shareholders who belonged to the same *keiretsu* (corporate grouping) as the bank. Relationship banking and cross shareholding prevented these shareholders from disciplining the bank managers. In financial systems where banks play a large role in corporate governance, the more effective the banks are in monitoring other companies, the more difficult it may become to monitor bank managers.

The modern financial intermediation theory emphasizes the monitoring role of banks over nonfinancial companies as part of their lending to and, wherever allowed, equity holding in, the latter companies.[1] Yet what is much less understood is the impact of these activities on monitoring the banks, in particular, the bank managers themselves. Does monitoring the managers of nonfinancial companies make disciplining bank managers themselves more complicated? Does corporate governance of banks become more difficult if the bank also lends to its shareholders and/or holds shares in its own shareholders? Put another way, how different is the corporate governance in banks from that in nonfinancial companies due to the particular role played by banks in the economy? This article studies these questions in the context of Japan, where banks play a very large role in the economy and where these problems seem to be especially acute.

The role of Japanese banks in monitoring other companies through their lending and shareholding has been well demonstrated.[2] These relationships are considered particularly, though not exclusively,

17.5.3 How to Record Bibliographical Data as You Go

Your best method for recording bibliographical data depends on where and how you do your research. But no matter your circumstances, always record everything you might need the first time you encounter a source.

If you are searching online:

1. Set up your computer:

    - Be sure that the history setting on your browser is set with no limit, so that it will record *all* the sites you visit and you can get back to each one.
    - Be sure that you have access to permanent storage. If you are using a public computer, bring blank, recordable CDs so that you can burn a record of everything you have found.

2. Save every web page or online document that has material you may use, including the pages that have bibliographical data.

3. Before you finish with a source, enter its data into a computer record. If your word processor has a citation database or if you are using citation software, enter the data there. Otherwise, enter the data in a file, one page per work (create a template for this).

If you are reading in a library with a laptop:

1. Before you finish with a source, enter its data into a computer record. If your word processor has a citation database or if you are using citation software, enter the data there. Otherwise, enter the data in a file, one page per work (create a template for this).

2. A good researcher checks twice so that she only has to find a source once. After you have entered all the data, go back and check each one against the text in front of you.

3. You might also consider photocopying title pages, copyright pages, and others with the bibliographical information you need. (This is also good advice for long quotations.)

If you are reading in a library without a laptop:

1. Before you head for the library, create a word-processing file with a template for the information you will record. Print more copies than you expect to need.

2. Before you finish with a source, write down its data on a template page. Check twice so that you only have to find the source once. Consider photocopying pages with the information you need.

3. Back at your computer, enter the information from your template pages either into a citation database or in the template file.

17.5.4 What to Do When You Can't Find the Data You Need

You can expect little trouble in finding the bibliographical data you need for most sources. But if your source lacks the usual information, you can almost always find information that will substitute. Be flexible and think about *why* readers might need each kind of information. For example, if you cite a TV show or a film, you won't have an author, but readers will be happy if you use the director instead. For a song, the songwriter is most like an author and the record company is most like the publisher. If you record the information that is most like the standards, you will be able to create adequate citations.

Experienced researchers know that proper citations require too many arbitrary details for anybody to keep them all in mind. So the secret to success here is to set up a system that will work and follow it without fail. Do that, and you'll find citations easy, perhaps even fun.

18: Chicago Style

This chapter shows you how to use the Chicago notes-bibliography style. In Chicago style, you use numbered notes for the citations in your text. Whenever you use the words or ideas of a source, you mark the place in your text with a raised number called a *superscript* and give the information about the source in a correspondingly numbered note. You then collect all of the sources you have cited into an alphabetical listing called a *bibliography*. This list should also include any works that you did not cite but that influenced your thinking. In special cases, you may include all sources you consulted, even if you did not use them in any way; but ask your teacher before you do so.

The forms for notes and bibliography entries are different for different kinds of sources, but for each kind of source a note and bibliography entry are similar:

Note for Journal Article

1. Tim Hitchcock, "Begging on the Streets of Eighteenth-Century London," *Journal of British Studies* 44, no. 3 (July 2005): 489.

Bibliography Entry for Journal Article

Hitchcock, Tim. "Begging on the Streets of Eighteenth-Century London." *Journal of British Studies* 44, no. 3 (July 2005): 478–498.

Note for Book

2. Philip Ball, *Bright Earth: Art and the Invention of Color* (New York: Farrar, Straus and Giroux, 2001), 99.

Bibliography Entry for Book

Ball, Philip. *Bright Earth: Art and the Invention of Color.* New York: Farrar, Straus and Giroux, 2001.

Although they look similar, these forms vary in small but important details such as order of elements, punctuation, capitalization, and abbreviations. So be sure you use the right kind of example and pay close attention to these details. To help you avoid confusing the note form with the bibliography-entry form, we have listed them in different sections (18.1 Notes and 18.2 Bibliography).

How to Use This Chapter

This chapter presents models for the most common kinds of sources. You will find models for notes in section 18.1 and for bibliography entries in 18.2. Within each section, the models are listed by kind of source: articles, reference works, websites and blogs, and books. Follow these steps:

1. **Find a model.**

    -   Find the model that matches your kind of source. For instance, if you need to cite a scholarly journal article in an online database, find the example for "Online Journal."
    -   Be certain that your source is in the same category as the example. If your source does not match any of the examples in this book, *do not guess.* Consult a more comprehensive guide, such as Kate. L. Turabian, *A Manual for Writers of Research Papers, Theses, and Dissertations,* 7th ed. (Chicago: University of Chicago Press, 2007).

2. **Match the model.**

- Create your citation by exactly matching the bibliographical information on your source to each detail in the model, point for point. Make
  sure that your note or bibliography entry corresponds to the model *in
  every detail*, including capitalization, abbreviations, punctuation, and
  spacing.
- If your source has multiple authors, consult the information on authors' names in section 18.1.2.1 (notes) or 18.2.1.1 (bibliography).

3. **Adjust, but only if necessary.**

- You may make reasonable small adjustments if your source is the
  same kind as a model but its bibliographic information is slightly
  different. For example, if the person who put together a book of collected material is called a "compiler" rather than an editor, you may
  use the form for an edited volume and use the word "compiler" or
  the abbreviation "comp." wherever the example uses "editor" or "ed":
  68. Henry Jones, compiler, *The Oxford Book of . . .*

Many of you will use software packages that format citations for you automatically. You may let your software create a first draft of your citations, *but
do not trust it to produce the correct form.* If you use an automatic citation builder,
recheck each note and bibliography entry. Find the appropriate example and
match it to the citation point by point. It is easy to miss small but important details when a citation is already formatted for you, so go slowly and be careful.

18.1 Notes

18.1.1 When and How to Add Notes

You must indicate in your text every place where you use the words or ideas
of a source. In most cases, you should cite a source in a numbered note, with
a corresponding number inserted in your text. The exact form of the note
depends on the kind of source you cite: journal article, website, book, and so
on. For sources you cite often, you can use parenthetical references.

For a quotation or paraphrase, insert the note number or parenthetical reference at the end of the quotation or at the end of the sentence that includes it:

The founding fathers' commitment to religious freedom was based on their commitment to the freedom of ideas. They were adamant that the "coercion of the
laws" cannot apply to "the operations of the mind" in the way that they must
apply to "the acts of the body."[3]

For ideas or methods, insert the note number at the end of the sentence in
which you first introduce or explain the borrowed material. *Be sure to cite every*

source that influenced your thinking, even if you do not quote or paraphrase from it. A reader might think you're guilty of plagiarism if you seem to reflect the ideas of a text that you do not cite. (See chapter 10.)

Notes are called *footnotes* if you put them at the bottom of the page or *endnotes* if they are in a separate list at the end. Most readers find footnotes easier to use because they can see the text and the note at the same time, without turning to the end of the paper. Ask your teacher what she prefers, but if you have a choice, use footnotes.

18.1.1.1 *Numbered Notes*

Most citations in your paper should be in numbered notes. Use your word-processing software to insert into your text a raised number, or superscript, that directs readers to a correspondingly numbered note.

Most Americans think of homelessness as a recent development, but it has always been part of the American heritage. Beggars had long been common in London,[1] which led early Americans to think of homeless beggars as a normal feature of city life. Of course, America's early cities . . .

1. Tim Hitchcock, "Begging on the Streets of Eighteenth-Century London," *Journal of British Studies* 44, no. 3 (July 2005): 489.

The superscript in your text must be *after* any punctuation:

NOT: . . . London[1], which . . .   BUT: . . . London,[1] which . . .

Your word-processing software should format the note for you. If not, do this:

- Number each note with a superscript. (It is acceptable if your software uses a number followed by a period: 1. Tim Hitchcock, "Begging . . .").
- Indent each note like a paragraph.
- Single-space notes with a blank line between notes.
- For footnotes, put a line between the body text and the first footnote on each page.
- For endnotes, list all notes starting on a new page after the text but before the bibliography; center the heading "Notes" at the top.

18.1.1.2 *Shortened Notes*

If you refer to the same source more than once, you can use a short form after the first note. The first note must give the full citation. After that, give enough information to identify the source, usually the author's last name and a word or two from the title. If you add page numbers, put a comma after the title and then the pages (but do not use *p.* or *pp.*).

Most Americans think of homelessness as a recent development, but it has always been part of the American heritage. Beggars had long been common in London,[1] which led early Americans to think of homeless beggars as a normal feature of city life. Of course, America's early cities did not have extensive slums, which were the source of most of London's beggars.[2] Nevertheless . . .

---

1. Tim Hitchcock, "Begging on the Streets of Eighteenth-Century London," *Journal of British Studies* 44, no. 3 (July 2005): 489.

2. Hitchcock, "Begging," 491.

18.1.1.3 *Parenthetical References in the Text*

Although most citations should be in notes, you can use parenthetical references if you have several citations to the same source. This is common when your paper analyzes one or two texts, as in many literary, philosophical, or historical essays.

In these cases, the first reference to the source should be a complete note:

---

3. Thomas Jefferson, *Notes on the State of Virginia*, ed. William Peden (New York: W. W. Norton & Company, 1954), 16.

After that, you can use a short parenthetical reference inserted into your text each time you cite this source. Give just enough information to match the reference to the full citation given in the note. In most cases, you should include only the author's last name and page number, separated by a comma:

The founding fathers' commitment to religious freedom was based on their commitment to the freedom of ideas. They were adamant that the "coercion of the laws" cannot apply to "the operations of the mind" in the way that they must apply to "the acts of the body" (Jefferson, 159).

If you mention the author's name in your text, you can give just the page number in parentheses:

. . . their commitment to the freedom of ideas. As Thomas Jefferson put it, the "coercion of the laws" cannot apply to "the operations of the mind" in the way that they must apply to "the acts of the body" (159).

If, however, your paper cites two works by the same author, you need to give both the author's name and a keyword or two from the title so that readers will know which work you are citing:

. . . the "coercion of the laws" cannot apply to "the operations of the mind" in the way that they must apply to "the acts of the body" (Jefferson, *Notes*, 159).

18.1.2 Elements Common to All Notes

When you create a note, you have to pay attention to the kind of source you are citing, because many elements of notes are different for different kinds of sources. But almost all notes consist of four basic elements—author's name, title of the work, publication facts, and page numbers.

18.1.2.1 Author's Name

The first element in a note is always the name of the author or authors. You should give the full name of the author *exactly* as it is shown in the source: use initials only if that's how the name appears. Do not include titles such as *Sir, Saint, Sister, Reverend, Doctor,* and so on. List all authors' names in regular order: first–middle–last. (*Note:* Authors are listed differently in bibliography entries; see 18.2.1.1.)

Single Author

4. Michael Pollan, *The Omnivore's Dilemma* . . .
5. J. K. Rowling, *Harry Potter and* . . .

Multiple Authors

If there is more than one author, list them in the order shown in the source. For three or more authors, put a comma between names and add *and* before the last name.

6. Steven D. Levitt and Stephen J. Dubner, *Freakonomics* . . .
7. Joyce Heatherton, James Fitzgilroy, and Jackson Hsu, *Meteors and Mudslides* . . .

If there is no author listed in the source, begin the note with the title of the work.

18.1.2.2 Title

Give the title *exactly* as it is shown in the source, including a subtitle if there is one. For articles and other short works, you will need both the article title and the title of the book, journal, or other work in which it occurs. If an online source does not have an obvious title, use the name of the site or any other reasonable replacement.

Capitalize titles headline style: capitalize the first and last words of the title and subtitle and all other words *except* articles (*a, an, the*), coordinate conjunctions (*and, but, or, nor, for, so, yet*), prepositions (*of, in, at, above, under,* and so forth), and the words *to* and *as*. If a title includes a subtitle, put a colon between the main title and the subtitle. With few exceptions, titles are set off in quotations marks or italics.

QUOTATION MARKS: ARTICLES, CHAPTERS, WEB PAGES, AND OTHER SHORT WORKS. Put the titles of short works that are part of longer ones in regular type, enclosed in quotation marks.

8. Tim Hitchcock, "Begging on the Streets of Eighteenth-Century London," . . .

9. Charlotte M. Porter, "Artist-Naturalists in Florida," Florida Museum of Natural History (website), accessed May 1, 2009, http://www.flmnh.ufl.edu/naturalists/.

ITALICS: BOOKS, JOURNALS, MAGAZINES, NEWSPAPERS, AND BLOGS. Put the titles of longer works in italics. If the title includes a title, put it in quotation marks and italics.

10. Thomas Jefferson, *Notes on the State of Virginia*, . . .

11. Tim Hitchcock, "Begging on the Streets of Eighteenth-Century London," *Journal of British Studies* . . .

12. John E. Sitter, *The Poetry of Pope's "Dunciad,"* . . .

18.1.2.3 Publication Facts

In addition to the author's name and title of the work, a note usually includes facts that identify *where* and *when* a source was published. Publication facts vary from one kind of source to another, so check each model carefully.

For online sources, you must also include the date you accessed the source and a complete online address or URL (uniform resource locator). In most cases, you should include the URL *exactly as it appears in your browser bar, even if it is very long.*

13. . . . . Florida Museum of Natural History (website), accessed May 1, 2009, http://www.flmnh.ufl.edu/naturalists/.

Most word processors will not break URLs if they spill over a line, but you can force a line break after a slash (/). If that still leaves a mostly empty line, you can force a break *before* a period, equal sign, or other punctuation.

18.1.2.4 Page Numbers

If you cite a specific passage in a source, you must indicate where readers can find that passage, usually by adding a page number. The page number (or numbers) may be preceded by either a comma or a colon, depending on the type of source. Do not include the word *page* or the abbreviations *p.* or *pp.* before the number.

14. Tim Hitchcock, "Begging on the Streets of Eighteenth-Century London," *Journal of British Studies* 44, no. 3 (July 2005): 489.

If you cite a range of pages, include all the digits in both numbers: do not abbreviate the second (*not* 127–32).

15. Philip Ball, *Bright Earth: Art and the Invention of Color* (New York: Farrar, Straus and Giroux, 2001), 98–99.

If you cite material from a table or lines from a poem, use the word *table* or *line(s)* and an identifying number(s).

16. Kenneth T. Jackson, *Crabgrass Frontier: The Suburbanization of the United States* (New York: Oxford University Press, 1985), table 1.

17. Ogden Nash, "Song for Ditherers," lines 1–4.

Many online sources do not have page numbers. If the source has a label for the section you quote, a heading, or a numbered paragraph, then use that as a locator. Otherwise, you can skip this element.

18.1.3 Notes for Periodical Articles

Most of the articles you will consult will be found in *periodicals*—journals, magazines, newspapers, and other works published at periodic intervals in print form, online, or both.

- **Journals** are scholarly or professional periodicals written for experts and available primarily in academic libraries. Journals often include the word *journal* in their titles (*Journal of Modern History*), but not always (*Postmodern Culture*).
- **Magazines** are not scholarly publications; they are designed for more general readers in both their content and their availability outside of academic settings. If you are unsure whether a periodical is a journal or a magazine, see whether its articles include citations; if so, treat it as a journal.
- **Newspapers** are generally daily or weekly publications whose articles are closely tied to recent events.

The Basic Pattern

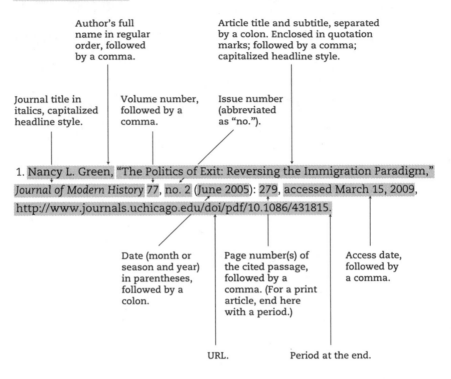

Author's full name in regular order, followed by a comma.

Article title and subtitle, separated by a colon. Enclosed in quotation marks; followed by a comma; capitalized headline style.

Journal title in italics, capitalized headline style.

Volume number, followed by a comma.

Issue number (abbreviated as "no.").

1. Nancy L. Green, "The Politics of Exit: Reversing the Immigration Paradigm," *Journal of Modern History* 77, no. 2 (June 2005): 279, accessed March 15, 2009, http://www.journals.uchicago.edu/doi/pdf/10.1086/431815.

Date (month or season and year) in parentheses, followed by a colon.

Page number(s) of the cited passage, followed by a comma. (For a print article, end here with a period.)

Access date, followed by a comma.

URL.

Period at the end.

Print Journal

If a journal lists both a volume and issue number, include both; list the date as it is printed on the journal (year, month + year, or season + year).

18. Ann Grodzins Gold, "Grains of Truth: Shifting Hierarchies of Food and Grace in Three Rajasthani Tales," *History of Religions* 38, no. 2 (November 1998): 150–151.

19. Garrett Cullity, "Decisions, Reasons, and Rationality," *Ethics* 119 (October 2008): 64.

20. Joshua Brown, "Historians and Photography," *American Art* 21, no. 3 (Fall 2007): 9–10.

Online Journal

If an online article has numbered pages, cite them. If not, look for headings, section numbers, or paragraph numbers. Otherwise, do not cite pages.

21. Jeremy Adelman, "An Age of Imperial Revolutions," *American Historical Review* 113, no. 2 (April 2008), accessed September 15, 2008, http://www.journals.uchicago.edu/doi/full/10.1086/ahr.113.2.319.

22. Alan Bass, "The Mystery of Sex and the Mystery of Time: An Integration

of Some Psychoanalytic and Philosophical Perspectives," *Postmodern Culture* 18, no. 1 (2007), accessed January 7, 2008, http://muse.jhu.edu/login?uri=/journals/postmodern_culture/v018/x.1.bass.html.

If an online article lists what it calls a "stable URL" or "permanent URL," use that instead of the URL in your browser bar.

23. Frank P. Whitney, "The Six-Year High School in Cleveland," *School Review* 37, no. 4 (1929): 70, accessed January 31, 2009, http://www.jstor.org/stable/1078814.

Print Magazine

24. William Langewiesche, "Rules of Engagement," *Vanity Fair,* November 2006, 50.

If the article is part of a "department" (a recurring section with the same title in each issue), add the department name in regular type without quotation marks between the article and magazine titles.

25. Hendrik Hertzberg, "Follow the Leaders," Talk of the Town, *New Yorker,* December 10, 2007, 41.

Online Magazine

If an online article has numbered pages, cite them. If not, look for headings, section numbers, or paragraph numbers. Otherwise, do not cite pages.

26. Stefan Theil, "In California, Green Means Growth," *Newsweek,* March 2, 2009, accessed April 24, 2009, http://www.newsweek.com/id/185792.

27. Nancy Goldstein, "The Economy Is a Feminist Issue," *Salon.com,* February 20, 2009, accessed February 26, 2009, http://www.salon.com/mwt/broadsheet/feature/2009/02/20/women_economy/index.html.

Print Newspaper

Omit page references for newspaper articles.

28. Lisa Guernsey, "Rewards for Students under a Microscope," *New York Times,* March 3, 2009.

Online Newspaper

29. Lisa Guernsey, "Rewards for Students under a Microscope," *New York Times,* March 3, 2009, accessed March 9, 2009, http://www.nytimes.com/2009/03/03/health/03rewa.html.

18.1.4   **Notes for Reference Works**
Reference works are sources such as encyclopedias and dictionaries; their entries usually do not have authors. (Cite an entry with an author as you would a chapter of a book; see 18.1.6.2.) If a reference work is arranged alphabetically, do not cite page numbers; list the entry in quotation marks, preceded by "s.v." (for the Latin *sub verbo,* or "under the word"). If you list more than one entry in the same note, use "s.vv."

Print Encyclopedia
If an encyclopedia has an edition number, give it.

30. *Encyclopaedia Britannica,* 15th ed., s.v. "Sibelius, Jean."

Online Encyclopedia

31. *Wikipedia,* s.v. "Martin Luther King, Jr.," accessed January 15, 2008, http://en.wikipedia.org/wiki/Martin_luther_king.

Print Dictionary
If a dictionary has an edition number, give it.

32. *Oxford English Dictionary,* 2nd ed., s.v. "hoot(e)nanny, hootananny."
33. *Dictionary of American Biography,* s.v. "Wadsworth, Jeremiah."

Online Dictionary

34. *Merriam-Webster OnLine,* s.v. "mondegreen," accessed September 19, 2008, http://www.merriam-webster.com/dictionary/mondegreen.

18.1.5   **Notes for Websites and Blogs**
You must cite *all* material you find on the Internet, even if it is not published by a journal, magazine, or newspaper. In a note, you should not cite a website as a whole (www.whitehouse.gov); cite the specific document or web page that you consulted (www.whitehouse.gov/agenda/energy_and_environment/). Similarly, do not cite an entire blog in a note, but the particular posting or comment that you use in your paper.

Web Page
Websites are unpredictable, so you may have to improvise, but as much as possible include the same kind of information you need for other online publications:

· author, if any
· web page title (in quotation marks)

- website title, if any (in italics)
- sponsoring organization, if any (in regular type)
- access date and URL

---

35. Charlotte M. Porter, "Mark Catesby's Audience and Patrons," *Florida Naturalists* (website), Florida Museum of Natural History, accessed May 1, 2009, http://www.flmnh.ufl.edu/naturalists/catesby01.htm.

36. "Code of Ethics," *City of Los Angeles* (website), accessed March 13, 2008, http://www.lacity.org/ita/urldoc2540.pdf.

37. "Biography," *The Charles Chestnut Digital Archive* (website), ed. Stephanie P. Browner, accessed March 10, 2009, http://www.chesnuttarchive.org/classroom/biography.html.

Blog Entry

Blog entries have relatively predictable bibliographical information:

- author
- title of posting (in quotation marks)
- title of blog (in italics)
- date of posting
- access date and URL

---

38. Rhian Ellis, "Squatters' Rights," *Ward Six* (blog), June 30, 2008, accessed August 1, 2008, http://wardsix.blogspot.com/2008/06/squatters-rights.html.

Web Page or Blog Comment

To cite a comment on a blog entry, begin with the name (or pseudonym) of the commenter, the title (if any), the date and time of the comment, and the words "comment on" followed by the standard entry for a blog entry or web page.

---

39. AC, July 1, 2008 (10:18 a.m.), comment on Rhian Ellis, "Squatters' Rights," *Ward Six* (blog), June 30, 2008, accessed August 1, 2008, http://wardsix.blogspot.com/2008/06/squatters-rights.html.

40. Philogenes, "Shocked, Shocked, I Tell You," March 16, 2009 (1:00 p.m.), comment on "Composition, Overcrowded," *Inside Higher Ed* (website), March 16, 2009, accessed March 17, 2009, http://www.insidehighered.com/news/2009/03/16/comp#Comments.

18.1.6   Notes for Books

The Basic Pattern

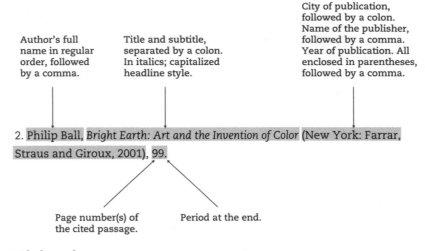

18.1.6.1   *Whole Books*

Print Book

41. Newton N. Minow and Craig L. LaMay, *Inside the Presidential Debates: Their Improbable Past and Promising Future* (Chicago: University of Chicago Press, 2008), 54.

If the book is produced by an organization rather than a person, list the organization as the author:

42. World Health Organization, *Health and Economic Development in South-Eastern Europe* (Geneva: World Health Organization, 2006), 92.

Book in Electronic Reader Format

Use the publication date of the e-book edition, and identify the e-book format. Do not use page numbers, but use chapters instead (abbreviate as "chap.").

43. Jane Austen, *Pride and Prejudice* (New York: Penguin Classics, 2007), Kindle edition, chap. 23.

Online Book

Most online books have page numbers. If not, identify the pages by section or chapter number.

44. Walt Whitman, *Leaves of Grass* (New York: self-published, 1855), 22, accessed November 22, 2009, http://www.whitmanarchive.org/published/LG/1855/whole.html.

Edited or Translated Book

If a book has an editor or translator but no author, put the editor or translator in place of the author, followed by the abbreviation "ed." or "trans."

45. Glenn Young, ed., *The Best American Short Plays, 2002–2003* (New York: Applause, 2007), 94.

46. Theodore Silverstein, trans., *Sir Gawain and the Green Knight* (Chicago: University of Chicago Press, 1974), 34.

If a book has an author as well as an editor or a translator, identify the editor or translator between the title and the publication facts.

47. Yves Bonnefoy, *New and Selected Poems,* ed. John Naughton and Anthony Rudolf (Chicago: University of Chicago Press, 1995), 64.

48. Georges Feydeau, *Four Farces by Georges Feydeau,* trans. Norman R. Shapiro (Chicago: University of Chicago Press, 1970), 122.

Revised Edition

If you consult a book labeled as a "revised" edition or a "second" (or subsequent) edition, place this information between the title and the publication facts, using abbreviations.

49. Karen V. Harper-Dorton and Martin Herbert, *Working with Children, Adolescents, and Their Families,* 3rd ed. (Chicago: Lyceum Books, 2002), 43.

50. Florence Babb, *Between Field and Cooking Pot: The Political Economy of Market-women in Peru,* rev. ed. (Austin: University of Texas Press, 1989), 199.

Multivolume Work

If you cite one book from a group of books with the same title (known as a *multivolume work*), indicate the volume number immediately before the page number, with the two numbers separated by a colon. Do not include the word "volume" or the abbreviation "vol."

51. Muriel St. Clare Byrne, ed., *The Lisle Letters,* 6 vols. (Chicago: University of Chicago Press, 1981), 4:243.

If the volume you cite has a different title from that of the whole group, give the volume title first, followed by "vol. X of" the group as a whole.

52. Jaroslav Pelikan, *Christian Doctrine and Modern Culture (since 1700),* vol. 5 of *The Christian Tradition: A History of the Development of Doctrine* (Chicago: University of Chicago Press, 1989), 16.

18.1.6.2 *Parts of Books*

Chapter in an Edited Book

If a book consists of chapters written by several different authors, cite the specific chapter you borrowed from.

53. Elizabeth F. L. Ellet, "By Rail and Stage to Galena," in *Prairie State: Impressions of Illinois, 1673–1967, by Travelers and Other Observers,* ed. Paul M. Angle (Chicago: University of Chicago Press, 1968), 275.

Introduction, Preface, or Afterword

If someone other than the author has written a supplemental part of a book, such as an introduction, preface, afterword, or epilogue, cite it separately. Do not capitalize a generic title such as "introduction"; put it in regular type, without quotation marks.

54. Francine Prose, introduction to *Word Court: Wherein Verbal Virtue Is Rewarded, Crimes against the Language Are Punished, and Poetic Justice Is Done,* by Barbara Wallraff (New York: Harcourt, 2000), 9.

Letter in a Collection

55. Adams to Charles Milnes Gaskell, London, 30 March 1868, in *Letters of Henry Adams, 1858–1891,* ed. Worthington Chauncey Ford (Boston: Houghton Mifflin, 1930), 141.

Short Story or Poem in a Collection

Put the titles of these works in regular type with quotation marks except for very long poems, whose titles are italicized.

56. Deborah Eisenberg, "Someone to Talk To," in *All around Atlantis* (New York: Farrar, Straus and Giroux, 1997), 61–92.

57. Seamus Heaney, "To George Seferis in the Underworld," in *District and Circle: Poems* (New York: Farrar, Straus and Giroux, 2006), 23.

58. Michael Wigglesworth, excerpt from *The Day of Doom,* in *The New Anthology of American Poetry: Traditions and Revolutions, Beginnings to 1900,* ed. Steven Gould Axelrod, Camille Roman, and Thomas Travisano (New Brunswick, NJ: Rutgers University Press, 2003), 71.

18.1.7 **Notes for Citing Citations in a Source**

When you find useful information quoted or reported in a secondary or tertiary source, you should always try to locate the original source. If you cannot, you must cite both the original source and the one you actually used. Cite the original source completely, including the page number(s), then add "quoted in" (for quotations) or "reported in" (for other borrowings), followed by the complete citation for the source you consulted. Put both sources in your bibliography.

59. Louis Zukofsky, "Sincerity and Objectification," *Poetry* 37 (February 1931): 269, quoted in Bonnie Costello, *Marianne Moore: Imaginary Possessions* (Cambridge, MA: Harvard University Press, 1981), 78.

18.2 Bibliography

If you have notes to more than four or five sources, you must list each source at the end of your paper in a section called a bibliography. You should also list other works you read but did not cite, if they influenced your thinking: a reader might think you're guilty of plagiarism if you seem to reflect the ideas of a text that you do not include in your bibliography (see chapter 10). Normally you should not include sources you consulted but did not use in any way, but your teacher might ask you to include them in order to see the scope of your research.

Start your list of sources on a new page. Center the heading "Bibliography" at the top of the first page. List the entries in alphabetical order, double-spaced, with a hanging indent. Alphabetize the sources according to the last name of the author or editor. Strictly follow the order of the letters, and ignore apostrophes and hyphens. Do not change the order for names that include abbreviations or internal capitals (such as McArthur or St. Helena):

Macally, Mack, Madden, McArthur, Mecks . . .
Saint-Beuve, Schwab, Selleck, Skillen, St. Helena, Stricker . . .

If you have to list more than one source by the same author, order those sources alphabetically by their titles. If a source does not have an author or editor, the first element in the bibliography entry will be the title, so use that to place the entry alphabetically among the authors' names.

See the sample bibliography in Chicago style on pages 181–82.

18.2.1 Elements Common to All Bibliography Entries

When you create a bibliography entry, you have to pay attention to the kind of source you are citing, because many elements are different for different kinds of sources. But most bibliography entries consist of three basic elements—author's name, title of the work, and publication facts.

18.2.1.1 *Author's Name*

Whenever possible, begin each bibliography entry with the name of the author(s). Spell out the full name of the author *exactly* as it is shown in the source: use initials only if that's how the name appears. Do not include titles such as *Sir, Saint, Sister, Reverend, Doctor,* and so on. However, list the author's name in *inverted* order: last name–comma–first name–middle name (if any). (*Note:* Authors are listed differently in notes; see 18.1.2.1.)

Single Author

Pollan, Michael. *The Omnivore's Dilemma* . . .
Rowling, J. K. *Harry Potter and* . . .

Multiple Authors

List all authors in the order they appear on the title page. List the *first* author with the last name first and a comma after the last and first name. List all other authors in regular order (first-middle-last). Put a comma after the name of the first author (even if there are only two); put *and* before and a period after the last author; and put a comma after all authors between the first and the last.

Levitt, Steven D., and Stephen J. Dubner. *Freakonomics* . . .
Heatherton, Joyce, James Fitzgilroy, and Jackson Hsu. *Meteors and Mudslides* . . .

If there is no author listed, begin the entry with the title of the work.

Multiple Works by One Author

If you cite multiple works by the same author or group of authors, you will have several entries that begin the same. For all entries after the first, replace the name(s) with three long dashes (em dashes). If the work is edited or translated, add the corresponding designation after the three em dashes and a comma. Note that the "ed." or "trans." is ignored in alphabetizing.

NOT	BUT
Schank, Roger C. *Dynamic Memory* . . .	Schank, Roger C. *Dynamic Memory* . . .
Schank, Roger C., ed. *Inside Multi-Media* . . .	———, ed. *Inside Multi-Media* . . .
Schank, Roger C. *Reading and* . . .	———. *Reading and* . . .
Schank, Roger C. *Tell Me a Story* . . .	———. *Tell Me a Story* . . .

18.2.1.2 Title

Give the title *exactly* as it is shown in the source, including a subtitle if there is one. For articles and other short works, you will need both the article title and the title of the book, journal, or other work in which it occurs. If an online source does not have an obvious title, use the name of the site or any other reasonable replacement.

Capitalize titles headline style: capitalize the first and last words of the title and subtitle and all other words *except* articles (*a, an, the*), coordinate conjunctions (*and, but, or, nor, for, so, yet*), prepositions (*of, in, at, above, under,* and so forth), and the words *to* and *as*. If a title includes a subtitle, put a colon between the main title and the subtitle. With few exceptions, titles are set off in quotations marks or italics.

QUOTATION MARKS: ARTICLES, CHAPTERS, AND OTHER SHORT WORKS. Put the titles of short works that are part of longer ones in regular type, enclosed in quotation marks.

Hitchcock, Tim. "Begging on the Streets of Eighteenth-Century London." . . .

ITALICS: BOOKS, JOURNALS, MAGAZINES, NEWSPAPERS, AND BLOGS. Put the titles of longer works in italics. If the title includes a title within it, put it in quotation marks and italics.

Jefferson, Thomas. *Notes on the State of Virginia.* . . .

Hitchcock, Tim. "Begging on the Streets of Eighteenth-Century London." *Journal of British Studies* . . .

Sitter, John E. *The Poetry of Pope's "Dunciad."* . . .

18.2.1.3 *Publication Facts*

In addition to author's name and title, a bibliographic citation usually includes facts that identify *where* and *when* a source was published. Publication facts vary from one kind of source to another, so check each model carefully.

For online sources, you must also include the date you accessed the source and a complete online address or URL (uniform resource locator). In most cases, you should include the URL *exactly as it appears in your browser bar, even if it is very long.*

Florida Naturalists (website). Florida Museum of Natural History. Accessed May 1, 2009, http://www.flmnh.ufl.edu/naturalists/.

Most word processors will not break URLs if they spill over a line, but you can force a line break after a slash (/). If that still leaves a mostly empty line, you can force a break *before* a period, equal sign, or other punctuation.

18.2.2 Bibliography Entries for Periodical Articles

Most of the articles you will consult will be found in *periodicals*—journals, magazines, newspapers, and other works published at periodic intervals in print form, online, or both.

- **Journals** are scholarly or professional periodicals written for experts and available primarily in academic libraries. Journals often include the word *journal* in their titles (*Journal of Modern History*), but not always (*Postmodern Culture*).
- **Magazines** are not scholarly publications; they are designed for more general readers in both their content and their availability outside of academic

settings. If you are unsure whether a periodical is a journal or a magazine, see whether its articles include citations; if so, treat it as a journal.

· **Newspapers** are generally daily or weekly publications whose articles are closely tied to recent events.

The Basic Pattern

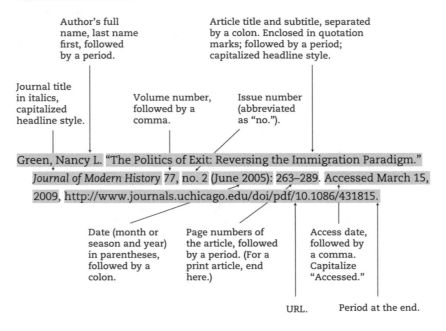

Author's full name, last name first, followed by a period.

Article title and subtitle, separated by a colon. Enclosed in quotation marks; followed by a period; capitalized headline style.

Journal title in italics, capitalized headline style.

Volume number, followed by a comma.

Issue number (abbreviated as "no.").

Green, Nancy L. "The Politics of Exit: Reversing the Immigration Paradigm." *Journal of Modern History* 77, no. 2 (June 2005): 263–289. Accessed March 15, 2009, http://www.journals.uchicago.edu/doi/pdf/10.1086/431815.

Date (month or season and year) in parentheses, followed by a colon.

Page numbers of the article, followed by a period. (For a print article, end here.)

Access date, followed by a comma. Capitalize "Accessed."

URL.   Period at the end.

Print Journal

If a journal lists both a volume and issue number, include both; list the date as it is printed on the journal (year, month + year, or season + year).

Gold, Ann Grodzins. "Grains of Truth: Shifting Hierarchies of Food and Grace in Three Rajasthani Tales." *History of Religions* 38, no. 2 (1998): 150–171.

Cullity, Garrett. "Decisions, Reasons, and Rationality." *Ethics* 119 (October 2008): 57–95.

Brown, Joshua. "Historians and Photography." *American Art* 21, no. 3 (Fall 2007): 9–13.

Online Journal

Bibliography entries for online journal articles are similar to those for print articles, except that online articles may not have identifiable page numbers.

Adelman, Jeremy. "An Age of Imperial Revolutions." *American Historical Review* 113, no. 2 (April 2008). Accessed September 15, 2008, http://www.journals .uchicago.edu/doi/full/10.1086/ahr.113.2.319.

Bass, Alan. "The Mystery of Sex and the Mystery of Time: An Integration of Some Psychoanalytic and Philosophical Perspectives." *Postmodern Culture* 18, no. 1 (2007). Accessed January 7, 2008, http://muse.jhu.edu/login?uri=/ journals/postmodern_culture/v0x/x.1.bass.html.

If an online article lists what it calls a "stable URL" or "permanent URL," use that instead of the URL in your browser bar.

Whitney, Frank P. "The Six-Year High School in Cleveland." *School Review* 37, no. 4 (1929): 267–271. Accessed January 31, 2009, http://www.jstor.org/stable/1078814.

Print Magazine

Magazine articles often jump across many pages with unrelated material, so do not include page numbers.

Langewiesche, William. "Rules of Engagement." *Vanity Fair*, November 2006.

If the article is part of a "department" (a recurring section with the same title in each issue), add the department name in regular type without quotation marks between the article and magazine titles.

Hertzberg, Hendrik. "Follow the Leaders." Talk of the Town. *New Yorker*, December 10, 2007.

Online Magazine

Theil, Stefan. "In California, Green Means Growth." *Newsweek*, March 2, 2009. Accessed April 24, 2009, http://www.newsweek.com/id/185792.

Goldstein, Nancy. "The Economy Is a Feminist Issue." *Salon.com*, February 20, 2009. Accessed February 26, 2009, http://www.salon.com/mwt/broadsheet/ feature/2009/02/20/women_economy/index.html.

Print Newspaper

Guernsey, Lisa. "Rewards for Students under a Microscope." *New York Times*, March 3, 2009.

Online Newspaper

Guernsey, Lisa. "Rewards for Students under a Microscope." *New York Times*, March 3, 2009. Accessed March 9, 2009, http://www.nytimes.com/2009/03/03/ health/03rewa.html.

18.2.3 Bibliography Entries for Reference Works

Bibliography entries for general reference works such as the *Encyclopaedia Britannica, Wikipedia,* the *Oxford English Dictionary,* and the *Dictionary of American Biography* should cite the work as a whole, not specific entries as in notes. List the title of the work, the edition number (if any), and for online works the URL for the home page. Do not include an access date.

Print Encyclopedia

Encyclopaedia Britannica, 15th ed.

OnlineEncyclopedia

Wikipedia. http://en.wikipedia.org/wiki/Main_Page.

Print Dictionary

Oxford English Dictionary, 2nd ed.

Online Dictionary

Merriam-Webster OnLine. http://www.merriam-webster.com.

18.2.4   **Bibliography Entries for Websites and Blogs**

Bibliography entries should cite websites and blogs as a whole, not specific web pages or blog entries / comments as in notes.

Website

Websites are unpredictable, so you may have to improvise, but as much as possible include the same kind of information you need for other online publications:

- author, if any
- website title, if any (in italics)
- sponsoring organization, if any (in regular type)
- URL of home page

City of Los Angeles (website). http://www.lacity.org.
Florida Naturalists (website). Florida Museum of Natural History. http://www
    .flmnh.ufl.edu/naturalists/.

Blog

Blog entries have relatively predictable bibliographical information:

- author
- title of blog (in italics)
- URL of home page

Ellis, Rhian, J. Robert Lennon, and Ed Skoog. *Ward Six* (blog). http://wardsix
    .blogspot.com/.

18.2.5   Bibliography Entries for Books

The Basic Pattern

Author's full
name, last name
first, followed by
a period.

Title and subtitle,
separated by a colon,
followed by a period.
In italics; capitalized
headline style.

City of publication,
followed by a colon.
Name of the publisher,
followed by a comma.
Year of publication.

Ball, Philip. *Bright Earth: Art and the Invention of Color.* New York: Farrar, Straus
and Giroux, 2001.

Period at the end.

18.2.5.1   *Whole Books*

Print Book

Minow, Newton N., and Craig L. LaMay. *Inside the Presidential Debates: Their Improbable Past and Promising Future.* Chicago: University of Chicago Press, 2008.

If the book is produced by an organization rather than a person, list the organization as the author:

World Health Organization. *Health and Economic Development in South-Eastern
Europe.* Geneva: World Health Organization, 2006.

Book in Electronic Reader Format

Use the publication date of the e-book edition; identify the e-book format.

Austen, Jane. *Pride and Prejudice.* New York: Penguin Classics, 2007. Kindle
edition.

Online Book

Use the URL for the main page (if there is more than one), and do not include
the access date.

Whitman, Walt. *Leaves of Grass.* New York: self-published, 1855. http://www
.whitmanarchive.org/published/LG/1855/whole.html.

Edited or Translated Book

If a book has an editor or translator instead of an author, put the name of
the editor or translator in place of the author's, followed by the abbreviation
"ed." or "trans."

Young, Glenn, ed. *The Best American Short Plays, 2002–2003.* New York: Applause,
2007.

Silverstein, Theodore, trans. *Sir Gawain and the Green Knight.* Chicago: University
of Chicago Press, 1974.

If a book has an author as well as an editor or a translator, identify the editor or translator between the title and the publication facts. Do not abbreviate the words "Edited by" or "Translated by."

Bonnefoy, Yves. *New and Selected Poems*. Edited by John Naughton and Anthony Rudolf. Chicago: University of Chicago Press, 1995.

Feydeau, Georges. *Four Farces by Georges Feydeau*. Translated by Norman R. Shapiro. Chicago: University of Chicago Press, 1970.

Revised Edition

If you consult a book labeled as a "revised" edition or a "2nd" (or subsequent) edition, place this information between the title and the publication facts, using abbreviations as in the following examples.

Harper-Dorton, Karen V., and Martin Herbert. *Working with Children, Adolescents, and Their Families*. 3rd ed. Chicago: Lyceum Books, 2002.

Babb, Florence. *Between Field and Cooking Pot: The Political Economy of Marketwomen in Peru*. Rev. ed. Austin: University of Texas Press, 1989.

Multivolume Work

If you cite one book from a group of books in a multivolume work, list only the specific volume you consulted. Identify the volume number ("Vol. X").

Byrne, Muriel St. Clare, ed. *The Lisle Letters*. Vol. 4. Chicago: University of Chicago Press, 1981.

If you consulted more than one volume in a group, list the whole group in a single entry. State the number of volumes after the title ("X vols.").

Byrne, Muriel St. Clare, ed. *The Lisle Letters*. 6 vols. Chicago: University of Chicago Press, 1981.

Pelikan, Jaroslav. *The Christian Tradition: A History of the Development of Doctrine*. 5 vols. Chicago: University of Chicago Press, 1971–1989.

If you cite a single volume with a distinct title, use both titles, starting with the title of the single volume.

Pelikan, Jaroslav. *Christian Doctrine and Modern Culture (since 1700)*. Vol. 5 of *The Christian Tradition: A History of the Development of Doctrine*. Chicago: University of Chicago Press, 1989.

18.2.5.2 *Parts of Books*

Chapter in an Edited Book

Cite the specific chapter, not the whole book, if you refer only to that one chapter in your notes. You may cite two specific chapters separately, if you specifically compare them in your text. Otherwise, cite the edited book as a whole.

Ellet, Elizabeth F. L. "By Rail and Stage to Galena." In *Prairie State: Impressions of Illinois, 1673–1967, by Travelers and Other Observers,* edited by Paul M. Angle, 271–279. Chicago: University of Chicago Press, 1968.

Introduction, Preface, or Afterword

If you have a note to a supplemental part of a book that was written by someone other than the book author, cite it separately. Put a generic title such as "introduction" in regular type, without quotation marks.

Prose, Francine. Introduction to *Word Court: Wherein Verbal Virtue Is Rewarded, Crimes against the Language Are Punished, and Poetic Justice Is Done,* by Barbara Wallraff, ix–xiv. New York: Harcourt, 2000.

Short Story or Poem in a Collection

Cite the specific work, not the whole book, if you refer only to that one work in your notes. You may cite two or more specific works separately, if you specifically compare them in your text. Otherwise, cite the collection as a whole.

Eisenberg, Deborah. "Someone to Talk to." In *All around Atlantis,* 61–92. New York: Farrar, Straus and Giroux, 1997.

Heaney, Seamus. "To George Seferis in the Underworld." In *District and Circle,* 22–23. New York: Farrar, Straus and Giroux, 2006.

Wigglesworth, Michael. Excerpt from *The Day of Doom.* In *The New Anthology of American Poetry: Traditions and Revolutions, Beginnings to 1900,* edited by Steven Gould Axelrod, Camille Roman, and Thomas Travisano, 68–74. New Brunswick, NJ: Rutgers University Press, 2003.

Sample

Bibliography

Adelman, Jeremy. "An Age of Imperial Revolutions." *American Historical Review* 113, no. 2 (April 2008). Accessed September 15, 2008, http://www.journals.uchicago.edu/doi/full/10.1086/ahr.113.2.319.

Babb, Florence. *Between Field and Cooking Pot: The Political Economy of Market-women in Peru.* Rev. ed. Austin: University of Texas Press, 1989.

Encyclopaedia Britannica, 15th ed.

Gold, Ann Grodzins. "Grains of Truth: Shifting Hierarchies of Food and Grace in Three Rajasthani Tales." *History of Religions* 38, no. 2 (1998): 150–171.

Goldstein, Nancy. "The Economy Is a Feminist Issue." *Salon.com,* February 20, 2009. Accessed February 26, 2009, http://www.salon.com/mwt/broadsheet/feature/2009/02/20/women_economy/index.html.

Harper-Dorton, Karen V., and Martin Herbert. *Working with Children, Adolescents, and Their Families.* 3rd ed. Chicago: Lyceum Books, 2002.

Langewiesche, William. "Rules of Engagement." *Vanity Fair,* November 2006.

Wikipedia. http://en.wikipedia.org/wiki/Main_Page.

World Health Organization. *Health and Economic Development in South-Eastern Europe.* Geneva: World Health Organization, 2006.

19: MLA Style

This chapter shows you how to use the MLA citation style. In this style, you use parenthetical references to cite every instance in which you use a source. You must also create a *bibliographical entry* for each source, listing its author, title, and publication data. At the end, you collect these bibliographical entries into an alphabetical list. This list must include every source you mention in your text or in a parenthetical reference. If it includes only sources you specifically cite, it is called a *works cited* list. That list may also include all sources you consulted in your research, even if you did not cite them in your text. In that case it is called a *works consulted* list. Ask your teacher which you should use.

How to Use This Chapter

This chapter presents models for the most common kinds of sources. You will find models of bibliographical entries in 19.2. The models are listed by kind of source: articles, reference works, websites and blogs, and books.

1. **Find a model.**

   - Find the model that matches your kind of source. For instance, if you need to cite a scholarly journal article in an online database, find the example for "Online Journal."
   - Be certain that your source is in the same category as the example. If your source does not match any of the examples in this book, *do not*

> *guess.* Consult a more comprehensive guide, such as the *MLA Handbook for Writers of Research Papers*, 7th ed. (2009).
>
> 2. **Match the model.**
>
>   · Create your citation by exactly matching the bibliographical information on your source to each detail in the model, point for point. Make sure that your bibliography entry corresponds to the model *in every detail*, including capitalization, abbreviations, punctuation, and spacing.
>   · If your source has multiple authors, consult the information on authors' names in section 19.2.1.1.
>
> 3. **Adjust, but only if necessary.**
>
>   · You may make reasonable small adjustments if your source is the same kind as a model but its bibliographic information is slightly different. For example, if the person who put together a book of collected material is called a "compiler" rather than an editor, you may use the form for an edited volume and use the word "compiler" or the abbreviation "comp." wherever the example uses "editor" or "ed.": Henry Jones, compiler. *The Oxford Book of* . . .

Many of you will use software packages that format citations for you automatically. You may let your software create a first draft of your citations, *but do not trust it to produce the correct form.* If you use an automatic citation builder, recheck each bibliographical entry. Find the appropriate example and match it to the citation point by point. It is easy to miss small but important details when a citation is already formatted for you, so go slowly and be careful.

19.1 When and How to Cite Sources in Your Text

19.1.1 Parenthetical References

You must indicate in your text every place where you use the words or ideas of a source (see chapter 10). The general rule is to insert a parenthetical reference that gives readers the minimum information they need to find the cited passage. Typically, that includes only the last name of the author and the page number(s) of the material in the source. The author's name tells readers how to find the details of that source in your works cited list, and the page numbers tell them where to look in the source. In some cases, however, you have to give more information to help readers identify a specific source (see 19.1.2).

You should insert the parenthetical reference immediately after the material borrowed from a source. For a quotation or paraphrase, insert the reference at the end of a sentence or clause (outside of quotation marks but inside a period or comma):

The founding fathers' commitment to religious freedom was based on their commitment to the freedom of ideas. They were adamant that the "coercion of the laws" cannot apply to "the operations of the mind" in the way that they must apply to "the acts of the body" (Jefferson 159).

If you quote or paraphrase several passages from the same work in a single paragraph, use only one parenthetical reference after the final quotation:

The founding fathers' commitment to religious freedom was based on their commitment to the freedom of ideas. They were adamant that the "coercion of the laws" cannot apply to "the operations of the mind" in the way that they must apply to "the acts of the body." The purpose of the law was, they believed, to protect us from injury. "But it does me no injury for my neighbor to say there are twenty gods, or no god" (Jefferson 159).

For a block quote, add the parenthetical reference to the end with no period after it.

According to Jared Diamond,

> Because technology begets more technology, the importance of an invention's diffusion potentially exceeds the importance of the original invention. Technology's history exemplifies what is termed an autocatalytic process: that is, one that speeds up at a rate that increases with time, because the process catalyzes itself. (301)

For ideas or methods, insert the reference at the end of the sentence(s) in which you first introduce or explain the borrowed material. *Be sure to cite every source that influenced your thinking, even if you do not quote or paraphrase from it.* A reader might think you're guilty of plagiarism if you seem to reflect the ideas of a text that you do not cite. (See chapter 10.)

19.1.2   Forms of Parenthetical References

Each parenthetical reference must point to one and only one source in your works cited list. The standard form includes the author's last name and a page number. (If the work is listed by an editor or translator rather than an author, use that name but do not add *ed.* or *trans.*) You may, however, need more or less information. If you mention the author when you introduce a quotation or paraphrase, you should not include the name again in the reference. If you list more than one work by an author in your works cited, add a short title to identify which work you are citing. If you refer not to a specific passage but to a whole work, do not include page numbers. There are other variants. These are most common:

Author Not Mentioned in Text

(Name Page)

The founding fathers' commitment to religious freedom was based on their commitment to the freedom of ideas. They were adamant that the "coercion of the laws" cannot apply to "the operations of the mind" in the way that they must apply to "the acts of the body" (Jefferson 159).

Author Mentioned in Text

(Page)

... their commitment to the freedom of ideas. As Thomas Jefferson put it, the "coercion of the laws" cannot apply to "the operations of the mind" in the way that they must apply to "the acts of the body" (159).

Author with Same Last Name as Others in Works Cited

(Initial Name Page)

... their commitment to the freedom of ideas. As Thomas Jefferson put it, the "coercion of the laws" cannot apply to "the operations of the mind" in the way that they must apply to "the acts of the body" (T. Jefferson 159).

More than One Work by Author

(Name, Short Title Page)

... their commitment to the freedom of ideas. They were adamant that the "coercion of the laws" cannot apply to "the operations of the mind" in the way that they must apply to "the acts of the body" (Jefferson, *Notes* 159).

Two or More Authors

(Name and Name Page) or (Name, Name, . . . , and Name Page)

A "family life map" illustrating the relationships between children and their parents or other caregivers can be instrumental in understanding the problems an adolescent faces at home (Harper-Dorton and Herbert 41).

19.1.3 Footnotes

In MLA style, you do not use notes to identify citations unless a citation is so long that it would disrupt the flow of your text. This situation typically arises when you cite many sources for a single idea. In that case, use the author + page form to refer to each source in the note:

Most Americans think of homelessness as a recent development, but it has always been part of the American heritage.[1] Beggars had long been common in London . . .

_____

1. For the British legacy of homelessness, see Hitchcock 491. For the American scene, see Armstrong 213-44; Cunard 55-58; Taylor 101-33; Unger, *Streets* 12-20; and Unger, *Spaces* 66-67.

You may, of course, also use notes for substantive comments, supplemental information, and so on.

Each note must be numbered with a corresponding raised number (or *superscript*) inserted in your text. Notes can be printed as footnotes, at the bottom of the page, or endnotes, on a separate page at the end. Because you are likely to have few notes, you should treat them as *footnotes,* which are easier for readers to find. List each footnote at the bottom of the page that includes the corresponding numbered reference. Use a line about two inches long to separate the body text and the footnote. (If your software does not add one automatically, do it yourself.)

19.2   Works Cited

Because you give readers only minimal bibliographical information in your text, you must give complete information for every source in the works cited list at the end of your paper. Normally you should not include a source you did not cite in your text, but your teacher may ask you to include all sources you consulted in order to see the scope of your research.

Start your list of sources on a new page. At the top of the first page center the heading "Works Cited." (If you include works you consulted but did not cite, use the heading "Works Consulted.") Skip a space and list all references in alphabetical order, double-spaced, each with a half-inch hanging indent. For a hyphenated last name, alphabetize by the first word in the compound. Strictly follow the order of the letters, and ignore apostrophes and hyphens. Do not change the order for names that include abbreviations or internal capitals (such as McArthur or St. Helena):

Macally, Mack, Madden, McArthur, Mecks . . .
Saint-Beuve, Schwab, Selleck, Skillen, St. Helena, Stricker . . .

If you have to list more than one source by the same author, order those sources alphabetically by their titles. If a source does not have an author or editor, the first element in the bibliography entry will be the title, so use that to place the entry alphabetically among the authors' names.

See the sample works cited list in MLA style on pages 196–97.

19.2.1   **Elements Common to All Bibliographical Entries**

When you create a bibliographical entry, pay attention to the kind of source you are citing, because many elements of citations are different for different kinds of sources. But all MLA-style entries consist of three basic elements—author's name, title of the work, and publication facts.

19.2.1.1 *Author's Name*

Whenever possible, begin each bibliographical entry with the name of the author(s). Spell the names exactly as they appear on the title page: use initials if that's how the name appears, but do not shorten names that are spelled out on the title page. Do not include titles such as *Sir, Saint, Sister, Reverend, Doctor,* and so on. However, list the author's name in *inverted* order: last name–comma–first name–middle name (if any).

Single Author

Pollan, Michael. *The Omnivore's Dilemma* . . .

Rowling, J. K. *Harry Potter and* . . .

Multiple Authors

List all authors in the order they appear on the title page. List the *first* author last name first with a comma after the last and first name. List all other authors in regular order (first-middle-last). Put a comma after the name of the first author (even if there are only two); put *and* before and a period after the last author; and put a comma after all authors between the first and the last.

Levitt, Steven D., and Stephen J. Dubner. *Freakonomics* . . .

Heatherton, Joyce, James Fitzgilroy, and Jackson Hsu. *Meteors and Mudslides* . . .

Multiple Works by One Author

If you cite multiple works by the same author or group of authors, you will have several entries that begin the same. For all entries after the first, replace the name(s) with three hyphens (not dashes). If the work is edited or translated, add the corresponding designation after the three hyphens and a comma. Note that the "ed." or "trans." is ignored in alphabetizing.

NOT	BUT
Schank, Roger C. *Dynamic Memory* . . .	Schank, Roger C. *Dynamic Memory* . . .
Schank, Roger C., ed. *Inside Multi-Media* . . .	---, ed. *Inside Multi-Media* . . .
Schank, Roger C. *Reading and* . . .	---. *Reading and* . . .
Schank, Roger C. *Tell Me a Story* . . .	---. *Tell Me a Story* . . .

19.2.1.2 *Title*

Give the title *exactly* as it is shown in the source, including a subtitle if there is one. For articles and other short works, you will need both the article title and the title of the book, journal, or other work in which it occurs. If an online source does not have an obvious title, use the name of the website or any other reasonable replacement.

Capitalize titles headline style: capitalize the first and last words of the title and subtitle and all other words *except* articles (*a, an, the*), coordinate conjunctions (*and, but, or, nor, for, so, yet*), prepositions (*of, in, at, above, under,* and so forth), and the words *to* and *as.* If a title includes a subtitle, put a colon between the main title and the subtitle.

ARTICLES, ENTRIES, WEB PAGES, AND OTHER SHORT WORKS. Put the titles of short works that are part of longer ones in regular type, enclosed in quotation marks.

Hitchcock, Tim. "Begging on the Streets of Eighteenth-Century London." *Journal of British Studies.* . . .

Porter, Charlotte M. "Artist-Naturalists in Florida." *Florida Naturalists.* . . .

BOOKS, JOURNALS, MAGAZINES, NEWSPAPERS, AND BLOGS. Put the titles of longer works in italics. If the title includes a title, put it in quotation marks and italics.

Jefferson, Thomas. *Notes on the State of Virginia.* . . .

Hitchcock, Tim. "Begging on the Streets of Eighteenth-Century London." *Journal of British Studies.* . . .

Sitter, John E. *The Poetry of Pope's "Dunciad."* . . .

19.2.1.3 *Publication Facts*

In addition to author's name and title, a bibliographical entry usually includes facts that identify *where* and *when* a source was published. Publication facts vary from one kind of source to another, so check each model carefully. All entries include the medium of publication (Print, Web, CD-ROM, DVD, etc.).

For articles obtained from an online database or similar provider, add the name of the online provider and the date you accessed the site. For other online materials, do not include a URL (uniform resource locator) but do include an access date.

For page ranges of three digits or more, abbreviate the second number to two digits (but not if the range crosses a hundreds boundary): 125-34, 1134-55, but 197-204.

For dates, use the day-month-year form, with no punctuation in the date: 4 May 2009. Abbreviate all months except May, June, and July: 6 Oct. 2008.

19.2.2   Bibliographical Entries for Periodical Articles

Most of the articles you will consult will be found in *periodicals*—journals, magazines, newspapers, and other works published at periodic intervals in print form, online, or both.

- **Journals** are scholarly or professional periodicals written for experts and available primarily in academic libraries. Journals often include the word *journal* in their titles (*Journal of Modern History*), but not always (*Postmodern Culture*).
- **Magazines** are not scholarly publications; they are designed for more general readers in both their content and their availability outside of academic settings. If you are unsure whether a periodical is a journal or a magazine, see whether its articles include citations; if so, treat it as a journal.
- **Newspapers** are generally daily or weekly publications whose articles are closely tied to recent events.

The Basic Pattern

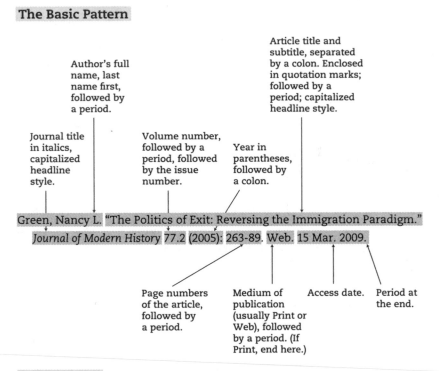

Print Journal

Green, Nancy L. "The Politics of Exit: Reversing the Immigration Paradigm." *Journal of Modern History* 77.2 (2005): 263-89. Print.

Gold, Ann Grodzins. "Grains of Truth: Shifting Hierarchies of Food and Grace in Three Rajasthani Tales." *History of Religions* 38.2 (1998): 150-71. Print.

Print Journal, Consulted Online

For articles obtained from an online database, include information on the print publication, followed by the database (in italics). If there are no page numbers, use "n. pag." instead.

Whitney, Frank P. "The Six-Year High School in Cleveland." *School Review* 37.4
      (1929): 267-71. *JSTOR*. Web. 9 Oct. 2008.

Adelman, Jeremy. "An Age of Imperial Revolutions." *American Historical Review*
      113.2 (Apr. 2008): n. pag. Web. 15 Sept. 2008.

Online Journal

If there are no page numbers, use "n. pag." instead.

Bass, Alan. "The Mystery of Sex and the Mystery of Time: An Integration of
      Some Psychoanalytic and Philosophical Perspectives." *Postmodern Culture*
      18.1 (2007): n. pag. Web. 5 Jan. 2009.

Print Magazine

Do not include volume or issue numbers, even if they are given. If the article is interrupted by other material, use only the first page number followed by "+."

Schapiro, Mark. "New Power for 'Old Europe.'" *Nation* 27 Dec. 2004: 33+. Print.

Print Magazine, Consulted Online

Include both the title of the magazine and the online provider, even if they are the same.

Castro, Janice. "Scientology's Largesse in Russia." *Time*. Time, 13 Apr. 1992. Web.
      6 Aug. 2007.

Online Magazine

Burton, Robert. "Should Johnny Play Linebacker?" *Salon.com*. Salon Media Group,
      13 Jan. 2009. Web. 20 Feb. 2009.

Newspaper

Include the edition (abbreviate as *ed.*) and the letter designation of the section if there is one. If the article is interrupted by material, use only the first page number followed by "+."

Bishop, Greg. "Favre Wins in Debut for Jets." *New York Times* 7 Sept. 2008, late ed.:
      D1. Print.

Online Newspaper

Include both the title of the newspaper and the online provider, even if they are the same.

Bishop, Greg. "Favre Wins in Debut for Jets." *New York Times*. New York Times, 7 Sept. 2008. Web. 11 Dec. 2008.

19.2.3 Bibliographical Entries for Reference Works

Begin with the entry, in quotation marks. If the reference work is a standard one, do not cite the author, editor, or publication data. List only the edition (if any), the year, and the medium of publication.

Dictionary or Encyclopedia

"Tool." Def. 3c. *Webster's Third New International Dictionary*. 1981. Print.

"Tool, n." Def. 2a. *OED Online*. 2008. Web. 22 Feb. 2009.

"Kabuki Drama." *The Encyclopedia Americana*. 2004. Print.

Specialized Dictionary or Encyclopedia

Cite a specialized reference work as you would a book. If it does not have an editor or an author, cite by its title.

Aulestia, Gorka. *Basque-English Dictionary*. Reno: U of Nevada P, 1989. Print.

Austin, Tim, comp. *The Times Guide to English Style and Usage*. Rev. ed. London: Times Books, 1999. Print.

Grossman, James R., Ann Durkin Keating, and Janice L. Reiff, eds. *Encyclopedia of Chicago*. Chicago Historical Society, 2005. Web. 4 July 2008.

Signed Entry in Encyclopedia

Masolo, Dismas. "African Sage Philosophy." *Stanford Encyclopedia of Philosophy*. Ed. Edward N. Zalta. Stanford UP, 14 Feb. 2006. Web. 5 Sept. 2008.

19.2.4 Bibliographical Entries for Websites and Blogs

Website

Websites are unpredictable, so you may have to improvise, but as much as possible include the same kind of information you need for other online publications:

- author, if any
- website title, if any (in italics)
- sponsor or publisher, if any (in regular type); if none put "N.p."
- date of publication; if none, put "n.d."
- medium of publication ("Web")
- access date

Evanston Public Library. Evanston Public Library Board of Trustees, n.d. Web. 19 July 2008.

Web Page

For individual pages, add the page title in quotation marks between the author and the site title. If there is no title, you may use a generic title *without* quotation marks, such as *Home Page, Introduction, Site Map,* and so on.

Porter, Charlotte M. "Mark Catesby's Audience and Patrons." *Florida Naturalists.*
    Florida Museum of Natural History, n.d. Web. 1 May 2009.

"Evanston Public Library Strategic Plan, 2000-2010: A Decade of Outreach."
    Evanston Public Library. Evanston Public Library Board of Trustees, n.d. Web.
    19 July 2008.

Blog

Blogs have relatively predictable bibliographical information:

- author
- title of blog (in italics)
- medium of publication ("Weblog")
- sponsor or publisher, if any (in regular type); if none put "N.p."
- date of publication; if none, put "n.d."
- access date

Ellis, Rhian, J. Robert Lennon, and Ed Skoog. *Ward Six.* Weblog. N.p., n.d. Web.
    10 Aug. 2008.

Blog Entry

For individual entries, add the entry title in quotation marks between the author and the blog title, followed by "Weblog entry."

Ellis, Rhian. "Squatters' Rights." Weblog entry. *Ward Six.* N.p., 30 June 2008. Web.
    10 Aug. 2008.

Comment on Blog Entry or Web Page

To cite a comment on a blog entry or web page, begin with the name (or pseudonym) of the commenter, the comment's title (if any), the words "Weblog comment" or "Comment," and the date of the comment, followed by the standard entry for a blog entry or web page.

AC, Weblog comment. 1 July 2008. Rhian Ellis, "Squatters' Rights." Weblog entry.
    Ward Six. N.p., 30 June 2008. Web. 10 Aug. 2008.

Philogenes, "Shocked, Shocked, I Tell You." Comment. 16 Mar. 2009. "Composi-
    tion, Overcrowded," *Inside Higher Ed,* 16 Mar. 2009. Web. 17 Mar. 2009.

19.2.5 Bibliographical Entries for Books

The Basic Pattern

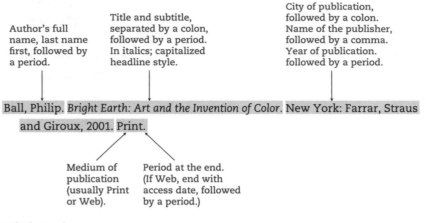

Author's full name, last name first, followed by a period.

Title and subtitle, separated by a colon, followed by a period. In italics; capitalized headline style.

City of publication, followed by a colon. Name of the publisher, followed by a comma. Year of publication. followed by a period.

Ball, Philip. *Bright Earth: Art and the Invention of Color.* New York: Farrar, Straus and Giroux, 2001. Print.

Medium of publication (usually Print or Web).

Period at the end. (If Web, end with access date, followed by a period.)

19.2.5.1 Whole Books

Print Book

For publishers' names, abbreviate "University" to "U" (no period) and "Press" to "P" (no period).

Minow, Newton N., and Craig L. LaMay. *Inside the Presidential Debates: Their Improbable Past and Promising Future.* Chicago: U Chicago P, 2008. Print.

If the book is produced by an organization rather than a person, list the organization as the author:

World Health Organization. *Health and Economic Development in South-Eastern Europe.* Geneva: World Health Organization, 2006. Print.

Book in Electronic Reader Format

Use the publication date of the e-book edition; identify the e-book format.

Austen, Jane. *Pride and Prejudice.* New York: Penguin Classics, 2007. Kindle edition.

Austen, Jane. *Pride and Prejudice.* New York: Penguin Classics, 2008. PDF e-book.

Online Book

Whitman, Walt. *Leaves of Grass.* New York, 1855. *The Walt Whitman Archive.* Web. 2 Jan. 2008.

Edited or Translated Book

If a book has an editor or translator but no author, put the editor or translator in place of the author, followed by the abbreviation "ed." or "trans."

Young, Glenn, ed. *The Best American Short Plays, 2002-2003.* New York: Applause, 2007. Print.

Silverstein, Theodore, trans. *Sir Gawain and the Green Knight*. Chicago: U Chicago
    P, 1974. Print.

If a book has an author as well as an editor and/or a translator, identify the
editor and/or translator in a separate section between the title and the publication data:

Bonnefoy, Yves. *New and Selected Poems*. Ed. John Naughton and Anthony Rudolf.
    Chicago: U Chicago P, 1995. Print.

Menchú, Rigoberta. *Crossing Borders*. Trans. and ed. Ann Wright. New York: Verso,
    1999. Print.

Adorno, Theodor W., and Walter Benjamin. *The Complete Correspondence, 1928-1940*.
    Ed. Henri Lonitz. Trans. Nicholas Walker. Cambridge: Harvard UP, 1999. Print.

Revised Edition

If you consult a book labeled as a "revised" edition or a "second" (or subsequent) edition, place this information between the title and the publication
facts, using abbreviations as in the following examples.

Harper-Dorton, Karen V., and Martin Herbert. *Working with Children, Adolescents,
    and Their Families*. 3rd ed. Chicago: Lyceum Books, 2002. Print.

Babb, Florence. *Between Field and Cooking Pot: The Political Economy of Marketwomen
    in Peru*. Rev. ed. Austin: U Texas P, 1989. Print.

Multivolume Work

If you cite one book from a group of books (called a *multivolume* work), list only
the specific volume you consulted. Identify the volume number ("Vol. X").

Byrne, Muriel St. Clare, ed. *The Lisle Letters*. Vol. 4. Chicago: U Chicago P, 1981.
    Print.

If the one volume you cite has a different title from that of the whole group,
cite the title of the volume. You do not need to add the title of the group.

Pelikan, Jaroslav. *The Emergence of the Catholic Tradition*. Chicago: U Chicago P,
    1971. Print.

If you consulted more than one volume in a group, list the whole group in a
single entry. State the number of volumes after the title ("X vols.").

Byrne, Muriel St. Clare, ed. *The Lisle Letters*. 6 vols. Chicago: U Chicago P, 1981.
    Print.

Pelikan, Jaroslav. *The Christian Tradition: A History of the Development of Doctrine*.
    5 vols. Chicago: U Chicago P, 1971-1989.

19.2.5.2 *Parts of Books*

Chapter in an Edited Book

Cite the specific chapter, not the whole book, if you refer only to that one
chapter in your text. You may cite two specific chapters separately, if you

specifically compare them in your text. Otherwise, cite the edited book as a whole.

Ellet, Elizabeth F. L. "By Rail and Stage to Galena." *Prairie State: Impressions of Illinois, 1673-1967, by Travelers and Other Observers.* Ed. Paul M. Angle. Chicago: U Chicago P, 1968. 271-79. Print.

Introductions, Prefaces, Afterwords

If you refer to a supplemental part of a book that was written by someone other than the book author, cite it separately. Put a generic title such as "introduction" in regular type, without quotation marks.

Prose, Francine. Introduction. *Word Court: Wherein Verbal Virtue Is Rewarded, Crimes against the Language Are Punished, and Poetic Justice Is Done.* By Barbara Wallraff. New York: Harcourt, 2000. ix-xiv. Print.

Letter in a Collection

Adams, Henry. "To Charles Milnes Gaskell." 30 March 1868. *Letters of Henry Adams, 1858-1891.* Ed. Worthington Chauncey Ford. Boston: Houghton Mifflin, 1930. 141. Print.

Short Story or Poem in a Collection

Cite the specific work, not the whole book, if you refer only to that one work. You may cite two or more specific works separately, if you specifically compare them in your text. Otherwise, cite the collection as a whole.

Eisenberg, Deborah. "Someone to Talk To." *All around Atlantis.* New York: Farrar, Straus and Giroux, 1997. 61-92. Print.

Heaney, Seamus. "To George Seferis in the Underworld." *District and Circle.* New York: Farrar, Straus and Giroux, 2006. 22-23. Print.

Wigglesworth, Michael. Excerpt from *The Day of Doom. The New Anthology of American Poetry: Traditions and Revolutions, Beginnings to 1900.* Ed. Steven Gould Axelrod, Camille Roman, and Thomas Travisano. New Brunswick, NJ: Rutgers UP, 2003. 68-74. Print.

Sample

Works Cited

Adelman, Jeremy. "An Age of Imperial Revolutions." *American Historical Review* 113.2 (Apr. 2008): n. pag. Web. 15 Sept. 2008.

Babb, Florence. *Between Field and Cooking Pot: The Political Economy of Marketwomen in Peru.* Rev. ed. Austin: U Texas P, 1989. Print.

Ellis, Rhian. "Squatters' Rights." Weblog entry. *Ward Six.* N.p., 30 June 2008. Web. 10 Aug. 2008.

Gold, Ann Grodzins. "Grains of Truth: Shifting Hierarchies of Food and Grace in Three Rajasthani Tales." *History of Religions* 38.2 (1998): 150-71. Print.

Green, Nancy L. "The Politics of Exit: Reversing the Immigration Paradigm." *Journal of Modern History* 77.2 (2005): 263-89. Web. 15 Mar. 2009.

Harper-Dorton, Karen V., and Martin Herbert. *Working with Children, Adolescents, and Their Families.* 3rd ed. Chicago: Lyceum Books, 2002. Print.

Masolo, Dismas. "African Sage Philosophy." *Stanford Encyclopedia of Philosophy.* Ed. Edward N. Zalta. Stanford UP, 14 Feb. 2006. Web. 5 Sept. 2008.

Menchú, Rigoberta. *Crossing Borders.* Trans. and ed. Ann Wright. New York: Verso, 1999. Print.

World Health Organization. *Health and Economic Development in South-Eastern Europe.* Geneva: World Health Organization, 2006. Print.

20: APA Style

This chapter shows you how to use the APA citation style. In this style, you use parenthetical references to cite every instance in which you use a source. You must also create a *bibliographical entry* for each source, listing its author, date, title, and publication data. At the end, you collect these bibliographical entries into an alphabetical list, called a *reference list*. This list must include every source you mention in your text or in a parenthetical reference: conversely, every source listed in your reference list must also be cited in your paper.

How to Use This Chapter

This chapter presents models for the most common kinds of sources. You will find models of bibliographical entries in 20.2. The models are listed by kind of source: articles, reference works, websites and blogs, and books.

1. **Find a model.**

    *   Find the model that matches your kind of source. For instance, if you need to cite a scholarly journal article in an online database, find the example for "Online Journal."
    *   Be certain that your source is in the same category as the example. If your source does not match any of the examples in this book, *do not guess*. Consult a more comprehensive guide, such as the *Publication*

> *Manual of the American Psychological Association,* 6th ed. (Washington, DC: APA, 2009).

2. **Match the model.**

   - Create your citation by exactly matching the bibliographical information on your source to each detail in the model, point for point. Make sure that your bibliography entry corresponds to the model *in every detail,* including capitalization, abbreviations, punctuation, and spacing.
   - If your source has multiple authors, consult the information on authors' names in section 20.2.1.1.

3. **Adjust, but only if necessary.**

   - You may make reasonable small adjustments if your source is the same kind as a model but its bibliographic information is slightly different. For example, if the person who put together a book of collected material is called a "compiler" rather than an editor, you may use the form for an edited volume and use the word "Compiler" where the model uses "Editor": Jones, Henry. (Compiler). (1994). *The Oxford Book of . . .*

Many of you will use software packages that format citations for you automatically. You may let your software create a first draft of your citations, *but do not trust it to produce the correct form.* If you use an automatic citation builder, recheck each note and bibliographical entry. Find the appropriate example and match it to the citation point by point. It is easy to miss small but important details when a citation is already formatted for you, so go slowly and be careful.

20.1 When and How to Cite Sources in Your Text

20.1.1 Parenthetical References

You must indicate in your text every place where you use the words or ideas of a source (see chapter 10). The general rule is to insert a parenthetical reference with the author's last name, the year of the publication, and the page number(s) in the source. The author's name and the date tell readers how to find the details of that source in your reference list, and the page numbers tell them where to look in the source. In some cases, however, you have to give more information to help readers identify a specific source (see 20.1.2).

In most cases, you should insert the parenthetical reference immediately after the material from a source. For a quotation or paraphrase, insert the reference at the end of a sentence or clause (outside of any quotation marks and before a period or comma):

Technology feeds on itself. In many cases, the "diffusion" of an invention is more important than the invention itself (Diamond, 1997, p. 301).

If you quote or paraphrase several passages from the same work in a single paragraph, use only one parenthetical reference after the final quotation:

Technology feeds on itself. In many cases, the "diffusion" of an invention is more important than the invention itself. For example, the peel-off adhesive on Post-it notes was a valuable invention, but it also set off a whole industry of temporary adhesives. Through this "autocatalytic process," the diffusion of a technology "speeds up at a rate that increases with time, because the process catalyzes itself" (Diamond, 1997, p. 301).

If you mention the author in your text, add the year after the author and the page numbers after the quotation or paraphrase:

Technology feeds on itself. As Diamond (1997) explains, the "diffusion" of an invention can be more important than the invention itself" (p. 301).

For a block quote, add the parenthetical reference to the end with no period after it.

According to Jared Diamond (1997),

> Because technology begets more technology, the importance of an invention's diffusion potentially exceeds the importance of the original invention. Technology's history exemplifies what is termed an autocatalytic process: that is, one that speeds up at a rate that increases with time, because the process catalyzes itself. (p. 301)

For ideas or methods, insert the reference at the end of the sentence(s) in which you first introduce or explain the borrowed material. *Be sure to cite every source that influenced your thinking, even if you do not quote or paraphrase from it.* A reader might think you're guilty of plagiarism if you seem to reflect the ideas of a text that you do not cite. (See chapter 10.)

20.1.2   Forms of Parenthetical References

Each parenthetical reference must point to one and only one source in your reference list. The standard form for these references includes the author's last name, the year of publication, and a page number (preceded by "p." or "pp."). If the work is listed by an editor or translator rather than an author, use that name but do not add *ed.* or *trans.* You may, however, need more or less information. If two or more authors have the same last name, add initials. If you refer not to a specific passage but to a whole work, do not include page numbers. There are other variants. These are most common:

Author Not Mentioned in Text

(Name, Year, Page)

Technology feeds on itself. In many cases, the "diffusion" of an invention is more important than the invention itself (Diamond, 1997, p. 301).

Author Mentioned in Text

(Year) . . . (Page)

Technology feeds on itself. As Diamond (1997) explains, the "diffusion" of an invention can be more important than the invention itself (p. 301).

Author with Same Last Name as Others in Reference List

(Initial + Name, Year, Page)

Technology feeds on itself. In many cases, the "diffusion" of an invention is more important than the invention itself (J. Diamond, 1997, p. 301).

Two Authors

(Name & Name, Year, Page)

A "family life map" illustrating the relationships between children and their parents or other caregivers can be instrumental in understanding the problems an adolescent faces at home (Harper-Dorton & Herbert, 2002, p. 41).

Three–Five Authors

First Citation: (Name, Name, . . . , & Name, Year, Page)

Most economists believe that expectations about inflation primarily determine the relationship between stocks and bonds (Yang, Zhou, & Wang, 2009, p. 670).

Subsequent Citation: (Name et al., Year, Page)

Most economists believe that expectations about inflation primarily determine the relationship between stocks and bonds (Yang et al., 2009, p. 670).

Six or More Authors

(Name et al., Year, Page)

When we look at developing countries, however, inflation seems to follow very different laws (Habermeier et al., 2009, p. 69).

Work without an Author

(Short Title, Year, Page)

College officials once thought that the way to reduce binge drinking was to scare students (*Drink and Die*, 2008, pp. 2–3).

Multiple Citations with Different Authors

(Cite; Cite; Cite)

Most economists believe that expectations about inflation primarily determine the relationship between stocks and bonds, with the exception of developing economies (Yang et al., 2009; Habermeier et al., 2009).

Multiple Citations with the Same Author

(Name, Year, Year, . . . Year)

Cognitive researchers have stressed the importance of stories in learning (Schank, 1990, 1994, 2004, 2005).

20.1.3 Footnotes

In APA style, you do not use notes to identify citations. You may use notes for substantive comments, supplemental information, and so on.

Each note must be numbered with a corresponding raised number (or *superscript*) inserted in your text. Notes can be printed as footnotes, at the bottom of the page, or as endnotes, on a separate page at the end. Because you are likely to have few notes, you should treat them as *footnotes,* which are easier for readers to find. List each footnote at the bottom of the page that includes the corresponding numbered reference. Use a line about two inches long to separate the body text and the footnote. (If your software does not add one automatically, do it yourself.)

20.2 Reference List

Because you give readers only minimal bibliographical information in your text, you must give complete information for every source in the reference list at the end of your paper.

Start your list of sources on a new page. At the top of the first page center the heading "Reference List." Skip a space and list all references double-spaced, each with a hanging indent. Use the same typeface as your main text. Put the list in alphabetical order by author and date. Strictly follow the order of the letters, and ignore apostrophes and hyphens. Do not change the order for names that include abbreviations or internal capitals (such as McArthur or St. Helena):

Macally, Mack, Madden, McArthur, Mecks, . . .
Saint-Beuve, Schwab, Selleck, Skillen, St. Helena, Stricker, . . .

If there is more than one entry for the same author in the same year, alphabetize them by title and add letters after the year: 2003a, 2003b, and so on.

See the sample reference list in APA style on pages 211–12.

20.2.1 Elements Common to All Bibliographical Entries

When you create a bibliographical entry, you have to pay attention to the kind of source you are citing, because many elements of citations are different for different kinds of sources. But all APA-style entries consist of four basic elements—author's name, date, title of the work, and publication facts.

20.2.1.1 Author's Name

Whenever possible, begin each bibliographical entry with the name of the author(s). Spell the last name of each author exactly as it appears on the title page: use initials for all first and middle names. Do not include titles such as *Sir, Saint, Sister, Reverend, Doctor,* and so on. The author's name is listed in *inverted* order: last name–comma–first initial–middle initial (if any).

Single Author

Pollan, M. (2006). *The omnivore's dilemma* . . .

Rowling, J. K. (2007). *Harry Potter and* . . .

Young, G. (Ed.). (2007). *The best* . . .

Multiple Authors

List all authors in the order they appear on the title page. List *all* authors in inverted order, last name first, followed by a comma followed by initial(s). Put an ampersand (&) before the name of the last author.

Levitt, S. D., & Dubner, S. J. (2005). *Freakonomics* . . .

Yang, J., Zhou, Y., Wang, Z., & Yang, J. (2009). The stock-bond . . .

More than Six Authors

If there are more than six authors, list the first six and then add "et al."

Habermeier, K. F., Otker-Rove, I., Jacome, L. I., Giustinani, A., Ishi, K., Vavra, D., et al. (2009). Inflation pressures . . .

20.2.1.2 Date

All bibliographical entries include a date in parentheses, immediately after the author. Most publications are identified by year: (2003). Monthly magazines or newspapers are also identified by month: (2003, June). Daily or weekly publications also include the day: (2003, September 5). Do not abbreviate months.

If your reference list includes more than one publication in the same year for the same author, alphabetize them by titles (ignoring *A* or *The*) and add a letter to each date.

Turner, M., & Fauconnier, G. (2008a). The origin of language as a product of the evolution of modern cognition. In B. Laks et al. (Eds.), *Origin and evolution of languages* . . .

Turner, M., & Fauconnier, G. (2008b). Rethinking metaphor. In R. Gibbs (Ed.), *Cambridge handbook of metaphor* . . .

20.2.1.3 *Title*

Whenever possible, identify a source by its title. For articles and other short works, include both the article title and the title of the book, journal, or other work in which it occurs. If an online source does not have an obvious title, use the name of the site or any other reasonable replacement for a title.

Capitalize all titles of articles and books sentence style: capitalize *only* the first word of the title and the subtitle and any proper nouns. If a title includes a subtitle, put a colon between the main title and the subtitle. Capitalize the titles of websites, blogs, and all journals, magazines, and other periodicals headline style (most will appear this way in the original): capitalize the first and last words of the title and subtitle and all other words *except* articles (*a, an, the*), coordinate conjunctions (*and, but, or, nor, for, so, yet*), prepositions (*of, in, at, above, under,* and so forth), and the words *to* and *as*.

ARTICLES AND OTHER SHORT WORKS. Put these titles in regular text. Do not enclose them in quotation marks. Italicize only those words that are italicized in the original. If the title includes quotation marks, copy them exactly as they appear in the original.

Hitchcock, T. (2005). Begging on the streets of eighteenth-century London. . . .

Gaskell, S. (2008, July 14). *New Yorker* mag's "satire" cover draws team
 Obama's ire . . .

BOOKS. Put these titles in italics. If the title includes a title, put it in quotation marks no matter how it appeared in the original. If any words in the original are italicized, leave them in italics.

Jefferson, T. (1954). *Notes on the state of Virginia.* . . .

Sitter, J. E. (1971). *The poetry of Pope's "Dunciad."* . . .

Porter, C. M. (2009). Artist-naturalists in Florida. *Florida Naturalists.* . . .

WEBSITES, JOURNALS, MAGAZINES, AND OTHER PERIODICALS. Put these titles in italics.

. . . *Journal of British Studies, 44,* 478–498.

. . . *New York Times,* D1, D4.

20.2.1.4 *Publication Facts*

In addition to the author's name and title, a bibliographical entry usually includes facts that identify *where* and *when* a source was published. Publication facts vary from one kind of source to another, so check each model carefully.

Note: The publication facts for books includes the city of publication. Do not include a state or country for large cities that are publishing centers. Do include a state or country for all other cities.

20.2.1.5 *Retrieval Information for Electronic Sources*

With few exceptions, you must include a *retrieval statement* for online sources, indicating where on the web you found it. Here are the elements of a retrieval statement:

- Date: Include a retrieval date.
- Website: Include the name of the site if you retrieve a named page from an institutional website, such as a university, city, or library site.

> ... Retrieved April 1, 2009, from University of California, Santa Barbara, website: http://vos.ucsb.edu/

- Database: If you obtain the text from an online database, include the name of the database (with no URL), followed by a period (and no access date).

> ... Retrieved from JSTOR database.

- URL: If you obtain the text from any source other than a database, include a URL (universal resource locator). If the source is an online newspaper, journal, or reference work, include just the home page (http:// www.salon.com, http:// encyclopedia.chicagohistory.org). Otherwise, include the complete URL exactly as it appears in the browser bar. If the URL is too long, break it *before* any internal punctuation or *after* a slash. Do not put a period after a URL.

> ... Retrieved January 22, 2009, from http://markturner.org/cinLEA.pdf
> ... Retrieved October 2, 2008, from http://muse.jhu.edu/login?uri=/journals/
>   postmodern_culture /v018/18.1.bass.html

When a URL directs readers to a home page with a search facility for finding the specific content you cite, replace "Retrieved from" with "Available from":

> Grossman, J. R., Keating, A. D., & Reiff, J. L. (Eds.). (2005). *Encyclopedia of
>   Chicago.* Chicago Historical Society. Available from http://encyclopedia
>   .chicagohistory.org

20.2.2 Bibliographical Entries for Periodical Articles

Most of the articles you will consult will be found in *periodicals*—journals, magazines, newspapers, and other works published at periodic intervals in print form, online, or both.

- **Journals** are scholarly or professional periodicals written for experts and available primarily in academic libraries. Journals often include the word *journal* in their titles (*Journal of Modern History*), but not always (*Postmodern Culture*).
- **Magazines** are not scholarly publications; they are designed for more general readers in both their content and their availability outside of academic

settings. If you are unsure whether a periodical is a journal or a magazine, see whether its articles include citations; if so, treat it as a journal.

- **Newspapers** are generally daily or weekly publications whose articles are closely tied to recent events.

The Basic Pattern

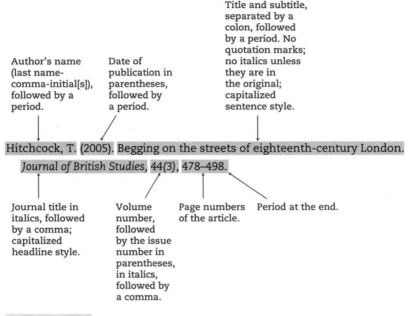

Author's name (last name-comma-initial[s]), followed by a period.

Date of publication in parentheses, followed by a period.

Title and subtitle, separated by a colon, followed by a period. No quotation marks; no italics unless they are in the original; capitalized sentence style.

Hitchcock, T. (2005). Begging on the streets of eighteenth-century London. *Journal of British Studies, 44(3),* 478–498.

Journal title in italics, followed by a comma; capitalized headline style.

Volume number, followed by the issue number in parentheses, in italics, followed by a comma.

Page numbers of the article.

Period at the end.

Print Journal

Green, N. L. (2005). The politics of exit: Reversing the immigration paradigm. *Journal of Modern History, 77(2),* 263–289.

Gold, A. G. (1998). Grains of truth: Shifting hierarchies of food and grace in three Rajasthani tales. *History of Religions, 38(2),* 150–171.

Print Journal, Obtained Online from the Publisher

If the publisher of an article provides copies that exactly match the print version (including page numbers), cite the information for the print version and add "[Electronic version]" after the article title but before the period.

Green, N. L. (2005). The politics of exit: Reversing the immigration paradigm [Electronic version]. *Journal of Modern History, 77(2),* 263–289.

Print Journal, Obtained from an Online Database

Include information on the print publication, followed by the retrieval information on the database; do not include the date retrieved.

Whitney, F. P. (1929). The six-year high school in Cleveland. *School Review, 37(4),* 267–271. Retrieved from JSTOR database.

Print Journal, Obtained Online

If you obtain a print article from an online source other than the publisher or a database, include information on the print publication, followed by the retrieval information, including the date retrieved and the exact URL.

Fauconnier, G., & Turner, M. (1998). Conceptual integration networks. *Cognitive Science, 22*(2), 133–187. Retrieved January 22, 2009, from http://markturner.org/cinLEA.pdf

Online Journal

Bass, A. (2007). The mystery of sex and the mystery of time: An integration of some psychoanalytic and philosophical perspectives. *Postmodern Culture, 18*(10). Retrieved October 22, 2008, from http://muse.jhu.edu/login?uri=/journals/postmodern_culture/v018/18.1.bass.html

Print Magazine

Do not include volume or issue numbers, even if they are given. If the article is interrupted by other material, list *all* page numbers.

Schapiro, M. (2004, December 27). New power for "old Europe." *Nation, 279*(22), 11–16.

Magazine, Consulted Online

Castro, J. (1992, April 13). Scientology's largesse in Russia. *Time.* Retrieved March 20, 2009, from http://www.time.com/time/magazine/article/0,9171,975290,00.html

Burton, R. (2009, January 13). Should Johnny play linebacker? *Salon.com.* Retrieved January 15, 2009, from http://www.salon.com/env/mind_reader/2009/01/13/sports_concussions/index.html

Newspaper

For print, include all page numbers, with letters identifying sections, if available.

Bishop, G. (2008, September 7). Favre wins in debut for Jets. *New York Times,* D1, D4.

Bishop, G. (2008, September 7). Favre wins in debut for Jets. *New York Times.* Retrieved December 10, 2008, from http://www.nytimes.com

20.2.3   Bibliographical Entries for Reference Works

Dictionary

Webster's third new international dictionary of the English language. (2002). Springfield, MA: Merriam-Webster.

Merriam-Webster's online dictionary. (n.d.). Available from http://www.m-w.com/dictionary/

Aulestia, G. (1989). *Basque-English dictionary.* Reno: University of Nevada Press.

Encyclopedia

Kabuki drama. (2000). *The world book encyclopedia.* Chicago: World Book.

Masolo, D. (2006). African sage philosophy. In E. N. Zalta (Ed.), *Stanford encyclopedia of philosophy.* Available from http://plato.stanford.edu

Grossman, J. R., Keating, A. D., & Reiff, J. L. (Eds.). (2005). *Encyclopedia of Chicago.* Chicago Historical Society. Available from http://encyclopedia .chicagohistory.org

20.2.4   Bibliographical Entries for Websites and Blogs

Website

Websites are unpredictable, so you may have to improvise, but as much as possible include the same kind of information you need for other online publications:

- author, if any
- date; if none use "n.d."
- website title, if any
- retrieval statement (or "Available from" and a home page)

Evanston Public Library Board of Trustees. (n.d.). Evanston Public Library. Available from http://www.epl.org

Web Page

Titles of web pages are in italics.

Evanston Public Library Board of Trustees. (n.d.). *Evanston Public Library strategic plan, 2000–2010: A decade of outreach.* Retrieved July 19, 2008, from the Evanston Public Library website: http://www.epl.org/library/strategic.html

Blog

Ellis, R., Lennon, J. R., & Skoog, E. (n.d.). *Ward six* [Web log]. Available from http://wardsix.blogspot.com

Blog Entry

Ellis, R. (2008, June 30). Squatters' rights. [Web log message]. Retrieved from http://wardsix.blogspot.com/2008/06/squatters.html

Comment on Blog Entry or Web Page

AC. (2008, July 1). Re: Squatters' rights. [Web log comment]. Retrieved from http://wardsix.blogspot.com/2008/06/squatters.html

Philogenes. (2009, March 16). Shocked, shocked, I tell you. Re: Composition, overcrowded. [Online forum comment]. Available from http://www .insidehighered.com/

20.2.5 Bibliographical Entries for Books

The Basic Pattern

| Author's name (last name-comma-initial[s]), followed by a period. | Date of publication in parentheses, followed by a period. | Title and subtitle, separated by a colon, followed by a period. In italics; capitalized sentence style. | City of publication, followed by a colon, followed by the name of the publisher. |

Ball, P. (2001). Bright earth: Art and the invention of color. New York: Farrar, Straus and Giroux.

Period at the end.

20.2.5.1 Whole Books

Print Book

Minow, N. N., & LaMay, C. L. (2008). *Inside the presidential debates: Their improbable past and promising future.* Chicago: University of Chicago Press.

If the book is produced by an organization rather than a person, list the organization as the author:

World Health Organization. (2006). *Health and economic development in Southeastern Europe.* Geneva: World Health Organization.

Print Book, Consulted Online

Whitman, W. (1855). *Leaves of grass.* Available from http://www.whitmanarchive.org

Book in Electronic Reader Format

Austen, J. (2007). *Pride and prejudice* [Kindle edition]. New York: Penguin Classics. (Original work published 1813).

Austen, J. (2008). *Pride and prejudice* [PDF e-book]. New York: Penguin Classics. (Original work published 1813).

Edited or Translated Book

If a book has an editor or translator but no author, treat the editor or translator as the author. If the original has an earlier date, indicate that in parentheses after the entry.

Young, G. (Ed.). (2007). *The best American short plays, 2002–2003.* New York: Applause.

Silverstein, T. (Trans.). (1974). *Sir Gawain and the green knight.* Chicago: University of Chicago Press. (Original work published in late 14th century).

If a book has an author as well as an editor and/or a translator, identify the editor and/or translator in parentheses after the title and before the period.

Bonnefoy, Y. (1995). *New and selected poems* (J. Naughton & A. Rudolf, Eds.). Chicago: University of Chicago Press.

Feydeau, G. (1970). *Four farces by Georges Feydeau* (N. R. Shapiro, Trans.). Chicago: University of Chicago Press.

Menchú, R. (1999). *Crossing borders* (A. Wright, Trans. & Ed.). New York: Verso.

Adorno, T. W., & Benjamin, W. (1999). *The complete correspondence, 1928–1940* (H. Lonitz, Ed., & N. Walker, Trans.). Cambridge, MA: Harvard University Press.

Revised Edition

If you consult a book labeled as a "revised" edition or a "second" (or subsequent) edition, place this information in parentheses, after the title and before the period, using abbreviations as in the following examples.

Harper-Dorton, K. V., & Herbert, M. (2002). *Working with children, adolescents, and their families* (3rd ed.). Chicago: Lyceum Books.

Bolt, P. J., Coletta, D. V., & Shackelford, C. G., Jr. (2005). *American defense policy* (8th ed.). Baltimore, MD: Johns Hopkins University Press.

Babb, F. (1989). *Between field and cooking pot: The political economy of marketwomen in Peru* (Rev. ed.). Austin, TX: University of Texas Press.

Multivolume Work

If you cite one book from a group of books (called a *multivolume* work), list only the specific volume you consulted. Identify the volume number "(Vol. X)."

Byrne, M. S. C. (Ed.). (1981). *The Lisle letters* (Vol. 4). Chicago: University of Chicago Press.

If the volume you cite has a different title from that of the whole group, use both titles, starting with the title of the group:

Pelikan, J. (1989). *The Christian tradition: A history of the development of doctrine: Vol. 5. Christian doctrine and modern culture.* Chicago: University of Chicago Press.

If you refer to more than one book in the group of books, you can cite all of them in one entry:

Byrne, M. S. C. (Ed.). (1981). *The Lisle letters* (6 vols.). Chicago: University of Chicago Press.

James, H. (1962–64). *The complete tales of Henry James* (L. Edel, Ed., 12 vols.). London: Rupert Hart-Davis.

20.2.5.2 *Parts of Books*

Chapter in an Edited Book

Cite the specific chapter, if you refer only to that one chapter. You may cite two specific chapters separately, if you specifically compare them in your text. Otherwise, cite the edited book as a whole.

Ellet, E. F. L. (1968). By rail and stage to Galena. In P. M. Angle (Ed.), *Prairie state: Impressions of Illinois, 1673–1967, by travelers and other observers* (pp. 271–279). Chicago: University of Chicago Press.

Introductions, Prefaces, Afterwords

If you refer to a supplemental part of a book that was written by someone other than the book author, cite it separately.

Prose, F. (2000). Introduction. In B. Wallraff, *Word court: Wherein verbal virtue is rewarded, crimes against the language are punished, and poetic justice is done* (pp. ix–xiv). New York: Harcourt.

Letter in a Collection

Adams, H. (1930). To Charles Milnes Gaskell. In *Letters of Henry Adams, 1858–1891* (W. C. Ford, Ed.). Boston: Houghton Mifflin. (Original was written March 30, 1868).

Short Story or Poem in a Collection

Cite the specific work, not the whole book, if you refer only to that one work. You may cite two or more specific works separately, if you specifically compare them in your text. Otherwise, cite the collection as a whole.

Eisenberg, D. (1997). Someone to Talk To. In *All around Atlantis* (pp. 61–92). New York: Farrar, Straus and Giroux.

Heaney, S. (2006). To George Seferis in the underworld. In *District and circle* (pp. 22–23). New York: Farrar, Straus and Giroux.

Wigglesworth, M. (2003). Excerpt from *The day of doom*. In S. G. Axelrod, C. Roman, & T. Travisano (Eds.), *The new anthology of American poetry: Traditions and revolutions, beginnings to 1900* (pp. 68–74). New Brunswick, NJ: Rutgers University Press.

Sample

Reference List

Babb, F. (1989). *Between field and cooking pot: The political economy of market-women in Peru* (Rev. ed.). Austin, TX: University of Texas Press.

Castro, J. (1992, April 13). Scientology's largesse in Russia. *Time.* Retrieved March 20, 2009, from http://www.time.com/time/magazine/article/0,9171,975290,00.html

Gold, A. G. (1998). Grains of truth: Shifting hierarchies of food and grace in three Rajasthani tales. *History of Religions, 38(2),* 150–171.

Green, N. L. (2005). The politics of exit: Reversing the immigration paradigm [Electronic version]. *Journal of Modern History, 77(2),* 263–289.

Hitchcock, T. (2005). Begging on the streets of eighteenth-century London. *Journal of British Studies, 44(3)*, 478–498.

Masolo, D. (2006). African sage philosophy. In E. N. Zalta (Ed.), *Stanford encyclopedia of philosophy*. Available from http://plato.stanford.edu

Whitney, F. P. (1929). The six-year high school in Cleveland. *School Review, 37(4)*, 267–271. Retrieved from JSTOR database.

World Health Organization. (2006). *Health and economic development in South-eastern Europe*. Geneva: World Health Organization.

PART III
Style

In part 3 we show you how to deal with issues of punctuation, matters of spelling not handled in dictionaries, and other matters of editorial style.

Read Me First: How to Use Part 3

We have designed this part not for reading but for reference. Use the contents at the beginning of each chapter to find the issue you need to address and consult the appropriate section. In some cases, you will find models to match; in others, directions to follow.

Go to www.turabian.org to find supplemental materials related to part 3.

21: Spelling: Plurals, Possessives, and Hyphenation

For most spelling questions, the rule is simple: Let your dictionary be your guide. But writers often face questions about spelling and related matters whose answers cannot be found in a dictionary. This chapter offers general guidelines and specific models for many of those questions. Many handbooks offer more extensive (and, in some cases, different) advice on spelling. If your teacher assigns one, let that guide take precedence over the advice offered here.

> **How to Use This Chapter**
> This chapter is organized by kinds of nouns. Find the section that corresponds to the kind of word you want to spell, find the appropriate model, and match your text to the model.

21.1 Spelling Basics

Model your spelling on standard American usage. When your spell-checker leaves you in doubt, consult a dictionary. Use standard spellings throughout your text, but copy the words in quotations and titles exactly as they appear in the original, even if the spelling differs from American standard English.

Be aware that dictionaries can differ on how to spell a word, and many dictionaries (especially online ones) are inaccurate or out-of-date. The most reliable dictionaries for current usage and spelling are

- *Webster's Third New International Dictionary* (2002)
- *Merriam-Webster's Collegiate Dictionary,* 11th ed. (2003)

The smaller *Collegiate Dictionary* is an abridged version of the *New International* and is easier to handle. It is also available on CD-ROM and online through many libraries. For the names of people and places, see the listings at the end of Webster's or the separate publications *Merriam-Webster's Biographical Dictionary* (1995) and *Merriam-Webster's Geographical Dictionary,* 3rd ed. (2007).

Most reliable dictionaries offer more than one acceptable spelling for some words. In those cases, you should use the first spelling offered. Under no circumstances use both in the same paper (spell-checkers will not catch this).

Use the spell-checking feature of your word-processing software. Spell-checkers are better than ever, and they will save you not only from misspellings but from typos as well. *But do not rely on a spell-checker alone.* Computer dictionaries are not entirely reliable, and it is easy for them to accept incorrect spellings that someone has added to a computer's custom dictionary (a serious problem for shared computers). Also, a spell-checker will not tell you when you have correctly spelled the wrong word: "Dad had *and* extra long nap because the kids were quite." A spell-checker is not a substitute for a good dictionary or careful proofreading.

21.2   Plurals

21.2.1   The General Rule
Most nouns form the plural by adding *s*.

dog	→ dogs	tree	→ trees
vehicle	→ vehicles	John	→ Johns

But there are many irregular nouns that form their plurals in different ways. When in doubt, consult a dictionary.

Do not confuse plurals with possessives. Do not use an apostrophe to make a standard plural:

Plural:	dogs, vehicles, Johns
Possessive:	dog's, vehicle's, John's

21.2.2   Special Cases

Nouns ending in *ch, j, s, sh, x,* or *z*
These nouns add *es*.

beach	→ beaches	glass	→ glasses
dish	→ dishes	Alex	→ Alexes

Common nouns ending in y

If the y is preceded by a vowel, add an s.

boy → boys   monkey → monkeys
day → days   decoy → decoys

If the y is preceded by a consonant, replaced it with *ies*.

baby → babies   family → families
story → stories   hobby → hobbies

Proper nouns ending in y

These nouns add s.

Harry → Harrys   Germany → Germanys
Sally → Sallys   Jay → Jays

Nouns ending in o

These nouns sometimes add s and sometimes es. If in doubt, check a dictionary.

hero → heroes   potato → potatoes
memo → memos   auto → autos

Nouns ending in f or fe

These nouns sometimes add s and sometimes replace the f with *ves*. If in doubt, check a dictionary.

leaf → leaves   knife → knives
roof → roofs   proof → proofs

Compound Nouns

If the compound is made of two nouns, make the last noun plural. (It does not matter whether the words are joined, hyphenated, or just together.)

bookkeeper → bookkeepers   district attorney → district attorneys
actor-singer → actor-singers   handyman → handymen

If the compound is made of a noun followed by an adjective or prepositional phrase, make the main noun plural. (It does not matter whether the words are hyphenated or not.)

sister-in-law → sisters-in-law   attorney general → attorneys general
man-of-war → men-of-war   president-elect → presidents-elect

Letters and Numerals

Numerals and capital letters usually form the plural by adding an *s* without an apostrophe.

R → Rs	1950 → 1950s	
ABC → ABCs	767 → 767s	

For lowercase letters or for instances where readers might mistake the plural combination for a word or common abbreviation, add an apostrophe before the *s*.

j → j's **not** js   I → I's **not** Is   A and B → A's and B's **not** As and Bs

Abbreviations

If an abbreviation has internal periods *or* includes both capital and lowercase letters, add an apostrophe plus *s*.

a.m. → a.m.'s   e.g. → e.g.'s   PhD → PhD's

Otherwise, add *s* without an apostrophe. If the abbreviation ends in a period, add the *s* before the period. (But remember that the plural of *p.* [page] is *pp.*)

URL → URLs   DVD → DVDs   ed. → eds.   vol. → vols.

Terms in Italics

For titles and other terms in italics, add *s* in roman type without an apostrophe.

Chicago Tribune → *Chicago Tribunes*   *New Yorker* → *New Yorkers*

Terms in Quotation Marks

Do not form the plural of a term in quotation marks; rephrase the sentence to avoid the need for a plural.

NOT: included many "To be continued's"
BUT: included "To be continued" many times

21.3 Possessives

21.3.1 The General Rules

Singular Nouns

For most singular nouns, including abbreviations, add an apostrophe and *s*, even if the word ends in *s*, *x*, or *z*.

the argument's effects   Jones's paper   Diaz's paper   JFK's speech

Plural Nouns Ending in s

For regular plural nouns, add an apostrophe without an additional *s*.

the arguments' effects   politicians' votes

the Davises' house   the Cavs' lineup

Plural Nouns Not Ending in s

For irregular plurals that do not end in *s*, add both an apostrophe and *s*.

the children's hour   the mice's nest

alumni's donations   the men's room

21.3.2   Special Cases

Exceptions for Singular Nouns Ending in s

For collective nouns that end in *s* but are treated as singular nouns, add an apostrophe without an additional *s*.

politics' true meaning   the United States' role

Nouns for Inanimate Objects

In most cases, you should not create possessives for inanimate objects.

NOT: the house's door   the hammer's handle   the shirt's color

Singular Compound Nouns

Add an apostrophe and an *s* to the last word in the compound.

bookkeeper's records   handyman's tools   district attorney's case

sister-in-law's children   attorney general's decision

Plural Compound Nouns

For compounds composed of two nouns, form the possessive based on the last word in the compound.

bookkeepers' records   handymen's tools   district attorneys' cases

Avoid possessive forms for compounds with a noun followed by an adjective or prepositional phrase; rephrase instead.

NOT: sisters-in-law's children   BUT: the children of the sisters-in-law

NOT: attorneys' general decisions   BUT: the decisions of the attorneys general

Multiple Nouns

To indicate that two or more nouns in a series each posses something separately, make all the nouns possessive.

New York's and Chicago's teams   historians' and economists' methods

To indicate that two or more entities possess something jointly, make only the last noun possessive.

Minneapolis and St. Paul's team   historians and economists' data

Terms in Italics
Add an apostrophe and an *s,* both in roman type.

the *Atlantic Monthly*'s editor   the *Chicago Tribune*'s readers

Terms in Quotation Marks
Avoid possessive forms for terms in quotation marks; rephrase instead.

NOT: the "Ode on a Grecian Urn"'s admirers
BUT: admirers of the "Ode on a Grecian Urn"

21.4 Hyphenated Words

A compound word or a compound modifier may be hyphenated, left open (with a space between elements), or closed (spelled as one word). To find out which form to use, check your dictionary first. If you cannot find a compound there, follow the principles in the following sections to decide whether or not to hyphenate. If you cannot find the form in either place, leave the compound open.

The patterns outlined below are not hard-and-fast rules. You will have to decide many individual cases on the basis of context, personal taste, or common usage in your discipline. Although much of the suggested hyphenation is logical and aids readability, some is only traditional.

21.4.1 Words Formed with Prefixes (and Prefix-like Prepositions)

21.4.1.1 *The General Rule*
Words formed with prefixes are normally closed (spelled as one word), whether they are nouns (*postmodernism*), verbs (*misrepresent*), adjectives (*antebellum*), or adverbs (*prematurely*). This pattern also applies to prepositions such as *over* and *under* that can be attached to words in the same position as prefixes (*overachiever, underhanded*).

21.4.1.2 *Special Cases That Call for Hyphens*
Use a hyphen between a prefix and the word it precedes in these cases:

Prefix + capitalized word:

sub-Saharan, pro-Asian, anti-American, un-American, trans-Siberian

Prefix + numeral:

pre-1950, mid-'80s, pro-3M, neo-'60s

Prefix + compound (hyphenated or open):

non-coffee-drinking, post-high school, pro-American dream

Stand-alone prefix in a compound phrase:

pre- and postwar, pro- and anti-Asian, over- and underachievers

Doubled prefix:

sub-sub-Saharan, sub-subclaim, post-postmodern, mega-megatrucks

Doubled letters at junction of prefix and root:

NOT: antiintellectual	BUT: anti-intellectual
NOT: megaandroid	BUT: mega-android
NOT: protooncologist	BUT: proto-oncologist
NOT: cyberrage	BUT: cyber-rage

Combinations that may be confused with other words:

re-cover (cover again) *vs.* recover, re-creation (created again) *vs.* recreation

21.4.2 Compounds Used as Adjectives

In most cases, hyphenate such a compound when it precedes the noun it modifies; otherwise leave it open.

Before Noun	After Noun
full-length treatment	treatment is full length
thought-provoking commentary	commentary was thought provoking
over-the-counter drug	drug sold over the counter
a frequently referred-to book	a book that is frequently referred to
spelled-out numbers	numbers that are spelled out

21.4.3 Compounds Used as Nouns

In most cases, compounds used as nouns are open.

master builder, middle class, decision making, cooking class

Many frequently used compounds are closed.

bookkeeper, handyman, birthrate, notebook

Only in special cases are compound nouns hyphenated (see 21.4.4).

21.4.4 ## Compounds Normally Hyphenated

The following compounds are normally hyphenated, no matter how or where they are used. In some cases, individual compounds that are especially common are closed (check your dictionary). Any exceptions are noted.

Age terms:

a three-year-old, three-year-old children, a fifty-two-year-old woman, eight- to ten-year-olds

all- (adjectives):

all-American player, all-out effort, all-encompassing rule, the rule is all-encompassing
Note: Adverbial *all-* forms are open: went all out, looked all around

cross-:

cross-checked pages, cross-referenced term, a cross-reference, go cross-country
Note: Some forms are closed: crossbow, crossover

e-:

e-marketing, an e-mail message, e-commerce, an e-book page

-elect:

president-elect, mayor-elect, chairwoman-elect
Exception: Multi-word elected offices are open: district attorney elect, county delegate elect

ever-:

ever-ready helper, ever-recurring problem
Note: everlasting

ex-:

ex-boyfriend, ex-marine, ex-CEO, ex-kindergarten teacher

Familiar phrases (standardized with hyphens):

Jack-of-all-trades, stick-in-the-mud

Fractions:

a two-thirds share, two-thirds done, four-fifths majority, seven-sixteenths
Exception: Use only one hyphen per fraction: one and three-quarters, three fifty-thirds
Note: Combinations of one-word fractions plus nouns follow the general rule: an eighth note, a half mile, a half-mile run, the run was a half mile long

Functional pairs (that could also be written with *and*):

city-state government (i.e., city and state), a nurse-practitioner, student-teacher internship, Arab-Israeli peace, Russian-English dictionary

great- (kinship):

great-grandmother, great-grandfather, great-aunt

-in-law:

son-in-law, mother-in-law, cousin-in-law

-odd:

twenty-odd points, 350-odd students, a hundred-odd dollars

on-:

on-screen, on-site
Note: Many *on-* words are closed: online, onboard, ongoing

Proper nouns, shortened:

Anglo-Saxon culture, Afro-American studies, the Franco-Prussian War, the Sino-Soviet bloc

self-:

self-realization, self-sustaining, self-conscious
Note: unselfconscious

-style:

Chicago-style pizza, '60s-style music, southern-style cooking, English-style riding

21.4.5 Compounds Normally Open

The following compounds are normally open (no hyphens), no matter how they are used. In some cases, individual compounds that are especially common are closed (check your dictionary). Any exceptions are noted.

-book:

reference book, coupon book, comic book
Note: checkbook, cookbook, textbook

Chemical terms:

hydrogen peroxide, sodium chloride solution

Colors:

bluish green water, the eyes are emerald green, red and green outfit
Note: Black and white follows the standard pattern: the print is black and white, a black-and-white print

Comparative constructions:

less prepared students, most talented athletes, those athletes are most talented
Note: Add a hyphen if readers might be confused over what the term modifies:
We hired more skilled workers to fill in for the holidays (i.e., more workers who are skilled).
Our training program produces more-skilled workers (i.e., workers who are more skilled).

-general:

attorney general, postmaster general

-ly adverbs:

highly regarded teacher, widely known singer, partially chewed food

Modified by a preceding adverb:

Without Adverb	With Adverb
thought-provoking commentary	extremely thought provoking commentary
ill-advised comment	highly ill advised comment

-percent:

5 percent, a 10 percent increase, your score was 86 percent
Note: Use Arabic numerals.

Proper nouns:

African American students, a Chinese American lawyer, the North Central Region, State Department employees, she is French Canadian

21.4.6   Compounds Normally Closed

The following compounds are normally closed. Any exceptions are noted.

-ache:

toothache, stomachache, heartache

-borne, -like, or -wide:

foodborne, childlike, doglike, systemwide, wordwide
Exception 1, proper nouns: Chicago-wide, Obama-like
Exception 2, three or more syllables: mosquito-borne, handkerchief-like
Exception 3, repeated letters: meadow-wide, bell-like

Directions:

Two directions: northeast, northwest, southwest, southeast
Three directions: east-northeast, north-northwest, south-southeast
Note: north-south, east-west, northeast-southwest, southeast-northwest

grand- (kinship):

grandfather, grandmother, granddaughter, grandnephew

step- (kinship):

stepmother, stepfather, stepson, stepgranddaughter

22: Punctuation

This chapter offers general guidelines for punctuation in the text of your paper. (For punctuation in citations, see part 2.) Some rules are clear-cut, but others are not, so you often have to depend on sound judgment and a good ear.

How to Use This Chapter
This chapter is organized not by kind of punctuation but by the kind of structure you need to punctuate: sentences, clauses, series, quotations, and so on.

Find the section that corresponds to the part of your writing you want to punctuate, find the appropriate model, and match your text to the model. If you find a grammatical term that you don't recognize or cannot define, look in the glossary (appendix B).

22.1 Complete Sentences

You must end every complete sentence with a *terminal punctuation* mark: a period (.), a question mark (?), or an exclamation point (!). Exclamations are rare in academic writing, and you should avoid them except in quotations.

22.1.1 Summary

You have three ways to end complete sentences:

1. Period
2. Question Mark
3. Exclamation Point

22.1.2 Three Ways to Punctuate Sentences

1. Period (for declaratory statements, imperatives, and indirect questions)

   He chose to use a graph.
   Consider the advantages of this method.
   The question was whether these differences could be reconciled.

2. Question Mark

   Did you consider the advantages of this method?

3. Exclamation Point

   Boy, am I surprised that you used this method!

22.1.3 Sentence Fragments

Experienced writers sometimes try to achieve a stylistic or rhetorical effect by punctuating incomplete sentences as though they were complete—called *sentence fragments.*

Which can be dangerous. Especially for students.

You should avoid fragments: teachers usually disallow them because they cannot distinguish intentional fragments from grammatical mistakes.
You can end fragments with any terminal punctuation.

Which can be dangerous.
For whom?
Especially for students!

22.2 Independent Clauses

A *compound sentence* is composed of two or more independent clauses that could be punctuated as complete sentences. You must separate the independent clauses within a sentence in one of eight ways. The following list groups them into the most common cases, less common cases, and cases for special effects. In all cases, you could end each clause with a period or question mark and make one compound sentence into two or more complete sentences.

22.2.1 Summary

You have eight ways to punctuate the independent clauses in a compound sentence:

1. Comma + Coordinate Conjunction
2. Semicolon
3. Semicolon + Coordinate Conjunction
4. Coordinate Conjunction (alone)
5. Comma (alone)—Caution!
6. Colon
7. Dash
8. Parentheses

22.2.2 Eight Ways to Punctuate Compound Sentences
Three common forms:

1. Comma + Coordinate Conjunction (*and, but, or, nor, for, so, yet*)

   This is the most common form. If the individual clauses are long or include internal punctuation, use a semicolon instead (see #3, below).
   Students around the world want to learn English, and many young Americans are eager to teach them.
   Three or more clauses. In this case, put a comma after each clause (including the one before the conjunction) and a conjunction before the last clause.
   The committee designed the questionnaire, the field-workers collected responses, and the statisticians analyzed the results.

2. Semicolon

   Students around the world want to learn English; many young Americans are eager to teach them.

Watch out for words that connect sentences but are not conjunctions: *however, thus, therefore, hence, then, indeed, accordingly, besides,* and so on. Because these are not conjunctions, you cannot use them with a comma in a compound sentence. Use a semicolon instead.

Productivity per capita in U.S. industry is much greater than that in China; however, China has an increasingly well-educated young labor force.

3. Semicolon + Coordinate Conjunction

    This form is generally reserved for sentences with complex clauses, especially those with internal punctuation. If the clauses are short, use a comma instead (see #1 above).

    Although productivity per capita in U.S. industry is much greater than that in China, China has an increasingly well-educated young labor force; but the crucial point is that knowledge—which is transferable between peoples—has become the most important world economic resource.

    Three or more complex clauses. In this case, put a semicolon after each clause (including the one before the conjunction) and a conjunction before the last clause.

    The committee designed the questionnaire, which was short but still took more than a month to be completed; the field-workers, who were forced to wait for the committee to finish its work, collected responses; and the statisticians analyzed the results, though not until several weeks later.

Two less common forms:

4. Coordinate Conjunction (alone)

    This form is reserved for sentences with two short, simple clauses. Do not use it if either clause has internal punctuation.

    The senator arrived at noon and the president left at once.

    The senator, who was late, arrived at noon, and the president left at once.

5. Comma (alone)—Caution!

    This form is used by many of the best writers when they want to emphasize the connection between two short independent clauses. But many teachers regard this construction as an error (called a *comma splice*). So avoid it unless you know your readers will accept it.

    The senator arrived, the president left.

Three forms for special effects:

6. Colon

    A colon suggests that the second clause follows closely from the first. Readers take it as shorthand for *therefore, to illustrate, for example, that is, let me expand on what I just said,* and so on. The second clause generally does not begin with a capital letter, but it can. Good writers rarely include a coordinating conjunction after a colon.

Dance is not widely supported: no company operates at a profit, and there are few outside major cities.

Only one question remains: What if we lose money?

Only one choice remained: He must confront his enemy.

A colon can also introduce a list of sentences.

Sally was faced with few good choices: She could risk revealing what she learned. Or she could let her best friend pay the price for something she did not do. Or was there a third way?

7. Dash

A dash can be used to signal the same relationships as a colon. It suggests a more informal style, and generally seems to readers like a longer pause. Writers often use a coordinating conjunction or another introducer in the clause after the dash.

NASA's moon program captured America's imagination—we were filled with pride.

Writing well may be hard—but it's worth the effort.

A perfect lawn requires constant diligence—after all, weeds are always poised to invade.

8. Parentheses

You can use parentheses in place of a colon or a dash if the second clause is short and serves as an explanation, illustration, or afterthought. Put the period outside the last parenthesis.

The first moon landing captivated America (the TV ratings were the highest ever).

Writing well may be hard (but it's worth the effort).

A perfect lawn requires constant diligence (after all, weeds are always poised to invade).

22.3   **Introductory Elements**

Sentences often begin with an introductory word, phrase, or subordinate clause before the main clause begins. When they are short these introducers pose little problem for readers, as in this sentence. But when (as in this sentence) an introducer becomes long enough that readers cannot keep it all in mind at once, especially if it includes multiple elements, readers need punctuation to help them keep the grammatical units straight in their minds. We can give you a few rules to guide you in punctuating introductory elements, but in many cases you will have to rely on your judgment to decide what readers need.

22.3.1 Summary

Use a comma to set off the following introductory elements:

1. Connecting adverb or adverb phrase (with some exceptions)
2. Commenting adverb or adverb phrase
3. Long introductory phrase or clause
4. Introductory element that might confuse readers

22.3.2 Four Ways to Punctuate Introductory Elements

1. Put a comma after an initial adverb or adverb phrase that connects the current sentence to previous ones.

   Connecting adverbs include such terms as *however, nevertheless, meanwhile, also, in addition, therefore,* and so on. Since readers tend to hear a mental pause after these terms, they usually expect a comma.
   In the meantime, the police were distracted by a noise in the alley.
   Conversely, binge drinkers tend to underestimate the risks of excessive drinking.
   Exception: You may omit the comma after a connecting adverb if it does not create a pause when you read aloud, especially for short terms like *now, thus, hence, perhaps,* and so on.
   Perhaps we will see you there.
   Now the evidence supports no such conclusion.

2. Put a comma after an initial adverb or adverb phrase that comments on the entire sentence.

   Commenting adverbs include such terms as *fortunately, surely, perhaps, of course,* and so on. Since readers usually hear a mental pause after these terms, they expect a comma.
   Happily, our investigation turned up no surprises.
   To be sure, some researchers offer conclusions that contradict this claim.

3. Put a comma after long introductory phrases or clauses.

   Although the Japanese have proved to be world leaders in industrial design, especially in consumer goods, they have largely failed to export goods that reflect that leadership.
   Despite the many concerns about the safety of nuclear power plants and their waste disposal, it seems inevitable that the United States will increase its nuclear footprint.
   This is not a hard-and-fast rule. You have to exercise judgment in deciding when an introductory phrase is long enough to need a comma. Consider adding a comma when an introducer reaches ten words. But two other factors are rel-

evant. Readers are less likely to expect a comma when two clauses have the same grammatical subject and are close in meaning. Compare

Once the IRS accepted our supporting documentation it agreed to allow the deductions for both the home office and the computer.

Although the IRS has few auditors and antiquated data processing, taxpayers remain fearful enough to be deterred from cheating.

You do not need a comma for short introductory phrases or clauses.

In a 2008 survey the CDC discovered fear of AIDS had become dangerously low.

To the untrained eye one cornfield looks like every other one.

If the inflow is reduced the pressure will remain within system tolerances.

4. Put a comma after an introductory element if it might confuse readers about the structure of the sentence.

NOT: When the speaker concludes her presentation will be all that most of the audience knows about her.

BUT: When the speaker concludes, her presentation will be all that most of the audience knows about her.

22.4 Trailing Elements

Many elements that can introduce a main clause can also trail it. In most cases, these trailing elements do not need punctuation. But in three cases they do.

22.4.1 Summary

Most trailing elements are not set off by punctuation. Here are three cases in which you can set them off.

1. Use commas to separate a trailer from a long main clause.
2. Use commas to separate one trailer from a previous one.
3. Use a comma or a dash to create an emphasizing pause.

22.4.2 Three Ways to Punctuate Trailing Elements

In most cases you do not need to set off a trailing element with a comma.

Introducer: Despite the many concerns about the safety of nuclear power plants and their waste disposal, it seems inevitable that the United States will increase its nuclear footprint.

Trailer: It seems inevitable that the United States will increase its nuclear footprint despite the many concerns about the safety of nuclear power plants and their waste disposal.

Introducer: Although the IRS has few auditors and antiquated data processing, taxpayers remain fearful enough to be deterred from cheating.

Trailer: Taxpayers remain fearful enough to be deterred from cheating even though the IRS has few auditors and antiquated data processing.

There are, however, three situations in which you may set off a trailing element—if, that is, you think it might help your readers.

1. Use a comma to set off a trailing element if the main clause is long and complex, especially if the trailer is also long.

Missile defense systems, which have an overwhelming number of variables that must be managed, make more sense in the abstract than in the reality,$_{main\ clause}$ because in the long run an engineering project can only be as successful as our understanding of the problem it is trying to solve.$_{trailer}$

2. Use a comma to set off one trailing element that follows another, especially if what has come before is long and complex.

Competitors will respond$_{main\ clause}$ when a new advertising campaign reframes the terms in which customers think about a product,$_{trailer\ 1}$ because they cannot be put out of the running for "share of mind."$_{trailer\ 2}$
Organic produce proved to sell primarily in luxury markets$_{main\ clause}$ despite the fact that the poor are in greatest need of its obvious health benefits,$_{trailer\ 1}$ as we predicted.$_{trailer\ 2}$

3. Use a comma or a dash to create a pause that emphasizes a trailing element.

I knew you would break your promise and go, because you always go.
I knew you would break your promise and go, as you always do.
There are, however, several situations in which you may set off a trailing element—if, that is, you think it might help your readers.

22.5   Elements Internal to Clauses

22.5.1   Summary

Adjective Strings

1. Use commas to separate adjectives when they independently modify the noun.
2. Do not use commas when the one adjective affects the meaning of the next.

Interrupting Elements

1. Enclose an interrupting element in paired commas, parentheses, or dashes.

Explanatory Elements

1. Set off most explanatory elements with paired commas.
2. Use dashes for a conversational tone or if the element has internal punctuation.
3. Use parentheses to make it seem like an aside or a footnote.

22.5.2 Adjective Strings

When two or more adjectives appear before a noun, not in a series connected by *and*, but as a string, you may need to separate them with a comma.

1. Use commas to separate a string of adjectives when each of them independently modifies the noun.

It was a large, well-placed, beautiful house.
They strolled out into the warm, luminous night.

2. Do not use a comma when the one adjective affects the meaning of the next.

She refused to be identified with a traditional political label.
Social network marketing is an innovative business strategy.

22.5.3 Interrupting Elements

Interrupting elements are words, phrases, or clauses that might have been located at the beginning or end of the current clause but that are located within the clause instead.

1. Enclose an interrupting element in commas, parentheses, or dashes, depending on how forceful you want the interruption to seem. Always use the punctuation marks in pairs.

The Quinn Report was, to say the least, a bombshell.
Alex Rodriguez is (according to reports) as tainted by steroids as Barry Bonds.
Happiness—especially when it comes through the graces of chance—is as fleeting as a hot streak at the craps table.

22.5.4 Explanatory Elements

Explanatory elements are modifiers that add useful information but are not essential to the core meaning of the clause: technically, they are called *nonrestrictive*. In contrast, *restrictive* modifiers add essential information that specifies who or what a word refers to. They answer the question "Which one?" The following modifiers (underlined) are restrictive because they add *specifying* details:

In cases of divorce, the parent <u>with custody</u> receives the tax deduction for child support. [*Which parent? The one with custody.*]

Binge drinkers, unlike most alcoholics, are attracted to bars <u>that have a party atmosphere</u>. [*Which bars? The ones that have a party atmosphere.*]

Nonrestrictive modifiers add explanatory details but they do not specify reference. They can be removed without changing the core meaning of the clause. They answer the question "What about it?" The following modifiers (underlined) are nonrestrictive because they add *explanatory* but not specifying details:

In this case, the mother—<u>the parent with custody</u>—receives the tax deduction for child support. [*What about the mother? She's the parent with custody.*]

My binge-drinking friends are attracted to the Main Street Bar, <u>which has a party atmosphere</u>. [*What about that bar? It has a party atmosphere.*]

Note that for relative clauses, the restrictive form uses *that* while the nonrestrictive one uses *which*.

Specifying, restrictive modifiers are never punctuated. Explanatory, nonrestrictive modifiers usually are.

1. Set off most explanatory elements with paired commas.

   These five books, which are on reserve in the library, are required reading.
   These five books, all required reading, are on reserve in the library.

2. Use dashes for a conversational tone or if the element has internal punctuation.

   Some characters in *Tom Jones* are "flat"—if I may use a somewhat discredited term—because they are caricatures of their names.
   The influence of three impressionists—Monet (1840–1926), Sisley (1839–1899), and Degas (1834–1917)—is obvious in her work.

3. Use parentheses to make it seem an aside or a footnote.

   The brain (at least the part that controls rational thinking) is a complex network of distinct units working in parallel.
   Kierkegaard (a Danish philosopher) once asked, "What is anxiety?"

22.6 Series and Lists

22.6.1 Summary

Two Coordinated Elements

1. Never use a comma to separate two coordinated words.
2. Use a comma to separate coordinated phrases or clauses *only* if readers might be confused about where one ends and the next begins.

Series of Three or More

1. Use commas after each item and a conjunction before the last.
2. Use semicolons instead of commas for long and complex items.

Run-in Lists

1. Put a colon or (to be informal or stylish) a dash before the list.
2. Punctuate the list as a series; do not capitalize the first word.
3. Never end the introducing clause with a verb.

Vertical Lists

1. Put a colon or period (but not a dash) at the end of a complete introductory clause; use no punctuation after an introductory subject or subject-verb.
2. If the items are complete sentences, capitalize the first word and use terminal punctuation at the end.
3. If the items are not complete sentences, omit terminal punctuation, even for the last item, and do not capitalize the first word.

22.6.2   Two Coordinated Elements

In most cases you should not put a comma between two coordinated words, phrases, or subordinate clauses. But you can add a comma if readers might be confused, which can happen when two phrases or clauses are long and complex or when the conjunction includes a confusing combination of words, such as several *ands* near one another.

1. Never put a comma between two words connected by a coordinate conjunction.

    NOT: the dogs, and cats ran   I saw John, and Sally   we ate, but didn't drink
    BUT: the dogs and cats ran   I saw John and Sally   we ate but didn't drink

2. Use a comma to separate two coordinated phrases or clauses if readers might be confused about where one ends and the next begins.

    NOT: Conrad's *Heart of Darkness* brilliantly dramatizes those primitive impulses that lie deep in each of us and stir only in our darkest dreams but asserts the need for the values that control those impulses.
    BUT: Conrad's *Heart of Darkness* brilliantly dramatizes those primitive impulses that lie deep in each of us and stir only in our darkest dreams, but asserts the need for the values that control those impulses.
    NOT: It is in the graveyard that Hamlet finally realizes that the inevitable end of

life is the grave and decay and that pride and all plotting and counter-plotting must lead to dust.

BUT: It is in the graveyard that Hamlet finally realizes that the inevitable end of life is the grave and decay, and that pride and all plotting and counter-plotting must lead to dust.

22.6.3 Series of Three or More

You must punctuate any series of three or more.

1. Put a comma after each item in a series except the last, and put a coordinating conjunction before the last item. Treat terms like *etc., and so forth,* or *and the like* as an item in the list.

   a red, white, and blue shirt
   run, walk, or crawl
   including pens, pencils, paper clips, tape, and the like
   You must go home, get your homework started, and stay off the Internet.

2. If the items in a series are long, and especially if they include internal punctuation, put a semicolon after each item in a series except the last, and put a coordinating conjunction before the last item.

   It was the project engineers who failed to consult the risk-management team, even though they worked in the same building; who designed the apparatus (though without user-testing or even without thinking about the needs of users); and who now have cost the company its good reputation with farmers.

22.6.4 Run-in Lists

1. Put a colon or (to be informal or stylish) a dash before the list.

   People expect three things of government: peace, prosperity, and respect for civil rights.
   Americans thrill to the sounds of baseball—the crack of ball on bat, the pop of ball on leather, the ump's cries of balls and strike, and the chilling silence of the pitcher staring down a batter.

2. Punctuate the list as a series (see 22.6.3). Do not capitalize the first word in the list.

3. Never end the introducing clause with a verb.

   NOT: The qualifications are: a doctorate in economics, industry experience, people skills, and an ability to communicate statistical data to a lay audience.
   BUT: The qualifications are as follows: a doctorate in economics . . .

22.6.5   Vertical Lists

1. Put a colon or period (but not a dash) at the end of a complete introductory clause.

    To be as clear as possible, your sentences must do the following:

    - Match characters to subjects and actions to verbs.
    - Begin with old information.
    - Use words that readers can picture.

    Use no punctuation after an introductory subject or subject-verb.

    To be as clear as possible, your sentences must

    - match characters to subjects and actions to verbs;
    - begin with old information;
    - use words that readers can picture.

2. If the items in the list are complete sentences, capitalize the first word and use terminal punctuation at the end.

    The report offered three conclusions.

    1. The securities markets will not soon recover.
    2. The securities industry is largely to blame.
    3. The economy will not recover until securities are better regulated.

3. If the items in the list are not complete sentences, omit terminal punctuation, even for the last item, and do not capitalize the first word.

    The report covers three areas:

    1. the securities markets
    2. the securities industry
    3. the effects on the economy

22.7   Quotations

22.7.1   Summary

1. Reproduce all quoted words exactly; indicate omitted words with an ellipsis; indicate added or changed words with square brackets.
2. Change the first letter of a quotation so that complete sentences start with a capital and incomplete sentences begin with a lowercase letter.
3. For the introduction to a quotation, follow complete sentences with periods, question marks, or colons; phrases with commas; *that* with no punctuation.

4. Run-in: Enclose all quoted words in pairs of quotation marks. Place the final quotation mark

   - *outside* periods and commas
   - *inside* colons and semicolons
   - *outside* question marks and parentheses that are part of the quotation
   - *inside* question marks and parentheses that are part of your sentence
   - *inside* a parenthetical reference

5. Block: Do not enclose the quotation in quotation marks; place a parenthetical reference after the final punctuation.

22.7.2 Punctuating Quotations

1. Reproduce all quoted words exactly as they appeared in the original. You may omit words if you replace them with an ellipsis (three dots); if an ellipsis comes at the end of a sentence, put the terminal punctuation of the original after the ellipsis. You may add or change words if you put them in square brackets.

   Original: Posner focuses on religion not for its spirituality, but for its social functions: "A notable feature of American society is religious pluralism, and we should consider how this relates to the efficacy of governance by social norms" (299).
   Changed version: In his discussion of religion, Posner says of American society that "a notable feature . . . is [its] religious pluralism" (299).

2. Change the first letter of a quotation so that complete sentences start with a capital and incomplete sentences begin with a lowercase letter. If you introduce the quotation with a clause ending in *that,* make the first letter lowercase. If you weave the quotation into your own sentence, change an initial capital to lowercase.

   Original: As a result of these earlier developments, the Mexican people were bound to benefit from the change.
   Lowercase changed to uppercase to begin complete sentence:
   Fernandez claims, "The Mexican people were bound to benefit from the change."
   "The Mexican people," notes Fernandez, "were bound to benefit from the change."
   Initial capital changed to lowercase following *that*:
   Fernandez points out that "as a result of these earlier developments, the Mexican people were bound to benefit from the change."
   Initial capital changed to lowercase to fit syntax of including sentence:
   Fernandez points out that the people "were bound to benefit" but only "as a result of these earlier developments."

3. If the introduction to a quotation is a complete sentence, put a period or a colon after it. If it is a phrase or incomplete clause, put a comma. If it is a clause ending in *that,* use no punctuation.

> Posner focuses on religion for its social functions. "A notable feature . . .
> Posner focuses on religion: "A notable feature . . .
> Posner says, "A notable feature . . .
> Posner says that "a notable feature . . .

4. Run-in: Enclose all quoted words in pairs of quotation marks. Place the final quotation mark

   - *outside* periods and commas

     > . . . now is the time."
     > . . . now is the time," but we also . . .

   - *inside* colons and semicolons

     > . . . now is the time"; but we also . . .

   - *outside* question marks and parentheses that are part of the quotation

     > He asked, "Is now the time?"
     > . . . now is the time (or so it seems)."

   - *inside* question marks and parentheses that are part of your sentence

     > Will he say, "Now is the time"?
     > . . . yesterday (as he said, "Now is the time").

   - *inside* a parenthetical reference

     > . . . now is the time" (Walker 210).

5. Block: Do not enclose the quotation in quotation marks. Place a parenthetical reference after the final punctuation.

   According to Jared Diamond,

   > Because technology begets more technology, . . . [t]echnology's history exemplifies what is termed an autocatalytic process: that is, one that speeds up at a rate that increases with time, because the process catalyzes itself. (301)

22.8   Punctuation Don'ts

1. **Titles and Headings.** Do not put a period after a title or heading, even if it is a complete sentence. You may put a question mark or exclamation point.

   4.3   Headings Can Be Sentences
   4.3   Can Headings Be Sentences?

2. **Subjects-Verbs-Objects.** Do not put a comma between a subject and its verb or a verb and its direct object, even if they are long. If a subject or verb is so long that you feel you must have a comma, revise the sentence.

NOT: A sentence whose subject goes on forever because it includes many complex subordinate clauses and long phrases that give readers no place to take a mental breath, may seem to some students to demand a comma to show where the subject ends and the verb begins.

For a subject that consists of a long list, put a colon or dash after the list and add a *summative subject* such as "all these."
The president, the vice president, the secretaries of the departments, senators, members of the House of Representatives, and Supreme Court justices—all these take an oath that pledges them to uphold the Constitution.

3. **Doubled Punctuation Marks.** Do not put two periods together.

NOT:　I work for Abco Inc..

　　　Rowling, J. K.. *Harry Potter and . . .*

BUT:　I work for Abco Inc.

　　　Rowling, J. K. *Harry Potter and . . .*

Omit a comma that occurs next to a question mark, exclamation point, or dash.

NOT:　When you ask yourself So *what?,* you find the significance of your research.

　　　While I cannot endorse your proposal—it just feels wrong to me—, I won't oppose it.

BUT:　When you ask yourself So *what?* you find the significance of your research.

　　　While I cannot endorse your proposal—it just feels wrong to me—I won't oppose it.

　　　While I cannot endorse your proposal (it just feels wrong to me), I won't oppose it.

23: Titles, Names, and Numbers

> **How to Use This Chapter**
> This chapter is organized for your reference. Find the section that deals with a specific form or issue and follow the instructions there.

23.1 Titles

The following conventions apply when you reproduce *in your text* the title of a book, article, poem, film, or other work. For titles in citations, see the appropriate sections of part 2.

23.1.1 Spelling

Reproduce a title exactly as it appears in the original. Preserve the original spelling (including hyphenation) even if it departs from your dictionary or standard usage.

23.1.2 Capitalization

In your text, capitalize titles headline style. In this style, you should capitalize the first letter of all words except the following:

- articles (*a, an, the*)
- coordinating conjunctions (*and, but, or, nor, for, so, yet*)

- prepositions (*of, in, at, above, under,* and so forth)
- the words *to* and *as*
- parts of proper nouns that are in lowercase (Ludwig van Beethoven, Charles de Gaulle)
- the second word of a hyphenated compound if it starts with a prefix (Anti-intellectual, Re-establishment)

Always capitalize the first and last words of the title and subtitle, even if they are on the list of words that are not capitalized.

The Economic Effects of the Civil War in the Mid-Atlantic States

To Have and to Hold: A Twenty-First-Century View of Marriage

All That Is True: The Life of Vincent van Gogh, 1853–1890

Four Readings of the Gospel according to Matthew

Self-Government and the Re-establishment of a New World Order

Note: The principles of capitalization have nothing to do with length. Capitalize all short words that are not on the do-not-capitalize list; use lowercase for all words that are on the list, no matter how long they might be.

For titles of works published in the eighteenth century or earlier, retain the original capitalization (and spelling), except that words spelled out in all capital letters should be given with an initial capital only.

A Treatise of morall philosophy Contaynyge the sayings of the wyse

23.1.3   Italics and Quotation Marks

Set off most titles either in italics or enclosed by quotation marks.

Italics

Most long, separately published works are printed in italics. If the first word of the title is *the,* do not capitalize or italicize it. Italicized works include

- books
  Culture and Anarchy   the *Chicago Manual of Style*

- plays and very long poems, especially those of book length
  A Winter's Tale   Dante's *Inferno*

- journals, magazines, newspapers, and other periodicals
  Signs   *Time*   the *Washington Post*

- long musical compositions such as operas and albums
  the *Marriage of Figaro*   *Kala* by M.I.A.

- paintings, sculptures, and other works of art, except for photographs
  Mona Lisa   Michelangelo's *David*

- movies, television shows, and radio programs

  Citizen Kane   *Sesame Street*   *All Things Considered*

Quotation Marks

Most short works are enclosed in quotation marks, especially those that are part of a larger work. Works set enclosed in quotation marks include

- chapters or other titled parts of books

  "The Later Years"

- short stories, short poems, and essays

  "The Dead"   "The Housekeeper"   "Of Books"

- articles or other features in journals, magazines, newspapers, and other periodicals

  "The Function of Fashion in Eighteenth-Century America"
  "Who Should Lead the Supreme Court?"
  "Election Comes Down to the Wire"

- individual episodes of television series

  "The Opposite"

- short musical compositions

  "The Star-Spangled Banner"

- photographs

  Ansel Adams's "North Dome"

Exceptions

For a few special types of titles, you should capitalize them but print them in regular type.

- book series

  Studies in Legal History

- scriptures and other sacred works
  the Bible
  the King James Bible
  the Upanishads
  the Koran
  Genesis
  Exodus

- websites mentioned in your text (in citations, they are in italics)

  twitter.com   Salon.com   aldaily.com

  Do not treat terms for the parts of books as titles; do not capitalize or set them off.

  your bibliography   the preface to *Style*   see chapter 4

23.2   Proper Names

23.2.1   People, Places, and Organizations

Capitalize the first letter in each element of the names of specific people, places, and organizations. Names that contain particles (such as *de* and *van*) or compound last names are capitalized unpredictably. When in doubt, consult *Webster's Biographical Dictionary* (1995) or another reliable authority. Do not capitalize prepositions (*of*) and conjunctions (*and*) that are parts of names. If *the* precedes a name, it is not capitalized.

Eleanor Roosevelt	the United States Congress
W. E. B. DuBois	the State Department
Ludwig van Beethoven	the European Union
Victoria Sackville-West	the University of North Carolina
Chiang Kai-shek	the Honda Motor Company
New York City	the National Conference of Christians and Jews
the Atlantic Ocean	the Roman Catholic Church
the Republic of Lithuania	the Allied Expeditionary Force

A professional title that immediately precedes a personal name is treated as part of the name and should be capitalized. If you use the title alone or after the personal name, it becomes a generic term and should be lowercased. This also applies to other generic terms that are in place of organization names.

President Harry Truman announced	the president announced
Professors Harris and Wilson wrote	the professors wrote
next to the Indian Ocean	next to the ocean

Names of ethnic and national groups are also capitalized. Terms denoting socioeconomic level, however, are not.

Arab Americans	the middle class
Latinos	blue-collar workers

Capitalize adjectives derived from names, unless they have become part of everyday language.

Machiavellian scheme	french fries
Roman and Arabic art	roman and arabic numerals

23.2.2 Historical Events and Periods

The names of many historical periods and events are traditionally capitalized; more generic terms usually are not, unless they include names.

the Bronze Age	ancient Rome
the Depression	the nineteenth century
the Industrial Revolution	the Shang dynasty
Prohibition	the colonial period
the Seven Years' War	the baby boom

23.2.3 Other Types of Names

Other types of names also follow specific patterns for capitalization, and some require italics.

Acts, Treaties, and Government Programs

Capitalize the formal or accepted titles of acts, treaties, government programs, and similar documents or entities, but lowercase informal or generic titles.

the United States (or U.S.) Constitution	the due process clause
the Treaty of Versailles	the treaty
Head Start	social programs

Brand Names

Capitalize the brand names of products, but do not use the symbols ® or ™ after the names. Unless you are discussing a specific product, use a generic term instead of a brand name.

Coca-Cola	cola
Xerox	photocopy

Electronic Technology

Capitalize names of computer hardware and software, networks, browsers, systems, and languages as well as shortened forms of these names.

Windows XP	the Internet; the net
Internet Explorer	the World Wide Web; the web

Ships, Aircraft, and Other Vessels

Capitalize and italicize the names of ships, aircraft, and the like. If the names are preceded by such abbreviations as USS (United States ship) or HMS (Her [or His] Majesty's ship), do not italicize these abbreviations or use the word *ship* in addition to the name.

| USS *Constitution* | *Spirit of St. Louis* |
| HMS *Saranac* | the space shuttle *Endeavor* |

23.3 Numbers

23.3.1 Words or Numerals?

23.3.1.1 *The General Rule*

Spell out numbers from one through one hundred. If the number has two words, use a hyphen (fifty-five). Also spell out round numbers followed by *hundred, thousand, hundred thousand, million,* and so on. For all other numbers, use arabic numerals. Follow this pattern for numbers that are part of physical quantities (distances, lengths, temperatures, and so on), and do not use abbreviations for the units in such quantities.

After seven years of war came sixty-four years of peace.
The population of the three states was approximately twelve million.
He cataloged more than 527 works of art.
Within fifteen minutes the temperature dropped twenty degrees.

If your topic relies heavily on numerical data, follow a different rule: spell out only single-digit numbers and use numerals for all others.

Use the same principles for ordinal numbers (*first, second,* etc.) that you use for standard ones. Add *st, nd, rd,* or *th* as appropriate.

On the 122nd and 123rd days of his trip, he received his eighteenth and nineteenth letters from home.

23.3.1.2 *Special Cases*

Initial Numbers

Never begin a sentence with a numeral. Either spell out the number or recast the sentence, especially when there are other numerals of a similar type in the sentence.

Two hundred fifty soldiers in the unit escaped injury while 175 sustained minor injuries.
Of the soldiers in the unit, 250 escaped injury and 175 sustained minor injuries.

When spelling out numbers over one hundred, omit the word *and* within the term (*two hundred fifty,* **not** *two hundred and fifty*).

Series of Numbers

Ignore the general rule when you have a series of numbers in the same sentence that are above *and* below the threshold, especially when those numbers are being compared. In these examples, all are expressed in numerals.

Of the group surveyed, 78 students had studied French and 142 had studied Spanish for three years or more.

We analyzed 62 cases; of these, 59 had occurred in adults and 3 in children.

23.3.2 Inclusive Numbers

To express a range of numbers, such as pages or years, give the first and last (or *inclusive*) numbers of the sequence. If the numbers are spelled out, express the range with the words *from* and *to;* if they are expressed in numerals, use either these words or a connecting hyphen with no space on either side. In citations, always use hyphens (see chapters 18-20).

from 45 to 50	NOT: from 45-50
45-50	NOT: forty-five-fifty

For inclusive numbers of one hundred or greater, use full numbers on both sides of the hyphen (245-280, or 1929-1994).

23.3.3 Percentages and Decimal Fractions

Use numerals to express percentages and decimal fractions, except at the beginning of a sentence. Spell out the word *percent,* except when you use many percentage figures and in the sciences, where the symbol % is usually preferred (with no intervening space after the number). Notice that the noun *percentage* should not be used with a number.

Scores for students who skipped summer school improved only 9 percent. The percentage of students who failed was about 2.4 times the usual rate.

Within this system, the subject scored 3.8, or 95%.

When you use fractional and whole numbers for the same type of item in the same sentence or paragraph, give both as numerals.

The average number of children born to college graduates dropped from 2.4 to 2.

Put a zero in front of a decimal fraction of less than 1.00 if the quantity expressed is capable of equaling or exceeding 1.00; otherwise, omit the initial zero.

a mean of 0.73

a loss of 0.08

$p < .05$

For fractions standing alone, follow the general rule for spelling out the parts (see 23.3.1). If you spell the parts, include a hyphen between them. Express in numerals a unit composed of a whole number and a fraction, with no intervening space between these items.

Trade and commodity services accounted for nine-tenths of all international receipts and payments.

One year during the Dust Bowl era, the town received only 15/16 of an inch of rain.

The main carving implement used in this society measured 2½ feet.

23.3.4 Money

If you refer only occasionally to U.S. currency, follow the general rule (see 23.3.1), and spell out the words *dollars* and *cents*. Otherwise use numerals along with the symbol $ or ¢. Omit the decimal point and following zeros for whole-dollar amounts, unless you refer to fractional amounts as well.

Rarely do they spend more than five dollars a week on recreation.
The report showed $135 collected in fines.
After peaking at $200.00, shares of the stock plummeted to $36.75.

Express large round numbers in a combination of numerals and words.
The deficit that year was $420 billion.

23.3.5 Time

For references to times of day in increments of an hour, half hour, or quarter hour, spell out the times. If necessary, specify *in the morning* or *in the evening*. You may use *o'clock,* although it is now rare in research writing.

The participants planned to meet every Thursday around ten thirty in the morning.

When emphasizing exact times, use numerals and, if necessary, *a.m.* or *p.m.* (lowercase, roman, no intervening space). Always include zeros after the colon for even hours.

Although scheduled to end at 11:00 a.m., the council meeting ran until 1:37 p.m.

In either situation, use the words *noon* and *midnight* (rather than numerals) to express these specific times of day.

23.3.6 Addresses and Thoroughfares

Follow the general rule (see 23.3.1) for the names of local numbered streets. State, federal, and interstate highways are always designated with numerals, as are street or building addresses and telephone and fax numbers. Note that the elements of a full address are separated by commas, except before a zip code.

The National Park Service maintains as a museum the house where Lincoln died (516 10th Street NW, Washington, DC 20004; 202-426-6924).

Ludwig Mies van der Rohe designed the apartments at 860-880 North Lake Shore Drive.

Interstate 95 serves as a critical transportation line from Boston to Miami.

23.3.7 Dates

23.3.7.1 *Month, Day, and Year*

Spell out the names of months when they occur in your text, whether alone or in dates. Express days and years in numerals, and avoid using them at the beginning of a sentence, where they would have to be spelled out (see 23.3.1.2). Do not abbreviate references to the year ("the great flood of '05").

Every September, we recall the events of 2001.
NOT: Two thousand one was a memorable year.

For full references to dates, give the month, the day (followed by a comma), and the year, in accordance with U.S. practices. If you omit the day, omit the comma. Also omit the comma for dates given with seasons instead of months; do not capitalize the names of seasons.

President John F. Kennedy was assassinated on November 22, 1963.
By March 1865 the war was nearly over.
The research was conducted over several weeks in spring 2006.

23.3.7.2 *Decades, Centuries, and Eras*

In general, refer to decades using numerals, including the century (1920s *not* 20s). If the century is clear, you can spell out the name of the decade. The first two decades of any century do not lend themselves to either style and should be described fully for clarity.

The 1920s brought unheralded financial prosperity.
During the fifties, the Cold War dominated the headlines.
Many of these discoveries were announced during the first decade of the twenty-first century.

Refer to centuries using either numerals or lowercase spelled-out names. If the century is spelled out and used as an adjective preceding a noun that it modifies, as in the second example, use a hyphen; otherwise, do not.

The Ottoman Empire reached its apex in the 1600s.
She teaches nineteenth-century novels but would rather teach poetry from the twentieth century.

Appendix A: Formatting Your Paper

A.1.1   **Title**

Every paper must have a title and identifying information. For papers of five or more pages, you should locate the title and identifying information (name and class) on a separate title page. For papers of four or fewer pages, you may omit a title page and locate this information at the top of page 1. Ask your teacher which he prefers.

- **Title page.** On a separate page, print the title about one-third from the top. Add your identifying information and the date about one-third from the bottom.
- **Title on page 1.** Print your title at the top of the first page of your paper. Skip two double-spaced lines and add your identifying information and the date. Skip two more double-spaced lines and begin the main text of your paper.

Print the title and identifying information in the same typeface as the main text, centered. If you have a subtitle, put the main title on the first line, followed by a colon, with the subtitle on the next line. Capitalize your title headline style (see 23.1.3). For identifying information, print on separate lines your name, your course and teacher, and the date you turn in the paper.

A.1.2   **Text**

Set up your word processor to print with the following characteristics:

- typeface: 12 point, roman, proportional serif font (such as Times or Palatino)
- double-spaced, including block quotations
- margins: at least 1 inch and no more than 1.5 inches
- paragraphs: first line indented .25 or .5 inch

A.1.3   **Header**

Create a header for all pages starting at page 2. Against the right margin put your name, followed by a hyphen, followed by the page number, all in 10-point type. The title page is page 0; the first page of text is page 1. Do not put a header on page 1.

A.1.4   **Notes**

Use the same format for individual notes, whether you print them as footnotes or endnotes. They should be single-spaced with 10-point type. Indent the first line the same amount as paragraphs. Note numbers can be superscripts or in regular type followed by a period. Print all notes as footnotes unless your teacher directs otherwise.

FOOTNOTES. If your software does not do it for you, place each footnote at the bottom of the page that includes its in-text reference. Use a two-inch line to separate footnotes from the main body of the paper.

ENDNOTES. Place endnotes on a separate page after the main text but before the bibliography. Center the heading "Notes" at the top of the page. Skip a line, then list the notes in numerical order. Skip a line between notes.

A.1.5   **Bibliography**

List all your sources on a separate page at the end. At the top of the page, center the title of the list appropriate to your citation style (Bibliography, Works Cited, or Reference List). Put bibliographical entries in the same typeface as the main text, double-spaced, with a hanging indent that matches the paragraph indentation. Consult part 2 for detailed information on how to create bibliographical entries.

Appendix B: Glossary of Grammatical Terms

In this section, we define some of the grammatical and other technical terms used in this book. These are not technical definitions, so don't be surprised if they differ from those in a reference book. We have created them simply to help you understand the discussions here, not to give you a theory of grammar.

acknowledgment and response: That part of argument that raises objections or other questions that you anticipate readers may have.

action: Traditionally, we say that action is expressed by a verb: *move, hate, think, discover*. But actions also appear in nominalizations: *movement, hatred, thought, discovery*. Actions are also implied in some adjectives: *advisable, resultant, explanatory*, etc.

active verb: A verb is in the *active voice* when its subject is the agent of its action and the direct object is the receiver of that action: *The dog chased the cat.*

adjectival clause: Adjectival clauses modify nouns. Also called *relative clauses,* they usually begin with a relative pronoun: *which, that, whom, whose, who.* There are two kinds: restrictive and nonrestrictive.

> **restrictive:** A restrictive clause modifies a noun whose referent you *cannot* identify without the added information in the clause. *I drove the car that was dirty.* Unless there is only one possible car in question, the noun phrase, *the car,* does not identify which car I drove, but with the added clause it does, the dirty one. We therefore call that clause *restrictive,* because it "restricts" or uniquely identifies what the noun phrase names.

> **nonrestrictive:** A nonrestrictive clause modifies a noun whose referent you *can* identify without the added information in the clause. *I drove my car, which was dirty.* The noun phrase, *my car,* identifies which car I drove, whether it is dirty or not. We therefore call that clause *nonrestrictive,* because it does not "restrict" or uniquely identify what the noun phrase names.

adjective: A word you can put *very* in front of: *very old, very interesting.* There are exceptions: *major, additional,* etc. Since this is also a test for adverbs, distinguish adjectives from adverbs by putting them between *the* and a noun: *The **occupational** hazard, the **major** reason,* etc. Some nouns also appear there—*the **chemical** hazard.*

adjective phrase: An adjective and what attaches to it: *so **full** that it burst.*

adverb: Adverbs modify all parts of speech except nouns: *especially old, walk quickly, very quickly.*

adverbial clause: A subordinate clause that modifies a verb or adjective, indicating time, cause, condition, etc. It usually begins with a subordinating conjunction such as *because, when, if, since, while, unless.*

adverb phrase: An adverb and what attaches to it: *as **soon** as I could.*

agent: Traditionally, we say that an agent is the person who performs an action (its "doer"). But for our purposes, an agent is the *seeming* source of any action, an entity without which the action could not occur: ***She** criticized the program in this report.* Often we can make the means by which we do something a seeming agent: ***This report** criticizes the program.*

appositive: A noun phrase that is left after deleting *which* and *be: My dog, ~~which~~ ~~is~~ a **Dalmatian**, ran away.*

article: They are easier to list: *a, an, the, this, these, that, those.*

character: The persons you talk about in your sentences. Also, things or ideas that you tell a story about by making them the subjects of several sentences in a passage.

chart: A graphic that presents quantitative evidences in bars, circles, points, or other shapes.

claim: The assertion that the rest of an argument supports. It must be something that a reader will not accept without support. A *practical claim* concerns what we do; a *conceptual claim* concerns what we think.

clause: A clause has at least one subject + verb, where the verb agrees with the subject in number and can be made past or present. These are clauses:

> She left   that they leave   if she left   why he is leaving

These next are not, because the verbs cannot be made past tense nor do they agree in number with the putative subject:

> for them to **go**   her **having gone**

comma splice: You create a comma splice when you join two independent clauses with only a comma.

complement: Whatever completes a verb:

> I am **home**.   You seem **tired**.   She helped **me**.

conjunction: Usually defined as a word that links words, phrases, or clauses. They are easier to illustrate than define (the first two are also categorized as subordinating conjunctions):

> adverbial conjunctions: *because, although, when, since*
> relative conjunctions: *who, whom, whose, which, that*
> coordinating conjunctions: *and, but, yet, for, so, or, nor*
> correlative conjunctions: *both X and Y, not only X but Y, (n)either X (n)or Y, X as well as Y*

data: The objects and raw observations from which you draw evidence.

dependent clause: Any clause that cannot stand alone as a sentence. It usually begins with a subordinating conjunction such as *because, if, when, which, that.*

direct object: The noun that follows a transitive verb and can be made the subject of a passive verb:

> I found **the money**.   **The money** was found by me.

evidence: That part of argument that reports on the objects or observations that you expect readers to accept as hard facts and that support your reasons.

figure: Any graphic except a table.

fragment: A phrase or dependent clause that begins with a capital letter and ends with a period, question mark, or exclamation mark:

> Because I left.   Though I am here!   Which is why I did that.

goal: That toward which the action of a verb is directed. In most cases, goals are direct objects:

> I see **you**.   I broke **the dish**.   I built **a house**.

graph: A graphic that presents quantitative evidences as continuous lines.

graphic: A visual image offered as evidence, including charts and graphs, tables, diagrams, photographs, and so on.

hypothesis: A provisional claim. An assertion that you think might be a good answer to your research question, but that you cannot yet support with reliable evidence.

independent clause: A clause that can stand alone as a sentence.

infinitive: A verb that cannot be made past or present. It often is preceded by the word *to: He decided to **stay**.* But sometimes not: *We helped him **repair** the door.*

main claim/point: The sentence that asserts the claim that a whole argument supports and that serves as the point around which an entire paper is organized.

main clause: A main clause is a part of a larger sentence that could stand alone as a sentence of its own.

nonrestrictive clause: *See* **adjectival clause.**

noun: A word that fits this frame: *The [   ] is good.* Some are concrete: *dog, rock, car;* others abstract: *ambition, space, speed.* The nouns that most concern us are abstractions derived from verbs or adjectives: *act/action, wide/width.*

noun clause: A noun clause functions like a noun, as the subject or object of a verb: *That you are here **proves** that you love me.*

object: There are three kinds:

1. **direct object:** the noun following a transitive verb

   > I *read* **the book**.   We *followed* **the car**.

2. **prepositional object:** the noun following a preposition

   > *in* **the house**   *by* **the walk**   *across* **the street**   *with* **fervor**

3. **indirect object:** the noun between a verb and its direct object

   > I *gave* **him** a tip.

passive: A verb is in the *passive voice* when its subject is the receiver of its action and the verb is preceded by a form of *be*; if the agent is named, it is in a *by* phrase: *The cat was chased by the dog.*

personal pronoun: Easier to list than define: *I, me, my, mine; we, us, our, ours; you, your, yours; he, him, his; she, her, hers; they, them, their, theirs.*

phrase: A group of words constituting a unit but not including a subject and a finite verb: *the dog, too old, was leaving, in the house, ready to work.*

point: The most important sentence in a document, section, or paragraph. It states the idea that everything else supports and develops.

possessive: *my, your, his, her, its, their,* or a noun ending with -*'s* or -*s'*: the **dog's** tail.

predicate: Whatever follows the whole subject, beginning with the verb phrase, including the complement and what attaches to it:

> He *left yesterday to buy a hat.*predicate

preposition: Easier to list: *in, on, up, over, of, at, by,* etc.

prepositional phrase: The preposition plus its object: *in + the house.*

reason: The part of argument that directly supports your claim. Reasons are based on evidence, but they are your judgments—subclaims—that you must support before you can expect readers to accept them.

relative clause: *See* **adjectival clause**.

relative pronoun: *who, whom, which, whose, that* when used in a relative clause.

restrictive clause: *See* **adjectival clause**.

run-on sentence: A punctuated sentence consisting of two or more grammatical sentences not separated by either a coordinating conjunction or any mark of punctuation this entry illustrates a run-on sentence.

subject: The subject is what the verb agrees with in number:

> **Two men** *are* at the door.   **One man** is at the door.

subordinate clause: A clause that usually begins with a subordinating conjunction such as *if, when, unless,* or *which, that, who*. There are three kinds of subordinate clauses: noun, adverbial, and adjectival.

subordinating conjunction: *because, if, when, since, unless, which, who, that, whose,* etc.

table: A grid with columns and rows that present data in numbers or words organized by categories.

theme: A concept that is important to the point of a paper or section and that is repeated through the body. It helps readers to organize their memory of the whole.

transitive verb: A verb with a direct object. The direct object prototypically "receives" an action. The prototypical direct object can be made the subject of a passive verb:

> We **read** the book.   The book **was read** by us.

By this definition, *resemble, become,* and *stand* (as in *He stands six feet tall*) are not transitive.

verb: The word that must agree with the subject in number and that can be inflected for past or present.

> The book **is** ready.   The books **were** returned.

warrant: The part of argument that states the principle of reasoning that connects a reason to its claim. Warrants are most explicitly stated in the form: Whenever this condition applies, we can conclude this.

whole subject: You can identify a whole subject once you identify its verb: Put a *who* or a *what* in front of the verb and turn the sentence into a question. The fullest answer to the question is the whole subject.

Appendix C: Resources for Research and Writing

There is a large literature on finding and presenting information. What we have listed here are those works that provide beginners with a useful overview (primarily specialized dictionaries and encyclopedias) and those that help beginners find sources. We have also included citation and writing guides for specialized research papers. If there is no date listed for an item, the publication appears annually. Sources available online or as a CD-ROM (in addition to or in place of traditional print formats) are so indicated. Online sources for which no URL is given are readily available from multiple online databases.

This list is divided as follows:

For most of those areas, six kinds of resources are listed:

1. specialized dictionaries that offer short essays defining concepts in a field
2. general and specialized encyclopedias that offer more extensive overviews of a topic
3. guides to finding resources in different fields and using their methodologies
4. bibliographies, abstracts, and indexes that list past and current publications in different fields
5. writing manuals for different fields
6. style manuals that describe required features of citations in different fields

Internet Databases (These Are All Bibliographies and Indexes)

General

ArticleFirst. Dublin, OH: OCLC, 1990–. http://www.oclc.org/.

Booklist. Chicago: American Library Association, 1969–. http://www.ala.org/booklist/.

Digital Dissertations. Ann Arbor, MI: UMI, [19—]–. http://www.proquest.com/en-US/catalogs/databases/detail/pqdt.shtml.

Electronic Resources Review. Bradford, UK: MCB University Press, 1997–2000. http://www.emeraldinsight.com/1364–5137.htm.

ERIC. Educational Resources Information Center. Ipswich, MA: EBSCO Pub., 1994–; Bethesda, MD: Cambridge Scientific Abstracts, 1998–. http://www.eric.ed.gov.

Essay and General Literature. Bronx, NY: H. W. Wilson, 1900–. http://www.hwwilson.com/databases/eglit.htm.

FirstSearch Dissertations. Ann Arbor, MI: University Microfilms. http://firstsearch.oclc.org.

General Reference Center Gold. Farmington Hills, MI: Gale Group, 1999–. http://www.gale.cengage.com.

InfoTrac OneFile. Farmington Hills, MI: Gale Group. http://www.gale.cengage.com/onefile.

ISI Web of Knowledge. Philadelphia: Institute for Scientific Information, 2000–. http://isi/webofknowledge.com.

ISI Web of Science. Philadelphia: Institute for Scientific Information, c. 1998–. http://isiknowledge.com.

LexisNexis Academic Universe. Dayton, OH: LexisNexis. http://
web.lexis-nexis.com/universe/.

Library Literature and Information Science Full Text. Bronx, NY: H. W. Wilson,
1900–. http://www.hwwilson.com/databases/liblit.htm.

Periodicals Index Online. ProQuest Information and Learning Company,
1990–. http://pio.chadwyck.co.uk/home.do.

ProQuest Research Library. Ann Arbor, MI: ProQuest Information and Learning,
1998–. http://proquest.umi.com/pqdweb?RQT=306&DBld=4138#sform.

Wilson Omnifile Full Text. Mega edition. Bronx, NY: H. W. Wilson, 1990–.
http://www.hwwilson.com/Databases/omnifile.htm.

WorldCat. Dublin, OH: Online Computer Library Center. http://www.oclc
.org/worldcat/.

Humanities

Arts and Humanities Search. Philadelphia: Institute for Scientific Information;
Dublin, OH: OCLC, 1990–. http://www.oclc.org.

Bibliography of the History of Art. Santa Monica, CA: J. Paul Getty Trust;
Vandoeuvre-lès-Nancy, France: Centre national de la recherche scienti-
fique, 1990–. http://www.getty.edu/research/conducting_research/bha.

History Resource Center U.S. Farmington Hills, MI: Gale Group, c. 2000–.
http://www.galenet.com/servlet/HistRC.

Humanities Full Text. Bronx, NY: H. W. Wilson, 1990–. http://www.hwwilson
.com/Databases/humani.htm.

Social Sciences

Anthropological Literature. Cambridge, MA: Tozzer Library, Harvard University, 1984–. http://hcl.harvard.edu/libraries/tozzer/anthrolit/anthrolit
.cfm.

PAIS Archive. Public Affairs Information Service. Dublin, OH: OCLC, 2004–.
http://www.oclc.org.

PAIS International. Public Affairs Information Service. Norwood, MA: Silver-
Platter International, 1900–. http://www.csa.com/factsheets/pais-set-c
.php.

Political Science Resources on the Web. Ann Arbor, MI: Document Center,
University of Michigan, 1996–. http://www.lib.umich.edu/government-
documents-center/explore/browse/political-science/254/search.

PsycARTICLES. Washington, DC: American Psychological Association,
2001–. http://www.apa.org/psycarticles.

PsycINFO. American Psychological Association. New York: Ovid Technologies, 1900–. http://www.apa.org/psycinfo/.

Social Sciences Citation Index with Abstracts. Philadelphia: Institute for Scientific

Information, c. 1992–. http://thomsonreuters.com/products_services/ science/science_products/a-z/social_sciences_citation_index.

Sociological Abstracts. Sociological Abstracts, Inc. Dublin, OH: OCLC, 1990–. http://www.oclc.org.

Natural Sciences

AGRICOLA (AGRICultural OnLine Access). Beltsville, MD: The Library, 1970–. http://purl.access.gpo.gov/GPO/LPS1292.

Applied Science and Technology Abstracts. Bronx, NY: H. W. Wilson; Dublin, OH: OCLC, 1983–. http://www.hwwilson.com/Databases/applieds.htm.

Science Citation Index. Philadelphia: Institute for Scientific Information, c. 1988–. http://www.thomsonreuters.com/products_services/science/ science_products/a-z/science_citation_index.

Web of Science. Philadelphia: Institute for Scientific Information, 1998–. http://isiknowledge.com.

Print Resources

General

1. Bowman, John S., ed. *The Cambridge Dictionary of American Biography.* Cambridge: Cambridge University Press, 1995.
1. Garraty, John A., and Mark C. Carnes, eds. *American National Biography.* New York: Oxford University Press, 1999.
1. Matthew, H. C. G., and Brian Howard Harrison, eds. *Oxford Dictionary of National Biography, in Association with the British Academy: From the Earliest Times to the Year 2000.* New York: Oxford University Press, 2004. Also at http://www.oxforddnb.com.
2. Jackson, Kenneth T., Karen Markoe, and Arnie Markoe, eds. *The Scribner Encyclopedia of American Lives.* 6 vols. covering 1981–2002. New York: Charles Scribner's Sons, 1998–c. 2004.
2. Lagassé, Paul, ed. *The Columbia Encyclopedia.* 6th ed. New York: Columbia University Press, 2000. Also at http://www.infoplease.com/encyclopedia.
2. *New Encyclopaedia Britannica.* 15th ed. 32 vols. Chicago: Encyclopaedia Britannica, 2005. Also at http://www.eb.com.
3. Balay, Robert, ed. *Guide to Reference Books.* 11th ed. Chicago: American Library Association, 1996.
3. Hacker, Diana, and Barbara Fister. *Research and Documentation in the Electronic Age.* 3rd ed. Boston: Bedford/St. Martin's, 2002. Also at http://www .dianahacker.com/resdoc/.
3. Kane, Eileen, and Mary O'Reilly-de Brún. *Doing Your Own Research.* New York: Marion Boyars, 2001.

3. Lipson, Charles. *Doing Honest Work in College: How to Prepare Citations, Avoid Plagiarism, and Achieve Real Academic Success.* 2nd ed. Chicago: University of Chicago Press, 2008.

3. Vitale, Philip H. *Basic Tools of Research: An Annotated Guide for Students of English.* 3rd ed., rev. and enl. New York: Barron's Educational Series, 1975.

4. *Alternative Press Index.* College Park, MD: Alternative Press Centre, 1969.

4. *Bibliographic Index.* New York: H. W. Wilson. Also at http://hwwilsonweb.com/databases/biblio.htm.

4. *Book Review Index.* Detroit: Gale Research, 1965–.

4. *Book Review Index: A Master Cumulation.* Detroit: Gale Research, 1980–.

4. Brigham, Clarence S. *History and Bibliography of American Newspapers, 1690–1820.* 2 vols. Westport, CT: Greenwood Press, 1976.

4. *Current Book Review Citations* [in English]. New York: H. W. Wilson, 1976–82.

4. Farber, Evan Ira, exec. ed., and Ruth Matteson Blackmore . . . [et al.], senior eds. *Combined Retrospective Index to Book Reviews in Scholarly Journals, 1886–1974.* Arlington, VA: Carrollton Press, 1979–.

4. Gregory, Winifred, ed. *American Newspapers 1821–1936: A Union List of Files Available in the United States and Canada.* New York: H. W. Wilson, 1937.

4. *Library of Congress Subject Catalog.* Washington, DC: Library of Congress. Also at http://catalog.loc.gov/.

4. *National Newspaper Index.* Menlo Park, CA: Information Access. Also online from multiple sources.

4. *New York Times Index.* New York: New York Times.

4. *Popular Periodical Index.* Camden, NJ: Rutgers University.

4. *ProQuest Digital Dissertations.* Ann Arbor, MI: University Microfilms International. Also at http://www.proquest.com/en-US/catalogs/databases/detail/pqdt.shtml.

4. *Readers' Guide to Periodical Literature.* New York: H. W. Wilson. Also at http://hwwilsonweb.com/databases/Readersg.htm.

4. *Reference Books Bulletin.* Chicago: American Library Association, 1984–.

4. *Serials Review.* San Diego: Pergamon, 1975–. Also by subscription through ScienceDirect.

4. *Wall Street Journal Index.* New York: Dow Jones. Also at http://www.il.proquest.com/products/pt-product-WSJ.shtml.

5. Strunk, William, and E. B. White. *The Elements of Style.* 4th ed. New York: Longman, 2004.

5. Tufte, Edward R. *The Visual Display of Quantitative Information.* Cheshire, CT: Graphics Press, 1983.

5. Williams, Joseph M. *Style: Toward Clarity and Grace.* Chicago: University of Chicago Press, 1990.

6. *The Chicago Manual of Style.* 15th ed. Chicago: University of Chicago Press, 2003.

Visual Representation of Data (Tables, Figures, etc.)

2. Harris, Robert L. *Information Graphics: A Comprehensive Illustrated Reference.* New York: Oxford University Press, 2000.

3. Cleveland, William S. *The Elements of Graphing Data.* 2nd ed. Summit, NJ: Hobart Press, 1994.

3. ———. *Visualizing Data.* Summit, NJ: AT&T Bell Laboratories, 1993.

3. Monmonier, Mark. *Mapping It Out: Expository Cartography for the Humanities and Social Sciences.* Chicago: University of Chicago Press, 1993.

3. Tufte, Edward R. *Envisioning Information.* Cheshire, CT: Graphics Press, 1990.

3. ———. *Visual and Statistical Thinking: Displays of Evidence for Decision Making.* Cheshire, CT: Graphics Press, 1997.

3. ———. *The Visual Display of Quantitative Information.* Cheshire, CT: Graphics Press, 1983.

3. Wainer, Howard. *Visual Revelations: Graphical Tales of Fate and Deception from Napoleon Bonaparte to Ross Perot.* New York: Copernicus, Springer-Verlag, 1997.

5. Kosslyn, Stephen M. *Elements of Graph Design.* New York: W. H. Freeman, 1994.

5. National Institutes of Health, Division of Research Services, Medical Arts and Photography Branch. *Graphics User Guide.* Bethesda, MD: The Branch, 1986.

5. Nicol, Adelheid A. M., and Penny M. Pexman. *Presenting Your Findings: A Practical Guide for Creating Tables.* Washington, DC: American Psychological Association, 1999.

5. Robbins, Naomi B. *Creating More Effective Graphs.* New York: John Wiley & Sons, 2004.

Humanities

General

3. Kirkham, Sandi. *How to Find Information in the Humanities.* London: Library Association, 1989.

4. *American Humanities Index.* Troy, NY: Whitston.

4. *Arts and Humanities Citation Index.* Philadelphia: Institute for Scientific Information, 1976–. Also at http://science.thomsonreuters.com/cgi-bin/jrnlst/jloptions.cgi?PC=H.

4. *British Humanities Index.* London: Library Association; Bethesda, MD: Cambridge Scientific Abstracts.

4. *Humanities Index.* New York: H. W. Wilson, 1974. Also at http://hwwilsonweb.com/Databases/humanities.htm.

4. *Index to Book Reviews in the Humanities.* Williamston, MI: P. Thomson, 1960–90.

5. Northey, Margot, and Maurice Legris. *Making Sense in the Humanities: A Student's Guide to Writing and Style.* Toronto: Oxford University Press, 1990.

Art

1. Chilvers, Ian, and Harold Osborne, eds. *The Oxford Dictionary of Art.* 3rd ed. Oxford: Oxford University Press, 2004. Also at http://www.enotes.com/oxford-art-encyclopedia/.

1. Myers, Bernard L., and Trewin Copplestone, eds. *The Macmillan Encyclopedia of Art.* Rev. ed. London: Macmillan, 1981.

1. Myers, Bernard S., and Shirley D. Myers, eds. *McGraw-Hill Dictionary of Art.* 5 vols. New York: McGraw-Hill, 1969.

2. Myers, Bernard S., ed. *Encyclopedia of World Art.* 17 vols. New York: McGraw-Hill, 1987.

3. Jones, Lois Swan. *Art Information and the Internet: How to Find It, How to Use It.* Phoenix: Oryx Press, 1999.

5. Barnet, Sylvan. *A Short Guide to Writing about Art.* 8th ed. New York: Pearson Longman, 2005.

History

1. Cook, Chris. *A Dictionary of Historical Terms.* 3rd ed. Houndmills, UK: Macmillan, 1998.

1. Ritter, Harry. *Dictionary of Concepts in History.* Westport, CT: Greenwood Press, 1986.

3. Benjamin, Jules R. *A Student's Guide to History.* 9th ed. Boston: Bedford/St. Martin's, 2004.

3. Brundage, Anthony. *Going to the Sources: A Guide to Historical Research and Writing.* 3rd ed. Wheeling, IL: Harlan Davidson, 2002.

5. Barzun, Jacques, and Henry F. Graff. *The Modern Researcher.* 6th ed. Belmont, CA: Thomson/Wadsworth, 2004.

5. Marius, Richard, and Melvin E. Page. *A Short Guide to Writing about History.* 5th ed. New York: Pearson Longman, 2005.

Literary Studies

1. Abrams, M. H. *A Glossary of Literary Terms.* 8th ed. Boston: Thomson/Wadsworth, 2005.

1. Baldick, Chris, ed. *The Concise Oxford Dictionary of Literary Terms.* 2nd ed. Oxford: Oxford University Press, 2001.

1. Brogan, Terry V. F., ed. *The New Princeton Handbook of Poetic Terms.* Princeton, NJ: Princeton University Press, 1994.

1. Groden, Michael, Martin Kreiswirth, and Imre Szeman, eds. *The Johns Hopkins Guide to Literary Theory and Criticism.* 2nd ed. Baltimore: Johns Hopkins University Press, 2005.

1. Preminger, Alex, and Terry V. F. Brogan, eds. *The New Princeton Encyclopedia of Poetry and Poetics.* Princeton, NJ: Princeton University Press, 1993.

2. Drabble, Margaret, ed. *The Oxford Companion to English Literature.* 6th ed. New York: Oxford University Press, 2000. Also at http://www.enotes.com/oce-encyclopedia/.

2. Hart, James David, and Phillip W. Leininger, eds. *The Oxford Companion to American Literature.* 6th ed. New York: Oxford University Press, 1995. Also at http://www.enotes.com/oca-encyclopedia/.

2. Lentricchia, Frank, and Thomas McLaughlin, eds. *Critical Terms for Literary Study.* 2nd ed. Chicago: University of Chicago Press, 1995.

2. Parini, Jay, ed. *The Oxford Encyclopedia of American Literature.* 4 vols. New York: Oxford University Press, 2004.

3. Harner, James L. *Literary Research Guide: An Annotated Listing of Reference Sources in English Literary Studies.* 4th ed. New York: Modern Language Association of America, 2002.

4. *MLA International Bibliography of Books and Articles on the Modern Languages and Literature.* New York: Modern Language Association of America. Also online from multiple sources.

5. Barnet, Sylvan, and William E. Cain. *A Short Guide to Writing about Literature.* 10th ed. New York: Longman Pearson, 2005.

5. Griffith, Kelley. *Writing Essays about Literature: A Guide and Style Sheet.* 7th ed. Boston: Heinle & Heinle, 2005.

6. Gibaldi, Joseph. *MLA Handbook for Writers of Research Papers.* 7th ed. New York: Modern Language Association of America, 2009.

Music

1. Randel, Don Michael, ed. *The Harvard Dictionary of Music.* 4th ed. Cambridge: Belknap Press of Harvard University Press, 2003.

1. Sadie, Stanley, and John Tyrrell, eds. *The New Grove Dictionary of Music and Musicians.* 2nd ed. 29 vols. New York: Grove, 2001. Also at http://www.grovemusic.com.

2. Netti, Bruno, Ruth M. Stone, James Porter, and Timothy Rice, eds. *The Garland Encyclopedia of World Music.* 10 vols. New York: Garland, 2002.

2. Sadie, Stanley, ed. *The Norton/Grove Concise Encyclopedia of Music.* Rev. and enl. ed. New York: W. W. Norton, 1994.

5. Herbert, Trevor. *Music in Words: A Short Guide to Researching and Writing about Music.* London: Associated Board of the Royal Schools of Music, 2001.

6. Bellman, Jonathan. *A Short Guide to Writing about Music.* New York: Longman, 2000.

6. Wingell, Richard. *Writing about Music: An Introductory Guide.* 3rd ed. Upper Saddle River, NJ: Prentice Hall, 2002.

Philosophy

1. Blackburn, Simon. *The Oxford Dictionary of Philosophy.* 2nd ed. Oxford: Oxford University Press, 2005. Also at http://www.oxfordreference.com/pages/Subjects_and_Titles__2E_R08.

2. Edwards, Paul. *The Encyclopedia of Philosophy.* 8 vols. New York: Macmillan, 1996.

2. Parkinson, George H. R. *The Handbook of Western Philosophy.* New York: Macmillan, 1988.

2. Urmson, J. O., and Jonathan Rée, eds. *The Concise Encyclopedia of Western Philosophy and Philosophers.* 3rd ed. London: Routledge, 2005.

3. List, Charles J., and Stephen H. Plum. *Library Research Guide to Philosophy.* Ann Arbor, MI: Pierian Press, 1990.

5. Martinich, Aloysius. *Philosophical Writing: An Introduction.* 3rd ed. Malden, MA: Blackwell, 2005.

5. Watson, Richard A. *Writing Philosophy: A Guide to Professional Writing and Publishing.* Carbondale: Southern Illinois University Press, 1992.

Social Sciences

General

1. Calhoun, Craig, ed. *Dictionary of the Social Sciences.* New York: Oxford University Press, 2002. Also at http://www.oxfordreference.com/pages/Subjects_and_Titles__2E_PS07.

1. *Statistical Abstract of the United States.* Washington, DC: U.S. Census Bureau. Also at http://www.census.gov/comendia/statab/.

2. Sills, David, ed. *International Encyclopedia of the Social Sciences.* 19 vols. New York: Macmillan, 1991.

3. Herron, Nancy L. *The Social Sciences: A Cross-Disciplinary Guide to Selected Sources.* 3rd ed. Englewood, CO: Libraries Unlimited, 2002.

5. Becker, Howard S. *Writing for Social Scientists: How to Start and Finish Your Thesis, Book, or Article.* Chicago: University of Chicago Press, 1986.

5. Bell, Judith. *Doing Your Research Project: A Guide for First-Time Researchers in Education, Health, and Social Science.* 4th ed. Maidenhead, UK: Open University Press, 2005.

5. Northey, Margot, Lorne Tepperman, and James Russell. *Making Sense: Social Sciences; A Student's Guide to Research and Writing.* Updated 2nd ed. Ontario: Oxford University Press, 2005.

Anthropology

1. Barfield, Thomas J., ed. *The Dictionary of Anthropology.* Oxford: Blackwell, 2000.

1. Winthrop, Robert H. *Dictionary of Concepts in Cultural Anthropology.* New York: Greenwood Press, 1991.

2. Barnard, Alan, and Jonathan Spencer, eds. *Encyclopedia of Social and Cultural Anthropology.* London: Routledge, 2004.
2. Ember, Melvin, Carol R. Ember, and Ian A. Skoggard, eds. *Encyclopedia of World Cultures: Supplement.* New York: Gale Group/Thomson Learning, 2002.
2. Levinson, David, ed. *Encyclopedia of World Cultures.* 10 vols. Boston: G. K. Hall, 1996.
2. Levinson, David, and Melvin Ember, eds. *Encyclopedia of Cultural Anthropology.* 4 vols. New York: Henry Holt, 1996.

Business
1. Friedman, Jack P. *Dictionary of Business Terms.* 3rd ed. Hauppauge, NY: Barron's Educational Series, 2000.
1. Link, Albert N. *Link's International Dictionary of Business Economics.* Chicago: Probus, 1993.
1. Nisberg, Jay N. *The Random House Dictionary of Business Terms.* New York: Random House, 1992.
2. Folsom, W. Davis, and Rick Boulware. *Encyclopedia of American Business.* New York: Facts on File, 2004.
2. McDonough, John, and Karen Egolf, eds. *The Advertising Age Encyclopedia of Advertising.* 3 vols. New York: Fitzroy Dearborn, 2003.
2. Vernon, Mark. *Business: The Key Concepts.* New York: Routledge, 2002.
2. Warner, Malcolm, and John P. Kotter, eds. *International Encyclopedia of Business and Management.* 2nd ed. 8 vols. London: Thomson Learning, 2002.
3. Amor, Louise, ed. *The Online Manual: A Practical Guide to Business Databases.* 6th ed. Oxford: Learned Information, 1997.
5. Farrell, Thomas J., and Charlotte Donabedian. *Writing the Business Research Paper: A Complete Guide.* Durham, NC: Carolina Academic Press, 1991.

Communications, Journalism, and Media Studies
1. Miller, Toby, ed. *Television: Critical Concepts in Media and Cultural Studies.* London: Routledge, 2003.
1. Newton, Harry. *Newton's Telecom Dictionary: Covering Telecommunications, Networking, Information Technology, the Internet, the Web, Computing, Wireless, and Fiber.* 21st ed. San Francisco: CMP Books, 2005.
1. Watson, James, and Anne Hill. *A Dictionary of Communication and Media Studies.* 4th ed. London: Arnold, 1997.
1. Weik, Martin H. *Communications Standard Dictionary.* 3rd ed. New York: Chapman & Hall, 1996.
1. Weiner, Richard. *Webster's New World Dictionary of Media and Communications.* Rev. and updated ed. New York: Macmillan, 1996.

2. Barnouw, Erik, ed. *International Encyclopedia of Communications.* 4 vols. New York: Oxford University Press, 1989.

2. Johnston, Donald H., ed. *Encyclopedia of International Media and Communications.* 4 vols. San Diego, CA: Academic Press, 2003.

2. Jones, Steve, ed. *Encyclopedia of New Media: An Essential Reference to Communication and Technology.* Thousand Oaks, CA: Sage, 2003.

2. Paneth, Donald. *The Encyclopedia of American Journalism.* New York: Facts on File, 1983.

2. Stern, Jane, and Michael Stern. *Jane and Michael Stern's Encyclopedia of Pop Culture: An A to Z Guide of Who's Who and What's What, from Aerobics and Bubble Gum to Valley of the Dolls and Moon Unit Zappa.* New York: HarperPerennial, 1992.

4. Blum, Eleanor, and Frances Goins Wilhoit. *Mass Media Bibliography: An Annotated Guide to Books and Journals for Research and Reference.* 3rd ed. Urbana: University of Illinois Press, 1990.

6. Goldstein, Norm, ed. *Stylebook and Briefing on Media Law.* 40th ed. New York: Associated Press, 2005.

Economics

1. Pearce, David W., ed. *MIT Dictionary of Modern Economics.* 4th ed. Cambridge, MA: MIT Press, 1992.

2. Eatwell, John, Murray Milgate, Peter K. Newman, and Sir Robert Harry Inglis Palgrave, eds. *The New Palgrave: A Dictionary of Economics.* 4 vols. New York: Palgrave, 2004.

2. Greenwald, Douglas, ed. *The McGraw-Hill Encyclopedia of Economics.* 2nd ed. New York: McGraw-Hill, 1994.

2. Mokyr, Joel, ed. *The Oxford Encyclopedia of Economic History.* 5 vols. Oxford: Oxford University Press, 2003.

5. McCloskey, Donald N. *The Writing of Economics.* New York: Macmillan, 1987.

5. Thomson, William. *A Guide for the Young Economist.* Cambridge, MA: MIT Press, 2001.

Education

1. Barrow, Robin, and Geoffrey Milburn. *A Critical Dictionary of Educational Concepts: An Appraisal of Selected Ideas and Issues in Educational Theory and Practice.* 2nd ed. New York: Teacher's College Press, 1990.

1. Collins, John Williams, and Nancy P. O'Brien, eds. *The Greenwood Dictionary of Education.* Westport, CT: Greenwood, 2003.

1. Gordon, Peter, and Dennis Lawton. *Dictionary of British Education.* 3rd ed. London: Woburn Press, 2003.

2. Alkin, Marvin C., ed. *Encyclopedia of Educational Research.* 6th ed. 4 vols. New York: Macmillan, 1992.

2. Guthrie, James W., ed. *Encyclopedia of Education.* 2nd ed. 8 vols. New York: Macmillan Reference USA, 2003.

2. Husen, Torsten, and T. Neville Postlethwaite, eds. *The International Encyclopedia of Education.* 2nd ed. 12 vols. Oxford: Pergamon, 1994.

2. Levinson, David L., Peter W. Cookson, and Alan R. Sadovnik, eds. *Education and Sociology: An Encyclopedia.* New York: RoutledgeFalmer, 2002.

2. Unger, Harlow G. *Encyclopedia of American Education.* 2nd ed. 3 vols. New York: Facts on File, 2001.

4. *The ERIC Database.* Lanham, MD: Educational Resources Information Center. Also at http://www.eric.ed.gov/.

Geography

1. Witherick, M. E., Simon Ross, and John Small. *A Modern Dictionary of Geography.* 4th ed. London: Arnold, 2001.

2. Dunbar, Gary S. *Modern Geography: An Encyclopedic Survey.* New York: Garland, 1991.

2. McCoy, John, ed. *Geo-Data: The World Geographic Encyclopedia.* 3rd ed. Detroit: Thomson-Gale, 2003.

2. Parker, Sybil P., ed. *World Geographical Encyclopedia.* 5 vols. New York: McGraw-Hill, 1995.

3. Walford, Nigel. *Geographical Data Analysis.* New York: John Wiley & Sons, 1995.

5. Durrenberger, Robert W., John K. Wright, and Elizabeth T. Platt. *Geographical Research and Writing.* New York: Crowell, 1985.

5. Northey, Margot, and David B. Knight. *Making Sense: A Student's Guide to Research and Writing: Geography and Environmental Sciences.* 2nd updated ed. Ontario: Oxford University Press, 2005.

Political Science

1. Robertson, David. *A Dictionary of Modern Politics.* 4th ed. London: Europa, 2005.

2. *The Almanac of American Politics.* Washington, DC: National Journal. Also at http://nationaljournal.com/members/almanac.

2. Hawkesworth, Mary E., and Maurice Kogan, eds. *Encyclopedia of Government and Politics.* 2nd ed. 2 vols. London: Routledge, 2004.

2. Miller, David, ed. *The Blackwell Encyclopaedia of Political Thought.* Oxford: Blackwell, 1998.

5. Biddle, Arthur W., Kenneth M. Holland, and Toby Fulwiler. *Writer's Guide: Political Science.* Lexington, MA: D. C. Heath, 1987.

5. Lovell, David W., and Rhonda Moore. *Essay Writing and Style Guide for Politics and the Social Sciences.* Sydney: Australasian Political Studies Association, 1992.

5. Schmidt, Diane E. *Writing in Political Science: A Practical Guide.* 3rd ed. New York: Pearson Longman, 2005.

6. American Political Science Association. *Style Manual for Political Science.* Rev. ed. Washington, DC: American Political Science Association, 2001.

Psychology

1. Colman, Andrew M. *Oxford Dictionary of Psychology.* Oxford: Oxford University Press, 2003. Also at http://www.oxfordreference.com/pages/ Subjects_and_Titles__2E_PS05.

1. Eysenck, Michael, ed. *The Blackwell Dictionary of Cognitive Psychology.* Oxford: Blackwell, 1997.

1. Hayes, Nicky, and Peter Stratton. *A Student's Dictionary of Psychology.* 4th ed. London: Arnold, 2003.

1. Wolman, Benjamin B., ed. *Dictionary of Behavioral Science.* 2nd ed. San Diego, CA: Academic Press, 1989.

2. Colman, Andrew M., ed. *Companion Encyclopedia of Psychology.* 2 vols. London: Routledge, 1997.

2. Craighead, W. Edward, Charles B. Nemeroff, and Raymond J. Corsini, eds. *The Corsini Encyclopedia of Psychology and Behavioral Science.* 3rd ed. 4 vols. New York: Wiley, 2002.

2. Kazdin, Alan E., ed. *Encyclopedia of Psychology.* 8 vols. Washington, DC: American Psychological Association; Oxford: Oxford University Press, 2000.

4. *PsycINFO.* Washington, DC: American Psychological Association. Also online from multiple sources.

4. *The Web of Science Citation Databases.* Philadelphia: Institute for Scientific Information. Also at http://isiknowledge.com.

5. Solomon, Paul R. *A Student's Guide to Research Report Writing in Psychology.* Glenview, IL: Scott Foresman, 1985.

5. Sternberg, R. J. *The Psychologist's Companion: A Guide to Scientific Writing for Students and Researchers.* 4th ed. Cambridge: Cambridge University Press, 2003.

6. *Publication Manual of the American Psychological Association.* 6th ed. Washington, DC: American Psychological Association, 2009.

Religion

1. Bowker, John, ed. *The Concise Oxford Dictionary of World Religions.* Oxford: Oxford University Press, 2000. Also at http://www.oxfordreference.com/ pages/Subjects_and_Titles__2E_R01.

1. Pye, Michael, ed. *Continuum Dictionary of Religion.* New York: Continuum, 1994.

2. Jones, Lindsay, ed. *Encyclopedia of Religion.* 15 vols. Detroit: Macmillan Reference USA, 2005.

2. Routledge Encyclopedias of Religion and Society (series). New York: Routledge.

Sociology

1. Abercrombie, Nicholas, Stephen Hill, and Bryan S. Turner. *The Penguin Dictionary of Sociology.* 4th ed. London: Penguin, 2000.
1. Johnson, Allan G. *The Blackwell Dictionary of Sociology: A User's Guide to Sociological Language.* 2nd ed. Oxford: Blackwell, 2002.
1. Scott, John, and Marshall Gordon, eds. *A Dictionary of Sociology.* 3rd ed. New York: Oxford University Press, 2005.
2. Beckert, Jens, and Milan Zafirovksi, eds. *Encyclopedia of Economic Sociology.* London: Routledge, 2005.
2. Borgatta, Edgar F., ed. *Encyclopedia of Sociology.* 2nd ed. 5 vols. New York: Macmillan Reference USA, 2000.
2. Levinson, David L., Peter W. Cookson, and Alan R. Sadovnik, eds. *Education and Sociology: An Encyclopedia.* New York: RoutledgeFalmer, 2002.
2. Ritzer, George, ed. *Encyclopedia of Social Theory.* 2 vols. Thousand Oaks, CA: Sage, 2005.
4. *Applied Social Sciences Index and Abstracts (ASSIA).* Bethesda, MD: Cambridge Scientific Abstracts. Also at http://www.csa.com/factsheets/assia-set-c.php.
4. *Social Science Research.* San Diego, CA: Academic Press. Also at http://www.sciencedirect.com.
5. Sociology Writing Group. *A Guide to Writing Sociology Papers.* 5th ed. New York: Worth, 2001.

Women's Studies

1. Mills, Jane. *Womanwords: A Dictionary of Words about Women.* New York: Henry Holt, 1993.
1. Uglow, Jennifer S., Frances Hinton, and Maggy Hendry, eds. *The Northeastern Dictionary of Women's Biography.* 3rd ed. Boston: Northeastern University Press, 1999.
2. Hine, Darlene Clark, Elsa Barkley Brown, and Rosalyn Terborg-Penn, eds. *Black Women in America: An Historical Encyclopedia.* 2 vols. Bloomington: Indiana University Press, 1994.
2. Kramarae, Cheris, and Dale Spender, eds. *Routledge International Encyclopedia of Women: Global Women's Issues and Knowledge.* 4 vols. New York: Routledge, 2000.
2. Tierney, Helen, ed. *Women's Studies Encyclopedia.* Rev. and expanded ed. 3 vols. Westport, CT: Greenwood Press, 1999.
2. Willard, Frances E., and Mary A. Livermore, eds. *American Women: Fifteen Hundred Biographies with Over 1,400 Portraits.* Rev. ed. 2 vols. Detroit: Gale Research, 1973.
3. Atkinson, Steven D., and Judith Hudson. *Women Online: Research in Women's Studies Using Online Databases.* New York: Haworth, 1990.

Natural Sciences

1. *McGraw-Hill Dictionary of Scientific and Technical Terms.* 6th ed. New York: McGraw-Hill, 2003. Also at http://www.accessscience.com.
1. Morris, Christopher, ed. *Academic Press Dictionary of Science and Technology.* San Diego, CA: Academic Press, 1992.
1. Porter, Ray, and Marilyn Bailey Ogilvie, eds. *The Biographical Dictionary of Scientists.* 3rd ed. 2 vols. New York: Oxford University Press, 2000.
1. *Science Navigator.* New York: McGraw-Hill, 1998. CD-ROM, version 4.0.
1. Walker, Peter M. B., ed. *Chambers Dictionary of Science and Technology.* London: Chambers, 2000.
2. Heilbron, J. L., ed. *The Oxford Companion to the History of Modern Science.* Oxford: Oxford University Press, 2003. Also at http://www.oxfordreference.com/pages/Subjects_and_titles__t132.
2. *McGraw-Hill Encyclopedia of Science and Technology.* 9th ed. New York: McGraw-Hill, 2002. Also at http://www.accessscience.com.
2. *Nature Encyclopedia: An A–Z Guide to Life on Earth.* New York: Oxford University Press, 2001.
2. *Van Nostrand's Scientific Encyclopedia.* 9th ed. New York: Wiley-Interscience, 2002.
3. *Directory of Technical and Scientific Directories: A World Bibliographic Guide to Medical, Agricultural, Industrial, and Natural Science Directories.* 6th ed. Phoenix: Oryx Press, 1989.
3. Hurt, Charlie Deuel. *Information Sources in Science and Technology.* 3rd ed. Englewood, CO: Libraries Unlimited, 1998.
5. Gilpin, Andrea A., and Patricia Patchet-Golubev. *A Guide to Writing in the Sciences.* Toronto: University of Toronto Press, 2000.
6. Rubens, Phillip, ed. *Science and Technical Writing: A Manual of Style.* 2nd ed. New York: Routledge, 2001.

Index